W9-CFF-358

EVERYDAY EXCHANGES

Marketwork and Capitalist
Common Sense

EVERYDAY EXCHANGES

Marketwork and Capitalist Common Sense

EVAN WATKINS

STANFORD UNIVERSITY PRESS

STANFORD, CALIFORNIA

Stanford University Press
Stanford, California
© 1998 by the Board of Trustees of the
Leland Stanford Junior University

Printed in the United States of America

CIP data are at the end of the book

FOR DIANE

Acknowledgments

There are a great many people who contributed a lot to this book. I especially want to thank Carolyn Allen and Susan Jeffords, and the cultural studies group at Penn State, for their discussions of the issues involved, and Helen Tartar, Ann Klefstad, and Nathan MacBrien at Stanford University Press for their many suggestions and careful work with the manuscript. Diane and Chris contributed their considerable knowledges as well as family support and encouragement.

Part of an earlier version of Chapter 1, under the title "The Dinosaurics of Size: Economic Narratives and Postmodern Culture," appeared in *The Centennial Review*, and part of an earlier version of Chapter 5, under the title "The Educational Politics of Human Resources: Humanities Teachers as Resource Managers," appeared in *the minnesota review*.

Contents

EVERYDAY EXCHANGES

Marketwork and Capitalist
Common Sense

Capitalist Common Sense

I'd like to begin by saying simply that this book is about economics, even if that statement is more grandiose than I can justify. My immediate reason for hesitating, however, is that I don't propose a renewed interest in economic issues by means of trashing most recent cultural studies directions as "merely" cultural, in order to get back to the real stuff. I think in fact there's been a lot of varied and remarkably useful attention to economics within the wide range of cultural studies, and while I don't rehearse its contribution often and at great length, it's because I'd like to think I can add something to all that I've learned from that work. But if your idea of an interest in economics involves shifting away from cultural phenomena to real, material economic analysis, then a "sort-of economics" is the best I can offer.

At the same time, I am suspicious of the contempt for economics evident in Laclau and Mouffe (and a great many others). They call economics, in *Hegemony and Socialist Strategy*, "the last redoubt of essentialism" in left politics. Depending on where you look in Laclau and Mouffe's own argument, economics offers not only such a vestigial reminder of hermeneutically imposed illusion, but also the most pervasive evidence of the exercise of hegemonic powers. Thus, despite the dangers of economic essentialism, they warn that "practically no domain of individual or collective life" (161) exists where you can imagine yourself safe from the relentless process of market commodification. Their anti-essentialism may not lead them to ignore economics, but they do sound pretty defeatist when it looms into view.

Cultural studies work generally is marked in any number of ways by similar bifocal intensities with regard to economics. Stuart Hall, for example, emphasizes the politics of cultural studies, and he has frequently expressed both astonishment and concern at its rapid growth in the United States, particularly in English departments. Unquestionably that growth has raised serious political questions. How is it that an ensemble of practices committed in whatever multiple ways to challenging dominant politics can become so academically successful? To what extent does that success both depend on and occlude the long histories of struggle to establish fields such as women studies and African American studies within the university? Has the expansion of cultural studies in fact created a new and more sophisticated form of cultural imperialism rather than transforming academic work in significant ways? Has cultural studies finally become just one more in a long list of names for university business as usual?

Alongside the force of such questions and the political difficulties they generate, however, economic lenses function as a reminder that over the last decade the labor market in English and related disciplines has undergone a massive transformation, one marked not only by the scarcity of jobs for recent Ph.D.'s, but more fundamentally by the proliferation of "temporary" and "part-time" positions and by the size and composition of the labor force. These changes have occurred within a complex of events that may well alter almost beyond recognition the organization, funding, demographics, and disciplinary divisions of the research university. In the short run, the processes of "downsizing" and "re-engineering" have become familiar management strategy in the university no less than in corporations, although in the former they go by different names. Meanwhile, throughout ongoing policy debates about educational reform and the experimentation with different mixes of funding and curricular reform, media representations of the necessity for getting a good education in today's world have begun to ring out like Baptist sermons.

There's not really any reason to think that such economic issues and the political debates about the academic success of cultural studies are mutually exclusive; indeed, they jostle everywhere in the practices of academic life. Nevertheless, the directions of their entrance into daily practices do appear polarized. It seems possible to generate the insights and the effects of political debate from the inside; in contrast, economic "realities" seem imposed from the outside as a limit on the realization of new political possibilities. And this perception of direction neatly translates the double focus evident in Laclau and Mouffe: it may be a mistake to imagine some underlying economic basis that determines either the political complexities of cultural studies work or its positioning in the university; but conversely, there is no place in the academy safe from the economic forces globally at work, and there seems little that can be done in economic terms to change the fact that four-fifths of the world's population live in conditions of devastating poverty. "We" can't even change the economic fate in store for far too many of our students in English and related fields.

English faculty don't exactly live in poverty, however. Even the exigencies of the current job market for students don't impose anything like the magnitude of poverty experienced by most people most places on the planet, and, principles of moral sacrifice aside, living in poverty is not a desirable experience. "When I think of poverty," Beverly Smith remarks to her sister in "Across the Kitchen Table: A Sister-to-Sister Dialogue" in *This Bridge Called My Back*, "I think of constant physical and material oppression. You know, you aren't poor one day and well-to-do the next. If you're poor it's a constant thing, everyday, everyday" (115). Constant physical and material oppression means economic resources also assume a primary importance in making sense of your life and estimating your powers of action as a social agent. Living in poverty, that is, you can't afford either half of the double vision registered in Laclau and Mouffe's argument. Countless everyday practices are understood by countless numbers of people worldwide in perfectly ordinary ways as economic practices, with little need for epistemological contortions to justify that understanding. Likewise, the thematics of a relentless market-imposed commodification of all social relations can no more appear as global threat than the celebratory image of "free market" universality arriving with the "collapse" of communism can appear as promise. Poverty reconstructs Lacan's psychoanalytic version of the Cogito in the form of a recognition that somehow you are always where The Market is not, and The Market is where you are not.

I can't easily escape that "sort-of economics" qualifier given the focus of this introduction: capitalist common sense. Even with a kind of Gramscian imprimatur, sense-making as I've alluded to it above and common sense as I will discuss it don't seem particularly material means of economic analysis. It's just the sort of thing a cultural studies type might dream up. Warnings such as Laclau and Mouffe's about an implacable marketplace expansion, however, express a kind of dystopian version of capitalist triumphalism, and thus seem to me to belong within the ensemble of effects produced by a capitalist common sense. While any such focus on common sense is perhaps only sort of economics, I think its effects are impossible to ignore.*

It is crucial to pursue the Smiths' attention, later in their dialogue, to ways of theorizing the intersections of different forms of oppression. Yet their equally urgent point is that understanding intersections depends on being able to think carefully about specific oppressions, beyond the commonsense limits imposed on attention to economics by arguments like Laclau and Mouffe's no less than by the chorus of capitalist triumphalism. Living in poverty tells you that "economics" always involves both material practices and sense-making operations, and it shouldn't take a first-hand experience of poverty to recognize that this isn't a particularly good time to give up on economics, in any sense. I will argue in the course of this book that there are some good reasons to look to new economic practices as, fundamentally, forms of political challenge.

❖

In a well-known passage in the first volume of *Capital*, Marx explains how in certain conditions of economic exchange some people find that the only economic resource they can bring to the exchange is their labor power. It's quite possible no one wants to be reminded of how many questions and how much debate this apparently simple formulation has occasioned. Thus, fortunately for my purposes, some of its simplicity can be preserved if you notice first what it suggests about a very familiar situation: working for pay. For some people what you actually do lies somewhere between the freedom of not having to work for pay and the bleakness of not being able to find paying work. Economic resources appear in terms of working practices, for pay. As Marx suggests, however, "for pay" can imply not only working but selling. And like going to work, selling something can also define economic resources. Going to work or not going to work, selling something or not selling something, make a big difference in how you think about what you can possibly do next. My "translation" of Marx avoids most of the crucially important issues raised by the idea of selling labor power, but it does this in order to emphasize how economic resources might be figured as complex bundles of practices. As economic resources,

---

* In "The Transgressive Knowledge of 'Ersatz' Economics," Jack Amariglio and David Ruccio emphasize the differences between academic discourses of economics and the every-day discourses of "ersatz" economics, at the same time that they also explain a great deal about the effects of those everyday discourses.

these practices help organize how you understand your daily experiences and what you can do in your circumstances.

Like Marx's notion of labor power, the familiar conception of economic resources as "purchasing power" can usefully be translated into what you're doing—here, buying stuff. Buying stuff, like going to work for pay or selling stuff, involves a complex of everyday practices configured as an economic resource. The "power" at issue is only a sort of shorthand that identifies somebody as doing these things—going to work (or not), buying stuff (or not), or selling stuff (or not). It links the practices to an agent for whom the practices help make sense of daily experiences. Economic resources in these terms are not aggregate units of possession to be differentiated across numerical indices by a "poverty line," but are instead defining organizations of insertion within or exclusion from specifically configured fields of everyday and familiar social practices.

As Marx sets up his argument in *Capital*, yet another concept seems necessary to make labor power a crucial feature of his structural description of an economic system: the concept of a market. He imagines labor power as something you sell in a market, just as the concept of purchasing power assumes a market where stuff can be bought and sold, and where the value of the stuff you can buy determines the level of your purchasing power. In these terms, a market appears less as an economic resource than as the field within which something can be identified as a resource that has a certain economic value.

Market theory assumes that beyond the activities of agents going to work, buying stuff, selling stuff, and so on lies "the market," the ultimate arbiter of what counts as a resource that would make sense of specific practices. Market is metasense. Beyond the many (often odd) reasons why classical and neoclassical economics is familiarly known as "free market" theory is that it tries to install its theorizing immediately at the level of market metasense, "freeing" the market from distractions that might clutter the picture. Market as metasense makes nonsense of any form of the question "For whom are markets an economic resource?" Such questions just confuse the issue.

In this context Marx's emphasis on a capitalist organization of production might best be understood as a way to resuscitate the meaningfulness of the question about markets as resource and supply some answers to it. He wasn't really out to deduce the specific operations of a capitalist market from the organization of production as a logically prior condition of possibility. His argument, I think, is that if you can recognize capitalist production as organized in this way, then you can recognize that markets operating in capitalist terms function as an economic resource for certain groups of the population and not for others. Market as metasense is an illusion. I like that conclusion well enough, but his schematic of labor power can introduce a treacherously circular path by which to reach it. His positive identification of labor power as itself something to sell already assumes market metasense, and, like the operators in certain forms of deconstruction, labor power as the operator of unraveling market metasense unravels itself right along with the idea of the market.

If markets are a form of economic resource, however, then markets are also sense-making practices. Depending on your sense of your resources in specific circumstances, you work, buy, sell—or market. There are practices specific to marketing as well as working practices, buying practices, and selling practices. At this point, however, market metasense might suggest I've simply invented an empty category. It's possible to imagine "buying" or "selling," like "working," as ensembles of practices, but apart from buying or selling what would you be doing if you were "marketing"? The market, as the field where buying and selling take place, again seems a metasense that defines what counts as an economic resource.

Yet the spatial metaphor can yield a plausible answer, without recourse to an operator like Marx's labor power. There's no magic or metaphysics about markets. When you're marketing you're not just inserted within or excluded from specific fields of everyday social practices. You're actively engaged in constructing a field of practices, and in configuring the ways you engage with other people as a complex of social relations that define economic resources. Some people can't find paying work much of the time, can't purchase or produce even basic necessities like food and shelter, have little if anything to sell, and can't sustain for very long (or very "legally") the construction of markets. In the contemporary social formation in the United States, that's poverty as an economic condition: an impoverished range of possible practices, a constant physical and material oppression.

Living in poverty is oppressive, but, as Beverly Smith points out, that doesn't imply you never think about anything except the conditions imposed by poverty: "Because of the fact of the education we had and the emphasis on cultural development and on intellectual development that has been in our family at least for three generations, makes people think, well, we must of come from a middle class background" (118). Coming from poverty doesn't mean that you never think about education or cultural development or whatever; it's just that how you make sense of your thinking is flooded with the visible, foregrounded, constant oppressiveness of your poverty. Such awareness may make it difficult to talk about economics without sounding deterministic. But I know from my own experience growing up that poverty makes it very easy to think continually about economic resources as everyday practices, even now, at a long remove from the people I grew up with.

Economics as everyday practices generates a kind of everyday economic common sense, and historically that common sense has been shaped in the United States by the designation of economic relations as "capitalist." Thus, in turn, representations of that capitalist-identified history are the points of articulation for a reservoir of common sense embedded in countless everyday practices. Economic changes are inevitably negotiated within a complex of representations elaborated as a capitalist common sense. Whether you see the present moment as "late" or "multinational" or even "post-" capitalism, one of the crucial characteristics of the present is the weight and density of capitalist common sense. That common sense doesn't create conditions of poverty, but it does impose limits on what can be done about it.

In what follows I'm not directly concerned with just how to define sense as "common" or "economic" or "capitalist." My procedure is more like an inquiry into definitional behaviors, where concepts like these, in all their discursive fluidity, could nevertheless be seen as articulated by a directional spine. Living in poverty means recognizing that economic resources do exist in abundance, if largely somewhere else. Thus conditions of poverty suggest one usefully heuristic question that might begin to reveal a spine of capitalist common sense in the United States: "Where do resources come from?"

❀

Common sense tells you that what capitalism does for a living is produce more, and newer, and different, and interesting economic resources. That is, common sense introduces "capitalism" as its central term of explanation for where resources come from, not by conceptual definition but as if responding to a familiar opener in casual conversation: "So what do you do?" Capitalism is doing its job, the common sense line continues, wherever and whenever lots of different economic resources appear all over the place.

In the United States, Cold War color imagery, for example, didn't define "capitalism." What it contributed to a history of capitalist common sense were details of a complicated web of circumstances that distinguished the effects of what capitalism does for a living across a political boundary line. In contrast to capitalist countries, communist countries were invariably represented in gray. Weather, buildings, the faces of the Politburo, people's hopes for the future, cars, turnips, now-unmarked churches, the shrouds covering artwork from the past—all appeared in tonally uniform gray. Nostalgia for its golden days aside, the grayness of black-and-white TV was a technology wonderfully suited to propaganda for the Cold War. Capitalism couldn't possibly be making a living *there*, in those uniform, cold, gray spaces televisually glimpsed behind the gray Curtain of Iron. Without capitalism at work, there's never economically enough, nothing to multiply and differentiate resources, nothing of much interest to do.

In another register of color, Cold War imagery saw the Third World as a rainbow riot of exotic "native" customs and costumes, often enough on islands, backed by the bluest of seas. (No wonder "Africa" was so often made to seem a Third World anomaly.) The plot twist was that while capitalism of course didn't produce this luxuriance of colored intensities, fortunately it was alive and working *here*, since its job was to make all this available for the first time to "ordinary people," dreaming their dreamy little dreams of resource enrichment in vacation leisure time. With pictures. Kodak and Polaroid, after all, were already here, supplying endlessly improved new indices of proof.

"Americans vote with their pocketbooks" became an increasingly familiar slogan of those color-polarized Cold War times, articulating a domestic counterpart to the global political divisions of First, Second, and Third Worlds by way of a job description of capitalism's responsibilities. In global politics "capitalism" identified the capacity to yield multiple, proliferating economic resources, thereby establishing the largest difference between First World and Second World and determining the available choice of directions for the Third World. Domestically, in contrast, capitalism's productivity founded citizen voting powers in a political democracy on incrementally variable levels of economic resources—the size of the pocketbook with which you voted. In fact you voted not once, but twice with your pocketbook: first at the ballot box for political leaders whose programs would best secure rising prosperity, and again at the store for businesses whose products offered the best and most desirable material. Whereas the ballot box seemed to put everybody's pocketbook on an equal level, voting at the store was directly dependent on the size of your pocketbook. Thus for "democratic" purposes, the distinction between the two forms of voting had simultaneously to be maintained and denied.

The distinction was necessary to ensure a separation of voting mechanisms and venue. How and where you voted depended on whether the issue was who should be president of the country or what should be the salary for General Motors's CEO. Historically, the common sense articulated as capitalism's job description had to make the difference between such questions so blindingly obvious that it couldn't possibly occur to anyone to ask for a ballot referendum on CEO salaries, as it couldn't occur to anyone that there would not be a ballot on who should be president—or, for that matter, on a bond issue to determine the salaries of police or teachers as state employees. That people in communist countries actually did sometimes vote on the salaries of business leaders was a gray sign not only of the absence of capitalism, but of the absence of democracy.

At the same time, it was necessary to efface the distinction between the two forms of voting. Unequal pocketbooks at the store had finally to mean the same thing as equal pocketbooks at the ballot box. This equation between apparent incommensurables takes us back to the magic of the market, the place where capitalism goes to work each day to ensure the productivity of resources. Common sense insists that the "freedom" implied by voting be quite capable of breathing an atmosphere of either ballot box or store without missing a heartbeat. You vote twice with your pocketbook. Market as metasense functions as the continual translation ensuring equivalent freedom between both forms of voting.

Political democracy at the ballot box doesn't just happen, however; it's more than a matter of people routinely going about their business. Democracy is assumed to require a great deal of effort, intelligence, idealistic values, and the shouldering of civic responsibility—and risk, by a great many people. Cold War slogans invariably pointed this out in memorializing those who had died to preserve democratic freedom. Market theory typically has offered what seems in contrast a stunningly painless form of realized freedom. "By a natural process," contemporary commentator Norman Barry notes in explaining Adam Smith's classic conception of market freedom, "Smith meant what would occur, or which pattern of events would emerge, from individual interaction in the absence of some specific human intervention, either of a political kind or from violence. The behavior of the market is an obvious example of such natural phenomena. The self-regulating properties of the market system are not the product of a designing mind but are a spontaneous outcome of the price mechanism" (quoted in Jameson, 271). The result is a "natural liberty" by which "every man . . . is left perfectly free to pursue his own interest in his own way and bring both his industry and capital into competition with those of any other man." What happens to women isn't exactly clear.

In his analysis of concepts of "the market" in *Postmodernism, or The Cultural Logic of Late Capitalism*, Fredric Jameson quotes the passage above as showing not only how market concepts are "totalizing" social theories, but also how a specific contradiction exists in recent conservative theorizing. "But obviously you can't have it both ways," Jameson points out; "there is no such thing as a booming, functioning market whose customer personnel is staffed by Calvinists and hard-working traditionalists knowing the value of the dollar" (271). More generally, however, that contradiction has emerged in a number of different forms throughout the modern formation of a capitalist common sense, because "freedom's" environmental amphibianism imposes a necessity to address in some way the discrepancy between the effort/responsibility/risk of political democracy on the one hand, and on the other the unentailed birth from market soil of the economic agent "left perfectly free," in Barry's words. Making your freedom, at the risk of life even, and being "left free" seem two rather different things. In any case, it's far from obvious why, if you could simply be "left free" by the market, so many people would use their freedom to begin constructing a regulated, nonmarket social prison.

The commonsense resolution to the dilemma has been to recognize that for all its prodigious power to produce economic resources—its job skills, in effect—capitalism not only has to go to work somewhere, but is ultimately dependent on an employer—namely, of course, the political democracy wise enough to hire capitalism for the job. The market, in other words, may leave you free, but only citizens who know the value of political democracy can appreciate and benefit from what that market freedom is all about. Thus in addition to the endlessly reiterated complaints about "political interference" and "regulation" of the market that are so much a part of capitalist common sense, there is also a complicated commonsense discourse involving what might be understood initially as a *positive* political component of economic marketplace democracy. While politics must not "interfere" with the market, democratic decision making must include an education in still a third form of voting with your pocketbook.

This form of voting has always seemed the most counterintuitive aspect of capitalist common sense to anyone living in poverty, for common

sense educated you to vote for savings and investment rather than immediate consumption. The market may operate "naturally" and freely, as
Smith advised, but capitalism doesn't work there and produce endlessly
proliferating economic resources from it for nothing, any more than the
freedom of political democracy can be had for nothing. Market capitalism's productivity requires the positive, reproductive maintenance of specific working conditions in order for capitalism to accomplish its job.

The reproduction of French workers, Marx famously remarked, requires
wine; the reproduction of English workers in contrast requires beer. The
reproduction of capitalism's effort of work likewise requires something:
precisely, a preference on the part of each individual agent for savings and
investment. The distinction between preferences for wine or beer signaled
to Marx the presence of a "moral component" in this process of reproducing specific conditions of work. The preference for savings and investment
over immediate consumption seemed necessary to reproduce capitalism's
doing its work of proliferating economic resources, and it involved an embedded moral injunction on a much vaster scale than beer or wine preferences. Occasionally that injunction had been made quite clear, as in the
following parable from twenties financier John J. Raskob, quoted in Dixon
Wector's *The Age of the Great Depression*: "If a man saves $15 a week, and
invests in good common stocks, and allows the dividends and rights to ac-
cumulate, at the end of twenty years he will have at least $80,000 and an
income from investments of around $400 a month. He will be rich. And
because income can do that, I am firm in my belief that anyone not only
can be rich, but *ought* to be rich" (4; my emphasis). Make capitalism rich
by your moral preference for savings and investments, and it will make you
rich; you and capitalism properly belong within a moral copula.

Thus in fact you vote three times in three different ways in capitalist
common sense: by choosing your political leaders; by choosing what and
how much to buy; and by choosing how much to save and invest. The first
is a sign of political freedom; the second a sign of economic freedom; and
the third a moral sign signifying the reproduction of necessary conditions
for both political democracy and the economics of the market. It is the
third and moral form of voting that explains why the painlessness of being
"left free" by the market is not immediately and enthusiastically embraced
by everyone. What poor people, welfare cheats, government planners and
regulators, and sundry other groups all have in common is the fundamental
immorality of wanting something for nothing. Being left free by the market isn't enough. Such groups want the immense benefits promised by cap-

italist productivity, without disciplining themselves to the moral behavior imposed by savings and investment.

"Keynesianism" has remained an anathema to this moral logic as expressed in the conservative versions of capitalist common sense alluded to in Jameson's remark above, because Keynesian principles seem to violate the moral education necessary to correct third-time voting. Whatever technicalities are involved, Keynesianism after all seems not only a license to spend but an imperative to do so. It may be obvious that unless a lot of people spend a lot a capitalist market might well grind to a halt, but the sinister quality of Keynesianism from this moral perspective involves more than the recognition of some necessary spending. The problem is the apparent shift Keynes performed on the grounds of "who spends." Out of the blue, as it were, government emerges mysteriously as a big spender, as if a parasitic "public" government rather than a productive "private" market could be capitalism's proper place of employment. And like in Plato's chain, such immoral behavior at the top is reflected in always more disgusting ways throughout the social formation. On viewing the "high" tragedy of profligate spending by a government parasitic on capitalist productivity, "low" welfare parasites simply catch available images of color TVs, big cars, and unlimited cigarettes from the fallout.

One shouldn't expect any form of common sense to be completely coherent, and capitalist common sense is no exception. Despite such conservative moral critiques, Keynesianism infiltrated the discursive currents of capitalist common sense in the United States on the level of economic theory, because it allowed a certain understanding of the problems of macroregulation. On the level of everyday consumer practices, it redefined consumer expectations by making consumption of government services a plausible thought. Keynesianism thereby redirected economic choices away from voting with one's pocketbook for political leaders who could ensure business prosperity, and toward voting with one's pocketbook for political leaders who would guarantee those government services. The "mimesis" at work here is how Keynesian-inspired theorizing of macroregulation inevitably reflected the dilemmas that emerged with this shift of consumer expectations.

Disturbances spread, however, and features of Keynesianism, as they became a part of economic policy decisions, continued to disturb the parameters of common sense in often unexpected ways. Keynes had targeted the potential vagaries of "private" savings and investment decisions as the cause of underconsumption, and policies during the New Deal and the recovery from the Depression had foregrounded his recommendations of government spending on public works projects as a way out of the underconsumption trap. In the postwar period, however, so-called commercial Keynesianism was embraced as potentially the least intrusive and hence the best means of addressing the original "problem," the autonomy of savings and investment decisions. By using monetary policy—varying interest and tax rates, for example—the government in effect could educate private decision makers about the best choice in the circumstances to achieve the general public goal of stabilizing the fluctuations in aggregate demand that could result in the underconsumption trap. Raising interest rates would be an incentive to save and invest; lowering rates would ripple out into an encouragement of immediate consumption, and so on.

State services are typically understood to result in specific material benefits for their citizen-consumers in many direct or indirect ways. This emphasis on monetary policy, however, made a general form of economic education itself a primary government service, and consequently an indispensable economic resource in everyday practices. That is, one way you made sense of everyday decisions involving economic resources was by going to school with government, learning the lessons available through its determinations of monetary policy. Like almost any form of "higher" education, the schooling in monetary policy had both its admission standards— in this case not intelligence but possession of a big pocketbook for saving and investment—and an increasingly elaborate hierarchy of differentiation among its "student" population. In other words, Keynesianism in this form made government not only a primary player in a capitalist market system but, equally important, a primary source of differential economic resources linked directly to educationally acquired skills. Tellingly enough, while monetarists continued to oppose Keynesian-inspired government intervention in a "free market" with respect to the direct distribution of material benefits, they also insisted unequivocally on the right to benefit from economic resources that accrued through a good education from the government: they insisted on a strictly determined federal control over the money supply, for example. Thus, recently, Alan Greenspan's decisions have made him seem the great chancellor of government education in these terms, and Wall Street uniformly reacted to congressional suggestions of a detailed review of his leadership of the Fed as an "absurd" request.

I've ignored whole regions of crucially important economic practices in this quick survey of recent history, because for the moment I want to stick very closely to what seems to me the spine of capitalist common sense. In the essay quoted above, Jameson argues that in their strongest forms—his example is Gary Becker's *An Economic Approach to Human Behavior*—market models of capitalism reveal, "scandalously," that market capitalism is "in reality a production model!" (267). The "scandal" for Jameson results from how such market theorizing is so dismissive of analyses like Marx's that begin instead in the organization of production. What I've been implying about capitalist common sense here, however, is that, more exactly, it involves a *productivity* model. That is, the spine that holds together the multiple forms of capitalist common sense is a belief in the exemplary productivity of capitalism. Whether the "secret" of that productivity is assumed to lie in the wonders of the market or in the efficiency of production, capitalist common sense always affirms that wherever economic resources exist in abundance, there you will find capitalism at work.

A sort of "high" intellectual critique of capitalist productivity, focusing attention on the evils of commodification that resulted from assuming productivity itself as a good thing, has rarely made much headway among people living in poverty. The perfectly sound reason is that it seems to translate in practice into an altogether mystifying and counterintuitive requirement to distinguish between "good" economic resources and "bad" (because commodified) resources. In practice it seems to be just another moral injunction, like the imperative to save and invest: consume only good stuff, not those nasty commodities. The visible spine of capitalist common sense has offered in contrast a compelling line of connection: abundant economic resources are nice to have, and productivity of resources is what capitalism is all about. Keynesianism spinal-tapped away, as it were, some of the accumulating moral fluid of "save and invest" from capitalist common sense, thereby restoring a wider potential of motion, and introduced the State as a kind of "second brain" in capitalism's tail to make sure the whole bulk could continue its steady momentum of productivity. Not surprisingly, Keynesianism attracted all kinds of moral criticism from conservative monetarists on one side, anxious to circumscribe that second brain's neural field strictly to monetary policy, and political criticism from radical critics on the other, quick to point out that in reality the state welfare capitalism Keynesianism introduced was just an under-the-table payoff to shut up and keep working.

Yet Marx himself had never denied that capitalism not only yielded immense economic resources, but also made it possible in principle for more people to have more resources. However, it seems to be a system that works only by exploiting the labor of a great many and concentrating abundant resources in the hands of a few. And Marx of course wasn't alone in that perception; capitalist common sense has always had to find ways of negotiating this objection's force in whatever terms it appeared. As I've implied indirectly by focusing first on Cold War imagery, however, the spine I've been tracing becomes more visible and insistent only at the point historically when it became possible for such countercapitalist perceptions to coalesce around "communism" as a potentially realizable and *progressive* alternative to capitalist productivity. It's in response to that potential, when alternatives to capitalism no longer could be uniformly cast as "backward" remnants of precapitalist formations, that it seemed so critical to emphasize productivity of economic resources as a good thing in and of itself and not merely a happy adjunct to capitalism's focus on the individual, its civilizing moral powers, or the rewards it makes available for individual initiative or innovation or whatever.

It was the world-historical appearance of communist countries more than anything else that made capitalist common sense take an insistently *economic* form, drawn down a line whose bone structure articulated a model of economic productivity. *Capital* in this register of meaning at least can be read as an attempt to show how capitalist common sense already depended, if in largely unacknowledged ways, on an economic form. And all the criticism that has been directed at the predictive power of Marx's specific economic analysis in *Capital* doesn't diminish what seems to me his altogether accurate anticipation of what would happen to capitalist common sense if ever communism was perceived as a realized possibility.

Keynesian policies are again of particular interest here, understood less as a sort of "payoff" of economic resources to maintain social equilibrium in the face of a communist alternative, however, than as a refocusing of sense-making attention away from resources as working practices and toward resources as buying practices—which is not quite the same as a shift from "production" to "consumption." What's involved is a shift that locates capitalist productivity first in the process of *constructing* the market rather than in the process of producing goods that can be brought to market. As if for the first time, the market appeared through a Keynesian lens as, precisely, something that must be constructed through specific relations among buying practices. The technical vocabulary surrounding "underconsumption" floated with it this immensely disorienting perception not only of market precariousness, but of a capitalist productivity whose primary job responsibility is the construction of the market. With the diminishment of Cold War intensities and the "collapse" of communism, the shift associated with Keynesian policies then also yields a way for capitalist common sense to respond in new terms to a Marxian critique of labor exploitation and concentration of resources at the top. I want to look briefly to this response as a key characteristic of "late" or "multinational" capitalist common sense.

❀

Once capitalist resource productivity comes to be understood as dependent on the work of constructing the market, the functionally crucial "working class" of a capitalist economy could no longer unequivocally be imaged in commonsense terms as the industrial production worker manufacturing durable goods—who might then be seen alternatively as exploited, alienated from the results of the labor, even her or his own labor power itself just another commodity, and so on. Whatever happens to workers in production, good or bad, depends on the work of constructing a field of market relations that can ensure rising productivity. The key to those market relations is the consumer. Consumers of course buy things, as they always have. But what's at stake in constructing the market is less consumer purchasing power, as registered in aggregate demand levels, than the intricacies of consumer buying practices as they construct, elaborate, and refine the potential field of market relations. Consuming is ultimately *marketwork*, the process of constructing the market. Consumers can then come into focus as in effect the primary "working class" of a capitalist economy.

It's necessary to distinguish this emergent commonsense picture I'm suggesting of consumer "workers" from two familiar left characterizations of late or multinational capitalism. The first is given symptomatic expression by Laclau and Mouffe in the passage from *Hegemony and Socialist Strategy* I alluded to earlier, with its imagery of capitalism implacably expanding beyond the economic into every space of everyday life:

> This penetration of capitalist relations of production, initiated at the beginning of the century and stepped up from the 1940s on, was to transform society into a vast market in which new "needs" were ceaselessly created, and in which more and more of the products of human labour were turned into commodities. This "commodification" of social life destroyed previous social relations, replacing them with commodity relations through which the logic of capitalist accumulation penetrated into increasingly numerous spheres. Today it is not only as a seller of labour-power that the individual is subordinated to capital, but also through his or her incorporation into a multitude of other social relations: culture, free time, illness, education, sex and even death. There is practically no domain of individual or collective life which escapes capitalist relations. (160–61)

The second familiar characterization derives from analysis, influenced by the Frankfurt School, of "the culture industry," and emphasizes the ostensible "choices" of always proliferating goods and services available to consumers as an illusion. In reality, you get to choose only from within a field of choice determined elsewhere. This direction of analysis thus rejoins the imagery of a capitalist "penetration" of the social field in Laclau and Mouffe's argument at the level of the commodity: every social relation is reduced to a commodity form determined by an omnipresent capitalist market exchange. As Jameson will often argue from a position at the intersection of these directions, there no longer seems anything left for capitalist economics to absorb. Even "nature" and "the unconscious" have been subsumed into the commodity web of capitalist enterprise.

What these arguments ignore, in their imagery of an implacable, "colonizing" economic expansiveness, is the conceptual rift within capitalist common sense occasioned by the perception of some foundational precariousness to the existence of the market. That perception is a different matter altogether than, for example, monetarist worries about the destabilizing effects of political "interference" with the market. Keynesian thinking had introduced the possibility that the market might not only admit but require active effort to sustain its equilibrium, and as I've suggested, recent forms of capitalist common sense extend that possibility into a recognition that, far from being a "natural process," the market itself must be constructed. The market doesn't naturally exist, in ways that can be relentlessly extended to other ensembles of social relationships, ultimately colonizing nature and the unconscious and everything else. It's only because the very existence of the market is always and everywhere up for grabs at any given moment that the possible conditions, for its emergence or failure to emerge, can appear absolutely anywhere in the totality of the social field. Thus the primary condition of possibility for the market is not the "commodification of social life," which assumes an existent market where commodification takes place, but the work of consumers who construct the market.

Likewise, then, the choices made by consumers must be understood in different terms than either the epistemological grid imposed by Frankfurt-style analysis—which turns on the question of whether consumer choices are "real" or "illusory"—or the imagery of a blank "mass" consumption passivity whose informing Frankfurt-School values Jean Baudrillard cheerfully inverts and celebrates. As Pierre Bourdieu recognizes in *Distinction*, the very process of consumer choice is work; "the consumption of goods," he argues, "no doubt always presupposes a labour of appropriation, to different degrees depending on the goods and the consumers, or, more precisely, that the consumer helps to produce the product he consumes, by a labour of identification and decoding which, in the case of a work of art, may constitute the whole of the consumption and gratification, and which requires time and dispositions acquired over time" (100). Consumer choice in this sense isn't simply a matter of arriving at alternatives and picking among them; like any form of work it requires time and effort, and it results in the construction of something.

Bourdieu's attention, however, is focused on the relation of consumers and goods, where the work becomes "a labour of appropriation . . . of identification and decoding." Without at all denying that such labor is part of consumer work, choices also involve the construction of market relations. As Marx endlessly reminds us, commodities are bearers of social relations as well as vehicles of identity. Choices are thus the matrix of work within which consumers configure forms of social relations as also, "ideally," market resources. This isn't a matter of commodities, but of the very field of the market as the location of capitalist productivity. That is, commodity relations don't "penetrate" and reconfigure previously existing social relations, as Laclau and Mouffe argue. Social relations in any form emerge through the work of consumer choice, and must be figured as market resources in order that commodities can continue to appear on the market at all. Or, in a current corporate vocabulary, social relations appear first as "human capital," simultaneously the sustaining force of market construction and the elementary dynamics of political democracy.

In Marx's analysis, exploitation involves the appropriation of surplus labor by someone other than the laborer. Consumers, however, can be assumed to work for themselves, not for a capitalist "owner." Whatever "appropriation" may go on, as Bourdieu remarks, becomes a labor "of identification and decoding" on the part of the consumer-worker, for the consumer-worker. Thus what's magical about the market in these terms is that the more consumers work for themselves in their increasingly elaborated practices of choosing and of identity formation, the more they can also do the marketwork necessary to construct and elaborate the social field of the market. The magic, in other words, doesn't lie *in* the market as an already existent "natural process" whose immanent "laws" automatically restore systemic equilibrium if people just naturally follow their interests. Rather, it involves the coincident symmetry between the complicated cultural efforts of working for yourself as consumer and constructing the market as consumer. No natural law determines the quality of work, guarantees the symmetry of effect, or automatically prevents the possibility of that symmetry going askew at any point. But correlatively, it's a symmetry that can be made to seem as if it requires neither exploitation of primary labor nor manipulation of consumer "desires" and "needs."

Corporate business practices play their role by creating new goods and services, ensuring that consumers have something to work on. Whether differences among goods and services are illusory or real, or whether by some labyrinthine ideological conspiracy you could impose normative boundaries on the range of goods and services available for choices, is a matter of indifference. What counts is that consumers work for themselves in ways that also shape the construction of the market. Thus as corporate motivational guru Tom Peters explains to would-be entrepreneurs, you must learn to ask yourself the really crucial question about anything you want to sell. This is not whether it creates a need or whether it falls safely within the parameters of the ideologically familiar; the question is rather "Is it weird enough?" (quoted in Newfield, "Corporate Pleasures," 41). Have you offered consumers a new occasion for innovative work that will in turn expand the field of market relations?

Of course for a great many people it's impossible to buy a lot, and hence engage in the marketwork of consumption, unless you have a job that pays you some money. The centrality of the work of market construction, however, assigns your "occupational" job, as it were, to the status of secondary rather than primary labor. Whatever you might do as an industrial laborer or in any other occupation is only a prologue to your real work, which begins when the "workday" ends. The primary conditions of capitalist productivity involve the labor of constructing the market; what you do "on the job," in your occupation, is simply part of reproducing the conditions of market productivity. As I will argue in Chapter 3, exploitation has by no means disappeared, but productivity as located in the market, and economic resources as figured in "human capital," require different ways of understanding exploitation. The more immediate point, however, involves the way consumer primary labor as market construction has begun to alter the moral economy of capitalist common sense in the United States.

Keynes's conception of an underconsumption trap targeted the private autonomy of savings and investment decisions as the random variable threatening the equilibrium of production capacity and aggregate demand. Thus Keynesian policies ran headlong into the imperative that had elevated savings to a sign of moral behavior and responsibility for economic resources. They violated a doubly segregated moral economy that had strictly divided work from responsibility, and responsibility in turn from pleasure. Crudely, you knew you were acting responsibly with the economic resources you had worked for if you felt the bite of denying yourself the immediate pleasures of consumption in order to save and invest.

In contrast to this morality, an emphasis on consumer practices offers a way to connect rather than to divide work, responsibility, and pleasure. Consumer practices may involve the work of market construction, but consumption also affords continually refined forms of pleasure. Far from being a temptation to irresponsibility, pleasure begins to appear in commonsense terms as simultaneously a sign of work getting done and responsibility shouldered. Pleasure isn't a violation of existent market laws; it yields an affective cement to hold together the coincident symmetry of working for yourself as consumer and working to construct the market. The familiar "greed is good" ethos inspired by Reaganism marked simply the first realization of how to take advantage of the changing moral dynamics of capitalist common sense. Likewise, Christopher Lasch's counter-perception of a "culture of narcissism" marked a nostalgia for an older and segregated morality, when work meant "real work" uncontaminated by any narcissistic pleasures of consumer self-identification. That initial rush has by now begun to modulate into far more refined indices of pleasure. So-called voluntary simplicity (and indeed some part of the affective intensities of "family values") is only the latest version of refinement, one that would eschew continuing to buy lots more stuff, however, only because more subtle pleasures require more complexly differentiated working practices as consumers. The driving force remains the identification of economic resources with consumer pleasures.

What generations of reformers had imaged as the immorality of an economic system that denied resources to a great many people could then be transposed in commonsense terms into a fundamentally different perception of immorality. An economic system would appear immoral only insofar as citizen-consumers were denied their appropriate pleasures for simultaneously engaging in the necessary, responsible work of market construction. Thus what Marxian thinking would understand as the exploitation of workers could be displaced to a "problem" existing for the most part only in so-called underdeveloped countries, and in the remnants of the Second World, whose citizens haven't yet learned "the American way," that is, the recognition that the market as the location of capitalist productivity is the only game in town.

It's worth stressing again that the process I'm describing represents a mutation (if, as I will argue in subsequent chapters, a conflicted one) of capitalist common sense and not a continued, implacable expansion of a capitalist economy. In commonsense terms the market as a constructed field of social relations is very different from the market as a "natural process," just as the location of capitalist productivity in the market differs from an image of the market as metasense, the arbiter of the value of economic resources. Whatever might best characterize the operations of a late or multinational capitalism must involve some recognition of how those operations negotiate the historical weight and densities of a changing formation of capitalist common sense.

My sense of the spine of capitalist common sense suggests that across these conflicted mutational shifts, the trajectory of connection is evidence of an assumption that multiple, proliferating forms of economic resources are what capitalism is all about. Where there are economic resources in abundance, there too you will find capitalism at work. What exactly this capitalism is, where it does its work, what it requires to work at peak efficiency, who should benefit, who is exploited, what is primary and what secondary labor, what is morally responsible and what irresponsible economic behavior—all these are questions to which capitalist common sense has given answers obviously and dramatically different. In one way or another, however, the answers have been articulated into motion by that flexibly shifting backbone that equates productivity of economic resources with capitalism.

Poverty is indeed a "constant physical and material oppression." But it does teach you to know better than that.

❋

There were good reasons for Marx's own insistence on the progressive capacity of capitalism to produce abundant economic resources. He knew all too well that predicating social change on conceptions that looked nostalgically to a precapitalist past for models of the future meant that the one thing that certainly wouldn't change was the position of remarkable privilege able to afford the luxury of such nostalgia. Nevertheless, for Marx as well as the economists he challenged, "precapitalist" and "capitalist" signified globally inflected temporalities, so that almost invariably the geography of Europe was conflated in his thinking with the global temporality of capitalism. As always, the "center" of "Eurocentrism" involves a consequent sleight-of-hand linking categories of time and space; colonialist mapping was everywhere an imperial temporality as well.

Current perceptions of an international capitalism, in contrast, imply that whatever its historical origins may have been in European economies and European colonialization, capitalism is now a global field. It assumes a great many different and often indigenous forms in "non-European" countries. Perceptions of internationalization have thus disturbed a familiar commonsense equation in the United States that had identified American *political* preeminence globally with the domestic history of an essential core of capitalist innovation and productivity distinguishing the United States from other countries. Unencumbered by the feudal past that had complicated and retarded the growth of capitalism in Europe, the United States had been free to develop the full potential of capitalist productivity. Yet with its new and often bewilderingly diverse temporalities of development, internationalization suddenly makes this domestic history reappear as an open question rather than a secure teleology of realization. While explicitly oriented to the future and the exigencies of economic planning for the twenty-first century, the theorizing of economic change that will occupy my attention in Chapter 1 nevertheless begins in an interrogation of the past, in the midst of a commonsense dilemma.

On the one hand, the collapse of communism "proves" there was indeed something radically wrong with the communist claim that something was wrong with capitalism. Rather than "buried," consigned at last to the dustbin of history, in the wake of the events of the last five years capitalism seems more obviously than ever the wave of the future; newspapers and television can hardly keep up with the scorecard of "free market" reforms occurring in country after country. On the other hand, however, all isn't quite right. Not only do communists seem to be returning to power in "liberated" economies, but the position of the United States itself looks precarious. If the United States *is* capitalism, then why is it "we" don't do better in the international market? Why is the national debt so large, the balance of trade so skewed, competition from abroad so intense, with unforeseen "tigers" appearing everywhere and jobs disappearing into other countries?

The tried and true conservative answer is of course "political interference" with the market, which suggests that nothing is wrong with capitalism that couldn't be fixed quickly if proponents of welfare-state thinking would stop living in the past. Unlike conservative politicians, able to afford this luxury of simply pointing fingers elsewhere, corporation executives of necessity learned to look inward as well, not only to corporate structure and organization, but more fundamentally to assumptions about corporate productivity and to the work of economists questioning those assumptions. I will argue in Chapter 1 that the history of capitalism in the United States thus has begun to appear in corporate eyes as something very different from the massive, uncomplicated progress of industrial modernization. Positive change isn't assumed to come from a return to precapitalist modes, but it does seem possible to rethink *capitalist* history itself in new and postmodern registers available through models like Piore and Sabel's influential concept of flexible specialization in *The Second Industrial Divide*.

Internationalization, however, creates political trouble as well as economic trouble for capitalist common sense, and again the effect is a double one. Robert Reich's redesigning of categories of labor and workers in *The Work of Nations*, relative to the organization of a global economy, recognizes a powerful relation between economic internationalization and internal political divisions. While population groups in the United States supplying what he calls "routine production services" and "in-person services" have a deep political investment in a national economy, those supplying "symbolic analyst services," the primary operators of global capital, see themselves first in the cosmopolitan role of international citizens. The result, he argues, has been a gradual secession from the nation by those citizens who are the most productive in a new global economy. For Reich, this challenge will require a new vision of national identity.

At the same time, however, a new conservative response has mobilized a domestic challenge to Reich's vision of an ethical renewal of "nation," and has thus begun to reorganize the dynamics of a Reaganite coalition of the right. The familiar racist symbolic embedded in a Reaganite "social issues" agenda is simultaneously mapped onto the economic practices of multinational corporations. As a result, economic internationalization and the assertion of national public policy directions such as those Reich offers are linked together as part of the same dangerous politics. This politics poses an even more frightening and insidious menace to the nation than the "Evil Empire" of the old Soviet Union.

Across these political disturbances in the range of commonsense assumptions, what's at stake economically remains a fundamental commonsense equation of capitalism with productivity of resources. With the "collapse" of communism, that is, the question of "whose capitalism? for whom?" thus emerges with renewed intensity as a primary political issue.

In Chapter 2, however, I want to rethink these conflicting narratives of economic change and internationalization otherwise than through the lens of that commonsense equation. Beginning with the distinction Masao Miyoshi draws between multinational and transnational corporations, I will argue that an emergent transnational organization of capital exists at an abstracting *remove* from the specific conditions of the production, marketing, and circulation of economic resources. Transnational capital is a political organization through and through. The international division of labor it produces is a division between labor engaged in economic practices, and a second-order symbolics of labor engaged instead in producing the political mobilities of capital worldwide. The multiplicity of markets (which I will address later, in Chapter 4), like the many distinct forms of economic production worldwide, exist in those multiple forms because transnational capital as a political organization is no longer directly engaged (as is multinationalism) in a totalizing organization of the economic. It is instead a political creation of diverse territories as economic colonies under the rule of transnational capital politics. The picture I show in Chapter 2 is then less a postcolonial world than a mutation of colonialism driven by the *separation* of politics from economic productivity.

In these circumstances even Marx's own carefully nuanced perception of a "progressive" capitalism becomes a disabling insight. It yields a hermeneutic of economic practices that makes nonsense of a whole range of potentially pertinent questions about domestic economies both in the United States and in "developing" countries. For anything you see by means of this Marxian hermeneutic that doesn't look like part of a historical development through a distinctively capitalist economics will appear as a now-"residual" pocket of a still surviving economic organization from the past. The meaning of such practices can only emerge across the backward glance that reminds you such circumstances used to be quite common, but are now rapidly vanishing. It's this hermeneutic that lends itself to that now familiar image of a completely successful global totalization of capital, eradicating the last remaining vestiges of precapitalist formations.

The implied temporality of this sense-making hermeneutic of global capitalism ignores the possibility of reading meanings from the adjacency of practices in a present configuration of social relations. Perhaps more important, it ignores the inventiveness of what I will call countercolonial economic practices that respond to specific, present forms of exclusion from a capitalist politics of transnationalism. Thus while a Marxian hermeneutic might let you see well enough the economic devastation visited on "developing" countries by the internationalization of capital, its imagery of victimhood would make it very difficult to recognize how not only the populations in "developing" nations but any number of groups in "developed" countries have of necessity constructed *new* and alternative economies that enable them to survive the colonizing political order of transnational capital.

Countercolonial economics is about survival, but also about leveraging economic practices into political powers. Poverty teaches you better than to think economic resources come from capitalist productivity; it breaks the linkages of capitalist common sense. Countercolonial economics adds the recognition that to the extent the politics of transnational capital depend on the productivity of economic colonies, then the multiplicities of economic conditions of production, marketing, and circulation in the colonies created by transnational capital become crucial resources with which to challenge transnational politics.

Marxist attention to economics and economic agents has always foregrounded an analysis of capitalist exploitation. In contrast to the "post-Marxism" of Laclau and Mouffe and others, it seems to me even more important to preserve that emphasis in circumstances where exploitation takes the form of transnational capitalist political practices visited on the economics of colonies. As figured politically, however, exploitation appears in multiple and shifting configurations of direction as well as in the unidirectional extortion of surplus labor at the workplace. Race and gender divisions, for example, can't be understood as economically exogenous social indices conveniently preserved from the past in order to yield a pool of exploited labor in the present. Within the terms of corporate "multiculturalism" and "diversity," the process by which such divisions are now being constituted and reconstituted will itself be a constitutive feature of exploitative social relations.

In Chapter 3, I will locate my analysis of new forms of exploitation at the conjunction of what seem to me two crucial components of a late capitalist common sense: a culture of conspiracy theorizing and an economy of information. "Conspiracy" has become the privileged epistemological instrument to read the process of information flow and circulation, and to project a vision of human capital agency at stake in controlling that process of circulation. In addition to the unidirectional extortion of surplus labor at the workplace, then, exploitation also functions multidirectionally, across the diversity of consumer practices. Those subject positions constructed and occupied by people engaged in the work of consumption are replaced by bodies as informational, yielding the accumulation of human capital for the agent of replacement. Thus exploitation as replacement is always situational, and the process of replacement can always be reinvented over and over through the epistemology of conspiracy stories.

Conditions of poverty, however, like a number of other conditions, are also a reminder that conspiracy can be made to tell a very different story. Conspiracy theorizing in these registers is pedagogical, not epistemological; the story it has to tell is the education of an agent capable of resisting replacement. Political agency in this sense doesn't then emerge as a subject position *in* the field, a position occupied in common with others, or as "equivalent to" the positions of other victims of exploitation in the kind of "democratic imaginary" projected by Laclau and Mouffe. In a pedagogical version of conspiracy theorizing, agency and position are not identical.

For Marx, the political "answer" to the capitalist economic exploitation he analyzed is generated from a class consciousness of union. That is, the political agency of unified class consciousness answers to the conditions of an exploited mass labor force imposed by capitalism. But the circumstances of human capital political exploitation, with their always shifting identifications of victims to be exploited, supply no comparable ground for unification. Pedagogies of conspiracy theorizing must first imagine the formation of a political agency against the capitalization of subjects as informational bodies on which human capital formation depends. Thus rather than the linkage of subjects in the consciousness of class unity, agency exists to preserve the irreplaceability of multiple subject positions. Conspiracy theorizing is the pedagogy of agent formation from within the complex of subject positions caught up in the practices of countercolonial economics.

A great many versions of left politics have long taught us that commodities are bad shit, and the "free market" nothing but an immense economic septic field leaching them into the rest of us. But "the market" targeted in this way by critique no longer functions even as an ideal descriptive metaphor of how markets ought to behave. Rather than an admitted idealization of what in actuality must be understood as a diverse, "mixed" economic field, the discourse of "the market" has begun instead to accomplish a metonymic condensation of field slippage. That is, metonymically, the politics of transnational capital appears as if it were simply the global expansion of marketplace economics. The double result is that the dependence of transnational capital on the economic productivity of the colonies disappears from view, while simultaneously the colonizing powers of transnational capital appear instead as if they were failures on the part of large groups of the population to adapt to the new and intensely competitive circumstances of a globalized economic market. As a metonymic field slippage, "the market" is about making actual economic practices invisible in commonsense terms.

Markets in contrast are complex ensembles of economic, political, and cultural practices, neither self-regulating entities nor alien impositions that frustrate the pleasures of commodity consumption. No market is a purely local ensemble, uncontaminated by the realities of global politics that drive the field metonymy of "the market." But markets nevertheless organize much of daily life for transnational colonized populations. They exist in multiple, often strikingly diverse forms, and they exist in the midst of the most highly "developed" nations no less than in the no-longer-remote enclaves of what used to seem a "third" world. Thus the point is not simply to pursue a deconstruction of economic fictions of "the market" that emphasizes—like Piore and Sabel, for example—the multiplicity and diversity of market organizations. Markets are the pedagogical home for the formation of political agency within the practices of countercolonial economics.

In Chapter 4, I've chosen to look at two different "home" markets at home in the social formation in the United States. I want to see across the trading in what are after all familiar commodity forms: literary scholarship and show dogs. My deliberately incongruous pairing of such specific and "atypical" commodity markets, if perhaps melodramatic, nevertheless serves well enough to emphasize the diversity among actual markets and market organizations. At the same time, often disturbing parallels between these disparate markets help make possible a recognition of the effects of market political discourse on both the organization of markets and the behaviors of marketplace agents. Likewise, the incongruity of thinking of both literary scholars and dog breeders and exhibitors as "professionals" serves not only to enlarge and differentiate "professional" as a category of social positioning, but also to reexamine how professionalization functions in narratives of political incorporation at the colonial borderlands of market economics and transnational capital politics.

Thus the identification of markets as "professional" homes both returns to and resituates the dilemmas of cultural studies politics with which I began. Cultural studies may well have become an institutional, (inter)disciplinary field of academic studies, but in my fifth and concluding chapter I want to look at cultural studies as also a market organization that in its economies of exchange everywhere borders on transnational capital politics. Issues of cross-cultural study, with its potentially colonizing absorption of "others," reemerge in the context of the ensemble of conditions linking academic practices and corporate "multiculturalism" and "diversity." Narratives of "opposition" and "co-optation" reemerge across the social positioning of humanities academics as managers in a university market of "human resources." Relations of institutional "centrality" and "marginalization" reemerge within the complex of demographics and selection practices as political technologies of colonialization.

A kind of cultural studies common sense that relegates economics to an external reality appearing everywhere as a globally imposed threat can offer little by way of political challenge to a capitalist common sense that continues to live the everyday equation of capitalism and economic productivity, even in the midst of now-devastating conflicts of direction whose effects have impoverished so many worldwide. In these circumstances to see cultural studies as itself a market organization and an ensemble of marketwork keeps it at the border of politics that matter, to be aligned wherever and whenever possible with the formations of political agency in the practices of countercolonial economics. Cultural studies politics might participate effectively in an economic reeducation of the university, directed not toward the corporate changes and "internationalization" of capital, but at the diverse economic practices that exist throughout the colonies of transnational capital.

ONE

Dinosaur Scale: Economic Narratives
of Postmodern Culture

Jurassic Park and its much publicized sequel are conveniently recent reminders of what a curious status dinosaurs have. In most traditional versions of an evolutionary narrative they have been the very emblem of failure, the most dramatic instance of inability to "adapt." Yet the failure is a specific kind of failure. Evolutionary history after all affords countless examples of life forms that proved unable to survive into different circumstances. Dinosaurs are special because of their size, which has also allowed them a prominent role in a modern imagery of monsters. Monsters are aberrant, and they project the potential for a recurrent aberrance, as it were, notoriously exploited by sequel after sequel in monster films. Dinosaurs as monsters, however, surround simple recurrence with the intensities made possible by playing recurrence against the linearity of the evolutionary narrative's insistence that once gone is gone forever. As *Jurassic Park* realizes, dinosaurs are thus doubly aberrant monsters. Their size signifies both materially and conceptually. Although perhaps still fanciful by scientific standards, the DNA plot mechanism of *Jurassic Park* faithfully follows out the logic of this doubleness by linking a material, genetic revival with the psychoanalytic story of a return of the repressed. Size has a crucial role in the linkage, as the barely visible in either case fills the screen with its immensity once released.

Social Darwinism involved a particular grafting of ideas of evolutionary progress onto "free market" economics, but the common matrix necessary for its emergence was the concept of "selection" in both strands of the grafting as a dynamic, ongoing process rather than the confirmation of an already existent, stable, hierarchical order. Like the shifting circumstances of a "natural" environment, marketplace competition was thus seen to re-

ward a capacity for often rapid adaptations and, in parallel fashion, to pe-
nalize a reliance on cultural inflexibility. While unequivocal versions of social Darwinism may have been short lived, the importance of competitive
selection and its dynamics in economic theory continued to be haunted by
this earlier grafting with accounts of natural selection.

Monopolies may have commanded the economic landscape, but even at
the apex of visible success their sheer size always contained a cautionary
tale, an echo of the fate of the dinosaur. The recent imagery of the difficulties of the Wang Corporation, for example—as having fed its immense
bulk on mainframe sales and consequently having been unable to compete
successfully in the new, quickened tide of fast-moving miniaturization—
is only a continuation of a story told many times. It's then hardly surprising
that optimistic economic accounts of how the present differs from the immediate industrial past eventually get around to size. Like the image of a
post-catastrophe world where the "little mammals" were freed from dinosaur dictatorships, the postmodern economic landscape will feature
smaller things, but there will be many more of them around than there
used to be, and they will be a lot more interesting.

Jurassic Park is not immediately an economic story. Nevertheless, the in-
terior narrative is set in motion by the plot dynamic of making money off a
theme park, and the film was surrounded by an elaborate merchandising
campaign involving a great many sectors of market potential. It was constructed to be, in Hollywood language, a "blockbuster"—or, in another
register, a dinosaur, a gamble on the return of Hollywood spectacle genetically updated for the present. Thus it both plays on and embodies the multiple status of the dinosaur as simultaneously an emblem of evolutionary
failure; a monstrous, threatening figure of "return" at home in both genetic
and psychoanalytic narratives; and an ambiguous sign of an economic pedagogy at work, since both marketplace control and marketplace obsolescence are disturbingly marked by the same immensities of size, the same
uniform gray skin. Yet in its use of dinosaur figures, the film can also function as a postmodern reminder that evolution, genetics, psychoanalysis, and
economic history all involve large master narratives of change.

In so many otherwise conflicting accounts, what identifies the "break"
between these modern master narratives and postmodernism is, precisely,
the breakup of size: the mass production of standardized goods gives way to
flexibly specialized production of high-value niche goods; the monopoly to
an endlessly shifting flux of merger activity and takeovers; the durable
commodity to the rapid flow of invisible, protean information; the urban

core to shopping malls; "totalizing" master narratives to pastiche and simulation; the molar to the molecular; the starkness of globally polarized class conflict to the proliferation of "new," often locally specific, social movements; "First World," "Second World," and "Third World" blocs to a patchwork fluidity of shifting cores and peripheries; monoculturalism to diversity; and of course the "Evil Empire" to a conglomerate of warring republics and ethnicities. The list goes on and on, since set against the immense figures of return striding threateningly across the screen in *Jurassic Park*—whose first target, not coincidentally, is an African American worker, perhaps the most typical film icon of a "new," "diverse" social world—all these multiple, conflicting accounts of postmodern multiplicity begin to blur together anyway.

I mean to suggest something simpler, however, than a reading of *Jurassic Park* as driven by fantasies of destroying a new social diversity and returning to the stable, patriarchal culture of the past. Doubtless it should be read that way, as its penultimate images of family snuggling around scientist-turned-father suggest. But I'm not really interested here in trying to read out all the intricacies of the film. I want to use it instead as a kind of symptomatic monitor, where the size represented in and by *Jurassic Park* can figure a nightmare conjured into existence by the thematics of postmodern "downsizing" in all its different forms. That is, for whatever hopes may be expressed through these accounts—and there are of course conservative as well as radical versions of the postmodern—size functions in common as a shared terror. The specific meanings of *Jurassic Park* may then assume a determinate conservative shape making use of size. But its imagery of size might equally well describe the familiar numb recognition that beyond the many locally informed sites of resistance celebrated in left politics, the linkages of some immense penumbric Power are always fatally at work. The threatening affect of size floats beyond the film, and continues to produce disturbances in the exchange rates of postmodern currencies of change.

Economics, however, is a relative latecomer to the many vocabularies of postmodern discourse in the United States. The officially designated historical continuity of "capitalism" as just economic common sense in the United States imposes an obligation to retrieve an origin somewhere in Adam Smith in order to enter "the true" and pronounce with authority on contemporary matters. Thus economics in this peculiar discursive context also affords perhaps the clearest example of having to deal directly, linearly, with a history of size. What in other sectors can often seem both a dramatic break with and a repudiation of the totalizing ambitions of modernist size, economically must be understood in some other way. As economic discourse begins, finally, to acquire something like a recognizably postmodern accent in the United States, it does so in terms that must nevertheless preserve a narrative continuity with an immediate past marked by nothing more obvious than the sheer size of economic institutions, from the manufacturing plant and its work force to corporate organization and the State itself. As a result, size has to be figured as benign, "normal," even necessary, while at the same time something to be superseded, a now obsolete relic in the present. I will give a certain precedence to economic discourse in what follows, not in accordance with an economic determinism, but largely because of the way its *cultural* latecomer status can bring into clearer focus the complex of effects monitored through the symptomatic lens of *Jurassic Park*.

Even in emphasizing economic narratives in this way, I am departing from a complex of political directions whose point of origin might conveniently be summed up in Laclau and Mouffe's phrase from *Hegemony and Socialist Strategy* characterizing economics as "the last redoubt of essentialism" on the left. Laclau and Mouffe's critique shares the general force of other familiar attacks on essentialism, but it also points specifically to the hermeneutic inadequacy of economic accounts of any sort to understanding oppositional politics as well as the ruling complex of dominant interests. As Michèle Barrett shrewdly points out in her reading of *Hegemony and Socialist Strategy*, one result of this refocusing of attention away from economics is that when Laclau and Mouffe do eventually get around to talking directly about contemporary economic conditions, "what is interesting about their constitution of 'capitalism' is that it remains an elemental and undefined agent in the argument" (75–76), as if you can't really talk about economics without first reinventing the dinosaur. In the passage Barrett refers to (*Hegemony*, 160–61), "capitalism" looks like nothing so much as a malevolent *Tyrannosaurus rex* swallowing up the globe.

In the next two sections, I want to construct an argument based on the premise that the politics of socialist "strategy" in Laclau and Mouffe can be translated into the terms of an economic narrative. This narrative has a remarkable congruity with certain already existing narratives of economic change, in particular Piore and Sabel's influential account of flexible specialization in *The Second Industrial Divide*, whose languages and concepts have become such an important part of corporate understanding in the decade since the book was published. Their argument is a complex instance of the dilemmas of a postmodern economics in the United States. They must negotiate a path between familiar challenges to totalizing narratives and foundational assumptions on the one hand, and on the other the imperatives to preserve a vision of continuity that can link the capitalism of the past, despite its size, to possibilities for the future. In this context, my *Jurassic Park* lens yields a way of understanding flexible specialization as something like a genetics of economic history, whose concluding figure of "yeoman democracy" invents as if for the first time the open political promise of a still-nascent capitalism.

For Piore and Sabel it is the persistence and revitalization of different forms of craft production that lead to the dissolution of industrial size and the deconstruction of a mass production paradigm of industrial modernization. For Laclau and Mouffe it is the emergence of "new" multiple social movements understood as a politics of radical democracy that marks an end to the mass movement, class-based collective politics of the industrial past. Radical democracy, like flexible specialization, is a reinvention, a retrieval of often forgotten elements of prisoned genetic material whose discursive matrices, once freed from a Marxian master narrative of economically based class conflict, yield a pluralized politics of the future. Published at roughly the same time, these two books share a great deal more than the fact that each continues to have a large and often unacknowledged sphere of influence.

Laclau and Mouffe's attenuated attention to economics prevents recognition of how a contemporary capitalism works in more complex and multiple ways than as some totalizing economic monster. Likewise, their account ignores the effects of other and conflicting narratives of change within a discursive matrix of the capitalist common sense I discussed in my introduction. I will argue in the third section of this chapter that the conjunction of three very different narratives powerfully informs a certain economic common sense of "late" capitalism in the United States. I want to think of capitalism as also a "common sense"—lifting the term from Gramsci—rather than as an "ideology," since I hope to make clear that these three narratives are ideologically very different indeed; they are produced in different ways and produce different effects. As I understand Gramsci's usage, common sense is neither ideologically coherent nor uniform in its effectivities. It functions rather as the liminal condition of possibility, like a plot copula that alerts you to connection, lifts events beyond random configuration, and supplies the scene of conflict where something is at stake, however differently the stakes may be understood ideologically.

Clearly capitalism as common sense is "larger" than what is suggested by the attempts of economists to construct accurate indices by which to measure economic resources as "capital" and "capital input"—attempts that, as I will suggest in later chapters, are increasingly meaningless. Yet capitalism is no dinosaur, that immense, inchoate, "penetrating" force that in Laclau and Mouffe's argument transformed "society into a vast market in which new 'needs' were ceaselessly created, and in which more and more of the products of human labour were turned into commodities" (180). *This* image of economic capitalism disguises the conflicted constructions of capitalism as common sense, with all their political effects.

❀

The attempt to preserve a narrative continuity in accounts of economic change means that concepts invented for the task of identifying the distinguishing features of a new, different, and postmodern present also project historical narratives that—not surprisingly—often seem driven by a certain nostalgia: capitalism's present as it unfolds will be better than the immediate past, because it resembles a "past" past, as it were, before big got "too big." Richard Crawford's *In the Era of Human Capital* affords a good example, in a section of the narrative appropriately borrowing the title "Small Is Beautiful": "Many Americans dream of owning their own business and being their own boss, but in the mature industrial economy most were employed by large organizations and had few opportunities to express their entrepreneurial drive. . . . Before the industrialization of the late nineteenth century, all U.S. business was small business. Farmers, merchants and skilled craftsmen all ran their businesses with a handful of employees or none at all" (52–53).

Nostalgia, however, implies a desire for a return to earlier and better times, which is not quite what Crawford has in mind. Looking even further into the past, he claims that every major economic change has produced a more affluent population generally: "An agricultural society is more affluent than a primitive society, an industrial society is more affluent than an agricultural society, and a knowledge society [of the present] is the most affluent of all" (9). Size then figures doubly in this narrative. In order for the size of an "affluent" population to continue to expand, the growth of economic institutions must be arrested and their size dismantled. Thus Crawford's is a nostalgia of resemblance rather than return, articulated across this flatly linear plot of always expanding affluence. The feeling of a present freedom and spaciousness requires the absence of any return motive, depending instead on the adjacency of resemblances thereby freed from any pressure toward identification. The transition from an "industrial" to a "knowledge" society preserves the linear narrative, while simultaneously acknowledging the pleasures of resemblance: small businesses became big businesses became *really* big businesses became downsized, flexibly specialized, regionally autonomous, entrepreneurial businesses—which resemble, but are by no means the same as, the small businesses that existed in the past.

While Piore and Sabel's argument seems to occupy an entirely different register of complexity than Crawford's, the pleasures of resemblance to a "preindustrial past," with its smaller size, function as crucially in their account as in Crawford's. Hence they carefully keep their distance from any claim that current instances of flexibly specialized production simply reflect the potential of new, computer-driven technologies. Such instances instead evidence a form of social and economic organization that makes it "hard to tell where society (in the form of family and school ties or community celebrations of ethnic and political identity) ends, and where economic organization begins. Among the ironies of the resurgence of craft production is that its deployment of modern technology depends on its reinvigoration of affiliations that are associated with the preindustrial past" (275). I want to argue in this section that "among the ironies" of economic discourse in the United States is the way a sophisticated and carefully nuanced analysis like *The Second Industrial Divide*, which I will suggest shares a number of assumptions with other forms of postmodernist discourse, also contrives to continue something very similar to Crawford's unabashed hymn to capitalism and capitalist progress.

In initial and striking contrast to Crawford, however, Piore and Sabel do not see industrialism with its associated technologies of mass production as having been a *necessary* phase of capitalist development. The "first" great divide in that long history of capitalism, marking the emergence of genuine industrial production from local centers of reorganized craft production, was neither necessary nor complete. For a number of historically contingent reasons, the industrializing of production appeared in certain sectors as an attractive option, for immediate gain in profit and in market control, and the results were successful enough to encourage emulation elsewhere. But rather than being the unfolding of some immanent logic of capitalist development—whose description, they argue, occupied Marx no less than Adam Smith—industrialism triumphed as something of a self-fulfilling prophecy. In fact industrial development always co-existed with (and often depended on) ostensibly marginal forms of small-scale craft production throughout the nineteenth and twentieth centuries.

Thus the "second" industrial divide that gives their book its title doesn't emerge, like Crawford's "knowledge" economy, as simply the inevitable next and even better chapter in a continuing story. It is identified rather by the rediscovery, rearticulation, and redeployment of production options always existent in any case in the very midst of industrial development, and its occasion is the massive combination of "crises" in the last third of the twentieth century that threw open to question a dominant assumption of continued industrial growth and progress. True to their earlier argument, however, this second divide is not to be understood as expressive of some deeper logic at work; the crises emergent in the seventies are not a working into visibility of Marx's inherent "contradictions" of capitalism. They might well mark certain limits to industrial expansion, and they correspond to a whole series of "accidents" and misguided policy decisions in reaction to political events. But since industrialization, even in the United States, was hardly complete anyway (there were always limits to its saturation of the social formation), the "divide" is as much a matter of the *perception* of crisis and change as of some subterranean seismic shifts in the material "base."

More specifically, the crises of the seventies signaled the breakdown of a mass production "paradigm" that had in the nineteenth century "won out in the realm of ideas" every bit as surely "as it won out in the realm of practice" (47). By way of Kuhn, they suggest that "technological branching points—or divides—mark not just the moments at which political contexts and their associated markets push industrial development down a divergent path; they also mark the consolidation of new visions of efficient production—new paradigms or trajectories" (44).

Thus with considerably greater sophistication than Crawford's argument, Piore and Sabel's critique is aimed not only at the sheer size of industrialized mass production, but more fundamentally at the totalizing narratives, from both "right" and "left," that had identified mass production with the global advance of capitalism. Indeed, "capitalism" makes no appearance at all in the index to the book, for it has everywhere been pluralized in the course of the argument. Capitalism can only be identified through multiple adjectival designators that recognize significant national and regional differences as well as diverse forms of production and of markets, and that inform the accumulation of detail around what in other contexts might well be dismissed as marginal "anomalies" or "survivals" from a disappearing past.

Piore and Sabel's argument seems to me to share a number of features with recognizably postmodern assumptions, and to bring economics in the U.S. within the orbit of postmodern discourses. Their emphasis on the local and the specific can't be read in conformity to any projection of an "inherent" logic of development. Nor can it be resolved into a focus on "microeconomic" adjustments, which typically characterizes the specific sectors of research engaged by professional economists. In marked contrast to such specialized research, Piore and Sabel aren't intent on filling in the spaces of a general outline that merely requires some fine-tuning to realize the full measure of its applicability. Local specificities function first in their argument as a blurring of field boundaries, where whatever might be identified as "the economic" slides insensibly into a complex ensemble of relations whose intricating strands refuse to be disentangled. In this sense one primary target of their anti-totalizing critique is, precisely, the prodigiously totalizing abstraction required by the disciplinary specialization of economics. Methodologically, the procedure yields less an interdisciplinary economics, informed by work in other fields, than a postdisciplinary insistence on the limits imposed by the abstraction of field constitution.

Such methodological self-reflexivity finds expression alternatively in the explicit recognition of "telling a story," in making visible the constructedness of their own periodizing narrative with its momentously identified "divides." That is, they understand very well the familiar postmodern lesson that the epistemological lure of the master narrative depends on the naturalizing powers of its teleology, as if direction, immanent and implacable, could be discerned just beneath the shimmering intensities that distress retinal clarity. The narrative of *The Second Industrial Divide* in contrast distributes its energy between a forbiddingly complicated and labyrinthine "plot"—which foregrounds historical figures like Proudhon, for example, in a new role as deconstructor in effect of Marx—and a recurrent trope of desire (what do you *want* to happen economically?) that is free at any point to seize on whatever in the plot seems relevant.

Twinned nicely in the title's break between "the second industrial divide" and "possibilities for prosperity," plot and desire thus cooperate to call attention everywhere to the construction of a narrative that positions flexible specialization as a telos in quotation marks—*as if* a resolution to an enormously complicated plot were simply what you wanted all along. It is a conclusion that could hear something like Crawford's "Many Americans

dream of owning their own business and being their own boss" as irre-
sistible affective charm when digitally remastered through the multinational sampling of capitalisms woven through the interminably available
complexities of their plot.

As I suggested initially, however, economic discourse in the United
States emerges into a peculiar relation with other forms of the postmodern,
which can be glimpsed most clearly in *The Second Industrial Divide* through
the very "hybrid" characteristics of the argument. On the one hand, the
pluralization of "capitalisms" is made possible by refusing to isolate any
single factor that determines economic direction, or indeed identifies the
specifically "economic" from other sectors of the social formation. Only a
hybrid discourse—tuned not only to the complexities of any given "instance," but more fundamentally to the multiple analytic strategies available for understanding such complexities—can hope to make local sense of
the "instance."

Yet on the other hand, with considerably more urgency than in other
examples of such postmodern hybridity, Piore and Sabel's argument raises
the question of what exactly might fall "outside" this pluralized field of
capitalisms. This is not quite the same kind of question as what was addressed to, say, a programmatic literary deconstruction in the form of "what
is outside of textuality?" Nor is there any bracingly postmodern daring
possible from recoding Derrida's familiar response "*il n'y pas de hors-texte*"
into "*il n'y pas de hors-capitalisme*." Derridean textuality could be seen as
liminally cooperating with an anti-totalizing postmodernism by fissuring
the textual into incommensurable loops, and by challenging the very sta-
bilities of "inside" and "outside." Piore and Sabel's narrative of multiple
capitalisms in contrast might well seem to rejoin at the other end that sin-
gular, depressing, thematic insistence of dominant Euro-American economics from at least the early decades of the century: there's really nothing
worth shit outside of capitalism, which has always been capable anyway of
flexibly accommodating itself to changing circumstances.

For all their emphasis on locally specific forms of production and of
markets, there's almost no attention in *The Second Industrial Divide* to self-
designated alternatives to capitalist economies. The only sustained discussion of the Soviet Union, for example, occurs in relation to the "wheat
deal" of the early seventies. China makes almost no appearance, and the
index as well as the text preserves the euphemism of "developing countries," with its implication of mere latecomers to the capitalist fold—albeit
with a footnote that records the difficulties "for leftist economists" of what

terminology exactly to deploy analytically. Granted, this is an argument directed at "the economies of advanced capitalist countries" and their "present deterioration of economic performance" (4). Yet surely one obvious option for understanding that "deterioration" would look for comparative terms from noncapitalist economies. That such an option isn't even raised for discussion suggests something more at work in their logic than the frequent inventories of diverse forms of capitalism. In their argument, such familiar conceptual operators as "capitalism," "socialism," and "communism" involve a more fundamental category mistake.

"Liberals and neo-Marxists agree," they argue early in their introductory chapter, "that the disruptions of the 1970s are the sign of a fundamental incompatibility between market capitalism and political democracy, at least in their existing forms" (7–8). Hence the persistent failure of political solutions to economic crisis would seem to validate this shared perception of incompatibility. "But why should the failure to find a political solution to the economic problem," they continue, "be taken as proof of its political origin? Indeed, the logjam of politics might be the effect of conflicts touched off by the deteriorating advanced economies—not the cause" (11). Economic problems might well be better understood as having economic causes, which become nearly impossible to identify when approached under the sign of categorical markers that have already linked economic organization and political direction together as defining a "capitalist" or "socialist" or "communist" *society*. These terms leave the analyst little option but to worry whether the historically realized forms of linkage have simply functioned to disguise what is now becoming apparent as "fundamental incompatibility."

Piore and Sabel's argument to this point might seem a rather simplistic form of economic determinism, but it soon becomes clear that what "economic causes" means in relation to seventies crises is the *paradigm* of mass production industrialization. The causes at stake are as much ideological as economic. The category mistake inherent in capitalism/socialism/communism is finally less a matter of how such terms simultaneously name economic organization and political direction than of how they disguise a prior ideological determination of what exactly counts as "economic content" in the first place. What mass production industrialization as a paradigm yields is first of all the identification of an essential economics of "capitalism." Thus looking for "economic causes" to the crises precipitated in the seventies doesn't lead to yet one more reinterpretation of available economic data that might reveal the "real" underlying forces of the economy. Rather, the search requires a sustained ideological critique of how a mass production paradigm identifies "the economic."

Such critique implies that a "fundamental incompatibility" between capitalism and political democracy is, strictly, an illusion imposed by the attempt to isolate *capitalism* itself as an object of analysis. It's an illusion that could only be compounded by engaging in comparative discussion of the "essential" features of capitalist and noncapitalist economies. Like that familiar deconstructed "subject" of bourgeois individualism, capitalism as the "object" of bourgeois economics is revealed through the lens of this postmodern economics as no more than a functional "center," a contradictory coherence whose balancing and organizing of an economic structure has no ultimate ground or referent. "Possibilities for prosperity" (the words of their subtitle) lie in learning strategically to reshape the political contours of a now decentered field of economic practices, in ways that always recognize a potentially infinite field of economic differences in which one's strategies are articulated.

Strategies, however, are to some great extent derived from rethinking economic history, and this postmodern version of a "political economy" requires very different analytic tools for the study of history. Rather than the attempt to discover underlying "tendential laws of motion," what informs the analyst's attention is an admittedly constructed premise of conceptual plausibility: "we must conceptualize a world in which technology can develop in various ways: a world that might have turned out differently from the way it did, and thus a world with a history of abandoned but viable alternatives to what exists" (38). Hence the terms of political choice become crucial indicators for distinguishing direction: "technological possibilities that are realized depend on the distribution of power and wealth: those who control the resources and returns from investments choose from among the available technologies the one most favorable to *their* interest. . . . This amounts to saying that economic development reflects politics" (38).

One important "abandoned but viable alternative" revealed in the complex of this strategic political approach to economic history is the formulation of the so-called American Plan during the pre-Depression twenties in the United States. It occupies a particularly crucial location in their analysis for a number of reasons. First, and most directly, it occurred within a context of increasingly polarized political relations between "labor" and "capital," that is, at a point when politics and economics most clearly and visibly intersected. Second, its details were formulated in direct response to a crisis in shop-floor relations, where questions of dispute resolution simultaneously affected the rights of workers and the very organization of tasks in mass production. And finally, the advent of the Depression marked a dramatic end to its implementation; it remains at best an inchoate experiment in welfare capitalism, "so much so that today it is hard to determine how it functioned in the economic climate for which it was designed" (125). By the same token, however, it lends itself to retrospective analysis as an enviably plastic shape, available to be rearticulated in some new form adaptable to the quite different "economic climate" of today.

The three key elements of the Plan were the possibility of favorably priced stock options for a firm's workers; participation by workers in long-term health and pension programs; and the establishment of "works councils" or "shop committees" involving both management and labor, and empowered not only to resolve grievances, but also to accomplish what the National Industrial Conference Board referred to as "welding together management and working force into a single, cohesive productive unit" (127). Remembering their initial postulate that "economic development reflects politics" and the choices made by politically dominant groups, Piore and Sabel stress the fact that management supported the Plan as very much in their own interests. In contrast to accounts by radical labor historians (see, for example, Green, *The World of the Worker*), however, Piore and Sabel argue that those interests were not simply a matter of containment, a way to prevent aggressively antagonistic union organization on the shop floor. A secure and relatively well-off work force was a requirement of expanded consumption; a cooperative work force with a stake in efficient production was a requirement of competitive market presence. Under the American Plan, both management and labor would necessarily engage in a process of substantive resolution of problems rather than in a process structured through the procedural rules of negotiation that were established in the wake of the Depression and the collapse of the American Plan. Following David Brody's argument, they conclude that "the American Plan was the victim of bad historical timing, not of capitalists' incapacity to make concessions to labor" (125). In larger terms, "the failure of the American Plan works councils and job sharing, and the rise of a system of layoffs and procedural justice, was largely an accident of economic history. If the recovery had come more quickly, welfare capitalism might have emerged strengthened from the Depression, and its shop-floor practices validated" (128).

What is unremarked in this analysis is the assumption that it's at least possible to imagine that management's and labor's interests were not *necessarily* and everywhere antagonistic. Workers aren't exactly against job se-

curity and salary levels that would enable them to buy more things, even if
their reasons may be different from those of management. Nor would the
collapse of a firm's competitive market presence be a desirable goal for
workers any more than for management. The potential for paralleling interests at strategic points creates conditions amenable to substantive discussion of specific direction. In contrast, the "procedural justice" that
emerged after the Depression begins, emerging from a premise that has already split spheres of interest in common from spheres of antagonistic interests, has set the task as a matter of adjudicating "rights" and negotiating
"concessions" within the spheres of antagonism. Thus ultimately Piore and
Sabel's fascination with the American Plan isn't tied to the detail of its policies, which given its short life are hard to determine anyway. Rather, they
value the fluidity of a refusal to determine in advance the boundary lines
between interests in common and interests that are antagonistic. Unlike in
a system of procedural justice, such determinations are part of what's at
stake in substantive discussion. The Depression in effect intervened to establish fixed boundaries, and hence brought the fluid experiment of the
American Plan to an abrupt end.

Yet even leaving aside any question of how much "substantive" discussion could actually occur in circumstances of unequal power distribution
between groups (a question that Piore and Sabel's own postulate—that political choices depend on the distribution of power and wealth—would encourage raising), there is still a further curiosity in their account of the
American Plan. "The major manufacturing companies," they argue, in the
immediate wake of the 1929 stock market collapse, "tried to maintain both
wage and employment at previous levels; when that proved impossible, they
shifted to work sharing. U.S. Steel and Ford abandoned wage maintenance
only in the fall of 1931, and most of the major corporations followed suit.
Work sharing, however [which had been encouraged by the American
Plan], continued into 1932. Up until October of that year, U.S. Steel employed 85 percent of its normal work force, even though production had
fallen 90 percent" (128). And this picture of hopeless persistence in the face
of sudden, overwhelming change is not quite what one has come to expect
from Piore and Sabel's narrative of multiple economic practices determined
"in the last instance" by local, contingent, even accidental political choices.

In this argument, the Depression is assumed to have arrived catastroph-
ically, in the midst of the Plan's emergent details, opening some seismic fis-
sure in the economic landscape that suddenly and irrevocably altered the
potential effect of every form of political decision and economic planning.

In the context of catastrophe, however, if the American Plan is acknowledged as simply a "victim of bad historical timing," how "viable" can *any*
alternative be that doesn't at least try to reckon with a "history" apparently
"timed" by a logic even "major manufacturing companies," let alone workers, are powerless to control? What point is there to imagining "a world
that might have turned out differently from the way it did, and thus a
world with a history of abandoned but viable alternatives to what exists" if
what exists turns out after all to be determined by catastrophic events like
the Depression? "The rise of a system of layoffs and procedural justice"
that followed the Depression "was largely an accident of economic history"
only in the sense that "real" economic history in any case is made by catastrophic irruptions, in the face of which any set of strategic alternatives
such as "procedural justice" or "substantive discussion" must appear merely
accidental indeed. The catastrophe of the Depression smashed the very matrix of possibility in which the American Plan was born.

When one turns back a chapter to their more direct discussion of the
Depression, however, what appears as irruptive catastrophe in the context
of the fortunes of the American Plan turns out to be eminently under-
standable: "The cause of the Great Depression and the nature of the reforms that sustained the postwar prosperity are subjects of enormous con-
troversy. . . . But whatever the factors immediately responsible for the crisis of the 1930s, our argument is that its fundamental cause was the
structural fragility of the economy that was associated with the rise of the
mass-production corporation" (75). On direct examination, a model of catastrophe yields quite easily to an understanding of the contradictory structural development of mass production. While corporations could control
both their immediate markets and their supplies of resources by a concentration in mass-produced consumer durables, this concentration simultaneously generated a mass *consumption* economy that made general national
prosperity a necessary condition for the market control possible to any corporation. That is, the contingent factors that had made it possible for corporations to assert immediate market control also led to a necessity for national prosperity that corporations alone could not determine.

Nevertheless, catastrophe hardly disappears in this calm explanation for
the structural causes of the Depression. It has been pushed further into the
past—or more exactly, further into still earlier chapters of their plot—until
implacable historical "catastrophe" rejoins the great contingent "accident"
that inaugurates the narrative in the first place, the emergence of a mass
production paradigm *as if* it were "destiny and blind decision" in their

chapter title. Rather than opposed, contingent "accident" and historically timed "catastrophe" are thus identified at an "in the Beginning" of mass industrialization. A mass industrialization paradigm, like the "reference myth" that stands at the beginning of Lévi-Strauss's immense mapping of mythic relations in *The Raw and the Cooked*, is an economic myth of size that functions as an arbitrary and necessary origin for the constructed narrative by which one is to understand the historical causes of the current crisis that identifies "the second industrial divide."

The parallel to Lévi-Strauss can suggest that their argument should be subjected to a critique on the order of Fredric Jameson's general indictment of the failures of postmodern historical thinking in *Postmodernism, or The Cultural Logic of Late Capital*. That is, what initially projects itself as historical explanation turns out to be merely a circular reflection of an origin acknowledged as always already arbitrary. At the same time, however, it is possible to draw a very different conclusion about the form of economic history in *The Second Industrial Divide* than what is implied by Jameson's critique. Without his attachment to a "realism" of historical trajectory, accident and catastrophe can be understood as indifferently available to furnish out a figure not of "History" in Jameson's sense but of desire, of what simultaneously motivates conceptualizing "a world that might have turned out differently from the way it did," and authorizes searching for "abandoned but viable alternatives" (38) like the American Plan. Troped as desire, accident and catastrophe shatter the iron logic of "what exists" into nothing more than a complex of "alternatives" where what appears as "abandoned" at any given moment can obligingly replay its "viability" the next. What "History" yields as the sad fate of the American Plan, now forever out of reach, can instead be genetically reassembled into a constituent theme of a vital and flexibly specialized production in the present.

Thus something like "genetics of economics" might well be a more appropriate terminology than "economic history" to characterize the combinatory structures of alternatives revealed through Piore and Sabel's analytic strategies. In any case, it is a terminology that serves my purposes well. I have been implying all along that what *The Second Industrial Divide* shares not only with Crawford, but more fundamentally with the economics of a Jurassic theme park, is the genetic reinvention of an impossible object, one that had been banished from the very outset of the narrative. In this case the impossible object that reemerges is a *nascent* capitalist society now, miraculously, arriving again in all its open fluidities.

As the motor force of narrative desire works to shatter the double helix

code inscribed throughout the molecular building blocks of a mass production paradigm, the complications of narrative plotting have also yielded
bits of prisoned genetic material from the multiple sectors of their exca-
vation. All this material can be brought finally to life in a concluding figure
of a newly arrived Capitalism whose nascent political promise is as immense as the *T. rex*, if also benign as Barney: "It is the ideal of yeoman
democracy, we think, that is most likely to catalyze American efforts to re-
build the economy on the model of flexible specialization. For the idea of
an economy of craft communities—some organized in large corporations;
many regionally based—speaks to the American tradition of localism. And
an economy that is based on skilled workers—many so versatile that alone
or with a few others they can function autonomously—appeals to American individualism: the sense that entrepreneurship is the source and product of personal liberty" (306).

❋

In the more overtly political context of Laclau and Mouffe's *Hegemony and
Socialist Strategy*, the initial originality of Piore and Sabel's argument would
lie in their direct attention to the status of "the economic." That is, rather
than once more supplying an inventory of what economic accounts leave
out, the "so much else" that seems irreducible to economic explanation, they
make it possible instead to understand economic factors themselves as belonging to the field of the symbolic. In the sense Laclau and Mouffe give
that much-used term, all economic indicators are inevitably overdetermined,
lacking an "ultimate literality which would reduce them to necessary moments of an immanent law" (98). Indeed, what Piore and Sabel refer to as a
mass production "paradigm" might be more adequately expressed in Laclau
and Mouffe's terminology as a kind of symbolic grammar of the economic, a
field of signifiers whose meanings involve an indeterminate surplus of signification at any point along a signifying chain rather than being gathered up
into a reference to some literal substratum of economic "reality."

Likewise, the crises of the seventies that supply the immediate occasion
for Piore and Sabel's analysis can be understood as the emergence of what
Laclau and Mouffe might describe as "antagonisms" external to that symbolic grammar of mass production economics. "Strictly speaking," Laclau
and Mouffe argue, "antagonisms are not *internal* but *external* to society [in
this case, to "the economic"]; or rather, they constitute the limits of society,
the latter's impossibility of fully constituting itself" (125; their emphasis).

In other words, the resurgence of craft production, for all that it may seem to occur in the margins of a mass production symbolics, is, "strictly speaking," a demonstration of the limits of a totalizing economic constitution of a mass production society.

While Laclau and Mouffe's argument thus leverages a more precise conceptual terminology by which to understand Piore and Sabel's critique of a mass industrialization paradigm, conversely the retrieval of marginalized economic options in *The Second Industrial Divide* supplies a useful explanatory context for Laclau and Mouffe's understanding of "radical democracy." What they propose, similar to the reinvention of craft production in *The Second Industrial Divide*, is a reinvention of democratic politics: "*The task of the Left*," they argue in italics, "*therefore cannot be to renounce liberal-democratic ideology, but on the contrary, to deepen and expand it in the direction of a radical and plural democracy*" (176). The genetic material of a radical democracy has been deposited in pockets throughout the historical formation in something of the same way as the instances of craft production that occupy Piore and Sabel's attention. It can be newly articulated to extend "a chain of democratic equivalences" (186) at once opposing the hegemony of capital's symbolic field, and constructing a new positivity of the political as flexible and open as the economics of flexible specialization that identifies for Piore and Sabel a viable alternative to the dominance of mass production.

My discussion of Piore and Sabel has implied numerous other parallels as well. Nevertheless, emphasizing congruities in this way, by translating back and forth between the two texts, must be arrested at the point where Piore and Sabel sketch a hypothesis of what an *international* economic order might look like that would permit active political commitment to flexibly specialized production in the United States:

> But it is conceivable that flexible specialization and mass production could be combined into a unified *international* economy. In this system, the old mass-production industries might migrate to the underdeveloped world, leaving behind in the industrialized world the high-tech industries and the traditional dispersed conglomerates in machine tools, garments, textiles, and the like—all revitalized through the fusion of traditional skills and high technology. . . . To the underdeveloped world, this hybrid system would provide industrialization. To the developed world, it would provide a chance to moderate the decline of mass production and its de-facto emigration from its homelands. Such a system would not last forever—any more than the corporate economy or the world of domestic macroregulation has proved immortal. But a hybrid of mass and flexible production would for a time create a universal interest in two basic goals: worldwide prosperity and a transnational welfare state. (280; their emphasis)

Almost regretfully, they acknowledge that it might not really work (although more recent economic policy decisions have certainly adopted the possibility with enthusiasm). This would be so not because such a hybrid system would mean condemning "the underdeveloped world" to a second-order status in this "worldwide prosperity," however, but because as yet "we" aren't in a position ourselves to achieve an escape from the negative consequences of industrial size and to construct a flexibly specialized economy. Thus, despite the congruities between the economics of flexible specialization and the politics of radical democracy, it's difficult to imagine that Laclau and Mouffe's argument would endorse in parallel fashion a hybrid global political order composed of a decidedly pre-radical and limited democracy operating in "underdeveloped" nations so that radical democracy could spread in the "developed" world. Nevertheless, the parallels are sufficient to suggest a couple of closely connected questions.

First, it's certainly convenient that Piore and Sabel can ignore the "unfortunate" effects of mass industrialization—which they themselves have emphasized—when those effects are imagined as localized in the context of "underdeveloped" nations. Nevertheless, they do recognize that challenges to totalizing industrial size don't preclude an awareness that the actual implementation of flexible specialization requires thinking at some point in some terms of a global economic organization, however necessarily "hybrid," historically contingent and multifaceted rather than homogeneously ordered. Wouldn't the actual achievement of radical democracy likewise require at some point a sustained attempt to think—if in very different form than that implied by Piore and Sabel—the configuration of a hybrid global *political* order that would radically alter the ensemble of interconnecting relations between "developing" and "developed" nations?

Second, in their deconstruction of capitalism as possessing any inherent defining logic or "essence," Piore and Sabel are continually engaged in elaborating a political account no less than an economic account of crisis, change, and potential new directions. Contingent political decisions are frequently adduced as "accidental" causes for economic phenomena, and the concluding appeal to yeoman democracy is openly and directly presented as a politics of flexible specialized economics. Laclau and Mouffe likewise work within a set of assumptions that teaches the fallacy of cleanly separating politics, culture, and economics. But in contrast to how Piore and Sabel follow through on these assumptions by projecting a political culture from their economics, it is remarkably difficult even to guess from *Hegemony and Socialist Strategy* what an economics of radical democracy would look like. Presumably, as I've implied, it could not involve some casual economic sacrifice of populations in the developing world similar to what Piore and Sabel suggest. Occasional, if brief, appeals to recent feminist studies hint that it would require radically reconceptualizing what is meant by "work" and "production." The question, however, remains wide open: what forms of economic organization could sustain and be sustained by a politics of radical democracy?

The reasons for the failure to supply coherent answers to these connected questions seem to me to have their source in what I called earlier the dinosaur model of the economic in Laclau and Mouffe's argument. When they attempt to think in global terms about an international economy, what emerges is the virulent, destructive force of an endlessly expansive capitalism, "penetrating" every corner of the social field. It's as if just beyond the contingent, intersecting cultural logics of "equivalence" and "autonomy" in all their local specificity, you still must find the implacable power of global capitalism. Likewise, the only image they offer of a sustained interpenetration of politics and economics is not one of radically democratic economies, but the terrifying hegemony of Thatcherism and Reaganism: "We are thus witnessing the emergence of a new hegemonic project, that of liberal-conservative discourse, which seeks to articulate the neo-liberal defense of the free market economy with the profoundly anti-egalitarian cultural and social traditionalism of conservatism" (175).

This globalizing monolith of capitalism prevents answers to the questions I've raised. It returns the oppositional politics of radical democracy to a familiar version of postmodern metaphysics that opposes Evil as totalization and closure to Good as multiplicity and contingency. The intersection of those spinning logics of "equivalence" and "autonomy," necessary to the social openness of radical democracy, is an intersection everywhere "overdetermined" by the affective threat of size in the background, the fear of totalization whose privileged vehicle is "the economic." The two logics *must* intersect, preserving the open contingency of each. At this level what one finds is no longer political critique, but a metaphysical faith that offers little help in understanding the effects of the conflicted dynamics of late capitalist common sense.

❖

As governor of California, Reagan was already emphasizing a new anticommunism as the cornerstone of foreign policy, and foreign policy in turn as key to domestic issues. Within the discursive mutation of communist regimes into the Evil Empire performed by the Reagan presidency, so-called Third World countries were increasingly identified with a fundamental immobility, in at least three different ways. Economically, they could not be expected to "develop" entirely on their own, without the intervention of foreign capital. Reagan's innovation was the intransigence of his demands for a direct economic as well as political return on U.S. investment in Third World development. Promises of alignment with U.S. rather than Soviet influence were no longer enough; countries had to demonstrate a political stability sufficient to guarantee an uninterrupted return on investment—hence the unqualified support of military dictators who would promise stability. Rationalizing such support meant that politically, Third World countries had to be represented as passive populations who without the authoritarian rule of a "strongman" would be helpless prey to communist takeover. And passivity of this sort could only result from a hopelessly backward, static, traditional culture that in no way prepared its citizens for democratic self-rule. Completing the circle, the source of such cultural ineptitude was of course the economic failure of independent capitalization. Economically, politically, and culturally, the Third World was an immobile bloc.

Reagan's foreign policy in this context may seem to have reinvented a nineteenth-century European colonial map. The significantly new operator, however, was a communist "Second World" bloc, and hence the intensities of imagery describing this Evil Empire should also be understood as indirect indicators of policy toward the Third World. That is, the Reaganite creation of the Empire was necessary to maintain the putative immobility of that third world. Functionally positioned as the incarnation of agency somewhere else than in Third World countries themselves, the Empire made possible a way to preserve the perception of the Third World "in itself" as immobile. Thus the Soviet Union as Evil Empire was not only a displaced image of the evils of Euro-American colonialism, but also a guarantee of irreducible difference between Third (immobile) and First (mobile) Worlds.

The highly publicized "disappearance" of Communism, however, has left that designation of Third World difference uncomfortably dangling in midair. No longer available to be schematized across a series of nodal points of immobility, simply the passive territory where First and Second World conflicts are fought out by proxy, the Third World dissolves into continually shifting adjacencies of "core," "periphery," "rim," "spheres of influence," "elastic" and "inelastic" economies, and so on. Thus for all its initial propaganda success, the Gulf War marked a limit to foreign policy in its Reaganite configuration, with the inescapable recognition that "we" were at war, not with the agents of Empire working by proxy, but simply with one particular Third World country, and one that was anything but immobile.

In contrast to Reagan's emphasis as California governor, Pete Wilson based his 1994 reelection campaign on first a promise to work for a constitutional amendment that would deny citizenship to the children of illegal aliens, and then his enthusiastic support for Proposition 187, which would deny social benefits to illegal aliens. The contrast to Reagan conveniently marks a dramatic shift, altering not only the relations of foreign and domestic policy, but also the constitutive urgencies that shape the understanding of both in conservative politics. For "illegal alien" is not quite the same kind of threat as "the Evil Empire," nor can illegal aliens appear as confirmation in any sense of Third World immobility. They are imaged as "carriers" of everything from drugs, gang culture, and AIDS, to the more vaguely enveloping menace of proliferating crime. But they are also economic signs—microscopically visible evidence of capillary leakage across the no longer assured boundaries between First World prosperity and affluence and the miseries of Third World poverty. In other words, even if it is rarely named in this emergent conservative imaginary, the conceptualization of something like a "Third World" nevertheless continues to function politically, as a now vague and anonymous territory leaking illegal aliens elsewhere. Indeed, it is perhaps too close now to be directly identified by means of the safety implied by that "third." Illegal aliens are the indicators of adjacency, the multiple signifiers of an immensity too near, too threatening, too *mobile*, to be distanced by name.

It's far from clear in conservative accounts what specific economic problems are caused by illegal aliens. For some time, after all, politicians in Wilson's own state didn't exactly discourage what "everyone knew" to be an increase of illegal aliens in the work force. They were a source of cheap labor whose "illegal" status helped preserve the cheapness of the labor pool as available to do the many jobs no one else "wanted" to perform anyway, and in at least certain circumstances they supplied, at the other end of the labor spectrum, a cheap source of highly skilled labor as well. Wilson, like others, now points to the burden on social services, the increase of the homeless population on the streets, and the spread of disease and drug-generated criminal violence as largely attributable to the influx of illegal aliens. But he has no ready answer to the claims of his opponents that such a picture could just as easily be attributed to the combination of legal spending limits, the withdrawal of corporate capital, and "white flight" that has left both local governments and the state unable to pay for any "solutions" to anything anyway, least of all crime.

What I want to suggest is that the vocabulary concerning illegal aliens has become central to a conservative construction of an economic counternarrative to the story business writers like Crawford tell of a globally expanding affluence in a postmodern "knowledge" economy. As counternarrative, it should function first as a reminder that, so far from the neutral, demographic sign of a uniformly expanding population Crawford imagines, "affluence" in the United States has had a class, a race, a gender, and a national identity, available to "others" only by permission. Rather than a familiarly nationalistic zero-sum game of "they" win, "we" lose, however, this conservative counter-narrative disarticulates the combinatory power of national identity across the evidence of the flood of illegal aliens. That is, the "we" of an assumed national identity in the United States is split in such a way that "the nation" has been forced to permit the existence of something very like a *Second* World, although obviously no longer the Evil Empire of the Soviet Union. Rather, the structural position of Second World is occupied by the menacing size that emerges into view once the apparatus of the state in the United States is understood as inextricably linked to the operations of *multi*national corporations. Together, state and corporations compose an unholy Second World that supports a population in the United States who benefit from, and whose affluence depends on, everything signified metonymically by illegal aliens as Third World. For example, in Buchanan's insistently expressed version of this counter-narrative throughout his 1996 campaign, the true identity of the United States as nation is gradually being destroyed by a Second World amalgam of national state institutions with the imperatives of multinational economics.

Unlike the positioning of the Evil Empire, this Second World as imaged in conservative counter-narrative can hardly identify an irreducible difference between First World affluence and mobility and Third World poverty and immobility. The First World is now itself imaged as an embattled conservative nation, rendered immobile even in its "own" home territory. The mobilities of illegal aliens likewise are a reminder of a disappearing difference, giving way to a uniformly bleak and forbidding landscape of poverty where the decaying expectations of First World communities are increasingly surrounded by the roving gang cultures of the illegal, the alien, the immigrant—all existing at a remove from the Second World high-plains citadels of multinational prosperity protected everywhere by the policies, and the employment potential, of the State.

Thus despite the efforts of old-line conservatives like George Will to subsume this picture into a familiar Reaganite attack on the "bloated" bureaucracy of the State, it's the newer language of commentators such as Rush Limbaugh who mobilize the intensities of counter-narrative. And while Robert Reich may find in *Wall Street Journal* editorials "a near perfect barometer of conservative pressure points," the following passage he quotes from the *Journal* would signify very differently within the conservative counter-narrative I've been describing, as simply one more familiar expression of Second World interests: "Our own view remains that the problem is not too many immigrants, but too few. . . . As long as we don't train enough [Americans] ourselves, immigration is a saving grace" (287). The failure of the California schools voucher campaign supplied for the counter-narrative still further evidence of First and Second World division of the nation; the failure is largely attributed to the withdrawal of corporate financial backing that in the past, during the Reagan years, unhesitatingly supported a conservative "social issues" agenda.

The politics of counter-narrative is thus articulated through the most virulently coded racist language, but the *meanings* of that language are configured in very different ways than in the conjunction of neoliberal economics and conservative authoritarianism that occupies Laclau and Mouffe's attention in *Hegemony and Socialist Strategy*. As Piore and Sabel also recognize, if in less politically pointed terms than Laclau and Mouffe, the importance of economics in that Reaganite conjuncture—and the justification for describing it as "neoliberal"—depended on the separation of "the economic" as a distinct sphere of activity. Hence the familiar Reagan mantra of "get government off our backs" always signified doubly within the uneasy tensions between supply-side economics and social issues agendas that existed even at the height of Reaganism's appeal. On the one hand, it meant less government interference with the operation of the "free market," but on the other it was a demand for *local* community autonomy in politically determining operative social norms and values to be expressed in a whole range of policy decisions, from legal definitions of "family" to school curricula and the designation of religious holidays. The linkage expressed by the mantra depended on an abstraction of individual "liberty" and "freedom," applied to both economics and social issues. The meanings of "race," however, are perhaps the best indicators of the level of abstraction that was necessary to hold the linkage together against the tensions always threatening to split it.

Economically, race didn't signify at all; the assumption of a genuinely "free" market was also and everywhere the assumption of a race-blind market, impartially rewarding hard work and competitive innovation, regardless of race. Socially, in contrast, race was a primary signifier, defining and constituting the uniqueness of each "local community" as distinct from others. The neoliberal separation of "the economic" was then simultaneously what marked the boundary lines of the social, in race terms. Economics "began" and the social context "ended" at the point where race was no longer a primary constitutive factor. The economic system, however, would automatically "adjust" for locally determined policy decisions expressive of social values that might seem to have negative economic effects on racial groups. There would be no need for state government political interference to counter potentially negative effects. In this context, there is an obvious accuracy in Laclau and Mouffe's recognition that the hegemonic "liberty" suturing neoliberal economics and conservative authoritarianism, and the racism that sustains it, is made possible ideologically by an insistence on the distinctness of the economic field.

The racism that codes illegal aliens as menace and as the ultimate source of the "criminalization" of everyday living spaces, however, is another matter altogether. As I've suggested, the "alien" seen as illegal, mobile, Third World population groups is also and increasingly figured as crucial to Second World economics. That is, in contrast to the neoliberal premise of economic separation from the social preserved by Reaganism, with the death of the nation counter-narrative the racial distinctness of the alien simultaneously signifies the collapse of the economic as a distinct sector. Hence right-wing opposition to NAFTA, for example, involved not only a protectionist, pro-American worker rhetoric, articulating fears of the loss of American jobs to other countries; equally important, it emerged as a critique of the politics of multinational corporations, for covertly attempting to remove the "illegal" from the influx of aliens, and thereby to identify the properly distinct racial territories of First and Third Worlds. Racial meanings in this context appear within the terms of an economic battle, on a global stage. While the "illegal alien" remains an impossible figure of displacement overdetermining this counter-narrative's imaginary, it is a narrative that also projects an ostensibly "literal" story that remains immediately located in a critique of the rising trajectory of a Second World. It is a racially coded symbolic, in other words, that produces the literal, economic story that Limbaugh, Buchanan, and others tell over and over: an intensifying class division between First and Second Worlds, with the very national survival of the United States at stake.

Laclau and Mouffe locate the political barriers to radical democracy in a neoliberal/conservative ideology that would locate radical democracy as the end of a process where an older liberalism has gradually eroded into anarchic ungovernability. In contrast to that neoliberal/conservative ideology, however, the counter-narrative of the death of a nation reads the signs of "radical democracy" as functioning in the very different and orginary role of cultural agency for the economics of multinationalism. That is, so far from the ungovernable anarchic survival described by Reaganism, any politics that might look like a radical democratizing appears in the post-Reagan conservative counter-narrative as the *dominant cultural form* of an emergent Second World menace. The war, as Limbaugh always reminds us, is also and everywhere a cultural war.

Politically, the stakes in a counter-narrative reconfiguration of First, Second, and Third Worlds involve more than the mobilizations of affective investment through appeals to the image of a dying nation. Among other things, its increasingly insistent articulation of sinister global forces at work creates conditions where corporations can construct still another and very different narrative of economic change. In this narrative, the new self-representations of corporate economic interests in multiculturalism and diversity anticipate a larger and profound democratizing of the social formation, with global no less than national implications. That is, in its affirmation of multicultural diversity, this narrative distances corporate policy from the "reactionary" racism coded into a conservative counter-narrative. Equally important, it transforms counter-narrative claims for the interpenetration of the economic and the cultural into the groundwork for a new and positive liberating force. It manages, then, to obliterate a corporate history of involvement with a Reaganite separation of the economic from the social. Like Piore and Sabel's account of flexible specialization, from which it borrows a great deal in addition to the economics of reorganizing production, the corporate narrative emphasizes the interconnected ensemble of cultural, political, and economic factors. That ensemble appears the more plausible the more it projects itself as a positive version of the fears instantiated in conservative counter-narrative. The latter is made to appear as simply a racist fear of the positive democratic process at work in corporate multiculturalism.

"Managing diversity" in this corporate sense is hardly what Laclau and Mouffe have in mind as a form of radical democracy. And I have relatively little interest in that range of left debates about their argument that turns on whether they've abandoned a "genuinely" radical Marxian politics or overemphasized "the cultural" or ignored the difference between "discursive" and "extra-discursive" reality, and so on, such that their project of radical democracy might become easily susceptible to such "co-optation" by corporate interests. My point is that the strategic politics of *Hegemony and Socialist Strategy* can no longer offer very good strategy in the circumstances of a conservative counter-narrative that would identify radical democratizing with multicultural corporate interests, and a corporate narrative of self-representation that quite happily accepts and makes use of the identification for its own ends. That is, the issue isn't whether there's something inherently skewed about Laclau and Mouffe's argument that makes it eminently "co-optable"; it's that in present circumstances, it doesn't need to be co-opted, or even addressed, in order for a *corporate* postmodern economics to begin a task of forging a new hegemonic articulation from an ostensibly democratic multiculturalism.

Because it has potentially far-reaching effects on institutions of higher education in the United States, I will return at length to this corporate narrative in Chapter 5. For now, however, I want to address a third narrative of economic change, which involves elements transposed from both corporate multiculturalism and conservative visions of national demise. This narrative is perhaps clearest in Robert Reich's *The Work of Nations*, published shortly before he became Clinton's Secretary of Labor. It is ultimately an argument about an ethical vision of "nation" and national identity, but it depends on how Reich reassembles U.S. Census Bureau occupational data into a set of new classificatory categories that he claims reflect much more accurately the realities of a global, multinational economy.

What Reich calls "routine production services" involve "the kind of repetitive tasks performed by the old foot soldiers of American capitalism in the high-volume enterprise" (174). While the work may then typically be associated with blue-collar jobs in manufacturing, for Reich this category would also include a number of jobs in emergent high-tech industries as well: "The 'information revolution' may have rendered some of us more productive, but it has also produced huge piles of raw data which must be processed in much the same monotonous way that assembly-line workers and, before them, textile workers processed piles of other raw materials" (175). "In-person servers," the second category he constructs, is similar in many respects, likewise involving "simple and repetitive tasks" (176) and wages directly related to labor time and amount of work produced. The main difference "is that *these* services must be provided person-to-person, and thus are not sold worldwide" (176). The third and final category of his classificatory scheme is identified as "symbolic-analytic services." This category is more nebulous, however, since Reich intends it to characterize generally much of what seems like "new" features of exchange in a burgeoning global economy. Like the products of routine production, symbolic analyst services sell worldwide. Rather than standardized commodities, though, what is traded are "data, words, oral and visual representations" (177) that "solve, identify, and broker problems" (178) in very specific circumstances. The work thus involves the manipulation of symbols rather than the production and circulation of material goods, and the services appear in the form of symbolic constructs rather than as the performance of tasks.

For Reich, this new classification is intended to overcome the assumptions inherent in an older classificatory scheme, initiated in the thirties, that maintained a picture of a distinctly American economy where all American workers are "in the same boat"—to borrow Reich's frequent metaphor. The older scheme recognizes that certain groups may at times benefit disproportionately from the success of an American economy, as others can be disproportionately hit by its failures. Nevertheless, everybody's fortunes are ultimately linked to the general, global success or failure of corporate America. Reich's categorical recomposition of census data is intended to reveal this picture as an illusion: "As we discard vestigial notions of the competitiveness of American corporations, American industry, and the American economy, and recast them in terms of the competitiveness of the American work force, it becomes apparent that successes or failures will not be shared equally by all our citizens. Some Americans [symbolic analysts], whose contributions to the global economy are more highly valued in world markets, will succeed, while others, whose contributions are deemed less valuable, fail" (172). In short: "We are now in different boats, one [routine production services] sinking rapidly, one [in-person services] sinking more slowly, and the third [symbolic-analytic services] rising steadily" (208).

While Reich is no classical Marxist, the general politics of nation he describes is articulated within a matrix of these class-based positions in the economy. Further, where Piore and Sabel record the resurgence of flexible forms of craft production, Reich focuses instead on shifting definitions of economic value in relation to *consumption*, for it is the determination of consumer value in global terms that ultimately decides what skills, and whose skills, will be rewarded in the market: "America's core corporations are gradually, often painfully, turning toward serving the unique needs of particular customers. By trial and error, by fits and starts, often under great stress, and usually without much awareness of what they are doing or why, the firms that are surviving and succeeding are shifting from high volume [based in conceptions of production capacity] to high value" (82), based instead on assessments of diverse consumer demands. The result may look like a version of flexibly specialized production, as the description of corporate America bumbling its way into something new and different is similar to Piore and Sabel's emphasis on the radical contingencies of corporate decision-making. But "high value" is driven by the requirements of consumption rather than by the reorganization of production.

Thus the division of "boats" Reich describes is a function of how consumers in a multinational information economy identify primary sources of "value added" to the world economy: "As the value placed on new designs and concepts continues to grow relative to the value placed on standard products [and, by extension, in-person services], the demand for symbolic analysts will continue to surge" (225). Value is directly linked to the *kind* of work one does, and the determination of social position derives from the equation between value added and work skills. Symbolic analysts fare well in terms of social position, as well as salaries and benefits, because their work skills are in high demand, and their work skills are in high demand because they add proportionately more value to the world economy. Further, the United States is in a relatively strong competitive position in a global economy that values symbolic analysis, as a result of the massive U.S. infrastructure of resources dedicated to education and research. In contrast, as "the value placed on standard products" declines, there is less financial reward available to be allocated to routine producers, with the result that corporations locate routine production in countries where workers can be paid less.

These economic "realities," however, don't necessarily determine the political configuration of an American work force for Reich. He acknowledges that "immigration policy," for example, "will become a point of growing contention between America's symbolic analysts and in-person

servers in coming years" (289). The former see an open immigration policy
as yielding access to a world market of in-person services; the latter see it as
opening the door to massive competition for already precarious jobs that
are less than desirable in any case. But there are alternatives for Reich to
such conflicts of interest. A genuinely progressive income tax would redis-
tribute incoming wealth to the United States from a global economy, off-
setting "the polarizing tendencies" (245) of that economy. Investment in
access to training and education for more people would both strengthen
the U.S. position in a global market for symbolic analytic services, and take
advantage of how, in Reich's analysis at least, a "global economy imposes
no particular limits upon the number of Americans who can sell symbolic-
analytic services worldwide" (247). Rethinking the very organization of
both routine production and in-person services would make these jobs
themselves more appealing and make the U.S. work force engaged in them
more globally competitive.

Realizing the potential of such alternatives is a matter of ethical choice
for Reich; ultimately, he holds, it is a matter of reconceiving the terms of
national identity in some way other than as grounded in the matrix of a
common economic fate: "We are, after all, citizens as well as economic ac-
tors; we may work in markets but we live in societies. How tight is the
social and political bond when the economic bond unravels?" (304). Rather
than "seceding" from the nation, as he argues symbolic analysts have been
doing as they follow their global interests, Reich argues instead for what
he calls a positive nationalism, "in which each nation's citizens take primary responsibility for enhancing the capacities of their countrymen for
full and productive lives, but who also work with other nations to ensure
that these improvements do not come at others' expense" (311). Positive
nationalism in this ethical sense offers for Reich a viable politics for the
future in a global economy. Against a conservative vision of national death,
it opens possibilities for rebirth.

As he's quite willing to admit, Reich's narrative is written by a symbolic analyst to other symbolic analysts, those he sees holding power given
them by current economic circumstances to make the kind of ethical
choices he describes. Thus positive nationalism isn't exactly a call to in-
person servers to be nice to immigrants, but an ethical imperative for symbolic analysts to use their economic power to work toward a nation where
conditions wouldn't polarize ethnically diverse population groups. Likewise, Reich doesn't expect a ground swell of support to carry a proposal
for a steeply graduated income tax if such a tax were opposed by symbolic

analysts. In fact political choices of any kind for other groups, he argues, are radically circumscribed by their *economic* condition of dependence on symbolic analysts: "In sum, because in-person servers and routine producers need symbolic analysts much more than symbolic analysts need them, the former have little political leverage over the latter. . . . The politics [of symbolic analysts' "secession" from the nation] are relatively peaceful, in other words, because the other side lacks any political artillery" (300). The task of saving the nation as a nation can only be undertaken by symbolic analysts, because they are the only agents holding the economic power to affect change.

The recent cultural politics of diversity and multiculturalism embedded in my second narrative of corporate democracy would doubtless take issue with Reich's generalizations about symbolic analysts' "secession." If anything, management consultants like John Fernandez and R. Roosevelt Thomas are even more emphatic than Reich about the necessity for massive public-funds investment in educational programs for larger groups of the population. To a great extent, their politics echoes Reich's own views on corporate change in his earlier book, *The Next American Frontier.* Management consultants may be more insistent than Reich on an economic payoff for corporate commitment to diversity; Reich, in *The Work of Nations* especially, argues for the primacy of an ethical conception of "nation" larger and more inclusive than such economic interests. The similarities in narrative point of view are nevertheless consistent. Both Reich's narrative and the narratives of corporate human resources management locate the agency for economic change in the group Reich identifies as symbolic analysts, and more specifically, in the classically masculine figure of the "good" (in the full ethical sense of that term) manager overseeing and "enabling" the diversity of his work force; in this narrative, this is the figure ultimately responsible for defining the terms of national identity. "Others" must depend on symbolic analysts, not only economically but for their very identity as citizens of the nation.

Surprisingly, however, Reich's vision of a national rebirth also has similarities to a conservative vision of a dying nation. His threefold division of economic trajectory within a U.S. work force structurally parallels the reconceptualization of First, Second, and Third Worlds in the death of a nation narrative. That is, in transposed terms, Reich's rapidly sinking boat of routine producers would be populated mainly by a First World remnant; the steadily rising boat of symbolic analysts by Second World multinationally affiliated "intellectuals" of all sorts, the infamously named "media

elite," and so on; the slowly sinking in-person servers boat by a heteroge-
neous mix of displaced First World workers and incoming, often "illegal"
aliens from the Third World who when "at home" are busily absorbing the
shift of routine production jobs outside U.S. borders. Thus while the parallel isn't exact by any means, the obvious differences in narrative point of
view and political goals shouldn't obscure certain fundamental structural
similarities. Nor should the Republican sweep of the recent off-year election be confusing. Republican candidates didn't alter the structure of Reich's narrative, but simply realized the folly of overtly locating their rhetoric
in the context of symbolic analyst positions, as Reich does. In a strategy
borrowed by Clinton in his reelection campaign, Republicans preferred instead to make use of the intensities of affect available from a conservative
counter-narrative.

❋

The three narratives I've been describing are produced from very different
discursive formations: the death of a nation by the racist symbolic of conservative counter-narrative; corporate democracy by a claim for aligning a
progressive cultural politics of diversity with corporate profit potential; rebirth of a nation by a vision of necessary ethical commitment to national
identity on the part of symbolic analyst managers. Further, these narratives
cast recent economic change in very different ideological colors—as politically threatening; politically progressive; and politically neutral, simply a
field where responsible ethical choices must be made. What they read *as
economic*, however, and what accounts for the frequent if idiosyncratic narrative parallels among them, is capitalism. That is, the economic stake in
narrative sense-making is everywhere the trajectory of capitalist change.
In the counter-narrative terms of death of a nation, the process of definition that emerges is a negative one; capitalism is a system rapidly being destroyed by the advent of a multicultural politics. But I'm not suggesting in
any case that all three narratives share any common definition of capitalism. Rather, they share a commonsense premise that abundant economic
resources are necessarily the result of a capitalist system of economic practices, however capitalism is defined.

Thus the issue is more than a matter of a name, for as I argued in my
introduction, understanding economic resources is also one way people organize how to make sense of their lives and estimate their powers of action
as social agents. "Capitalism" as I'm using it in this context is then a

"name" for a kind of economic common sense, for making sense of powers of action. What Piore and Sabel project through their deconstruction of "the economic" is a benign multiplicity of capitalisms, where optimally each functions as an entrepreneurial reinvention of local possibilities and resources. What the conjunction of the three narratives of economic change I've described suggests in contrast is a global force field of intense conflicts around commonsense identifications of economic productivity and capitalism. For in commonsense terms, the *distribution* of economic resources is then inevitably a matter of whose capitalism, for whom. Alternatives to capitalism can only signify across this conflicted intersection of narratives as simply the absence of economic resources to be distributed.

In the conclusion to his outline for alternative economic directions in *Postindustrial Possibilities*, economic sociologist Fred Block remarks that in "earlier moments in American history, powerful social movements have emerged—usually unexpectedly—to transform both the form and the content of domestic politics. Such movements have also been able to win significant reforms even in the face of considerable elite resistance. The fact that considerable time has passed since the last such occurrence is no reason in itself to doubt the possibility that this could happen once again" (218). It's not quite clear to me how in looking back over the last three decades Block would fail to see what Laclau and Mouffe like so many others argue persuasively, that new social movements *have* in fact emerged, which differ in any number of ways from oppositional social movements in the past. Further, it is arguably true that all three narratives I've been describing—if also in different ways—are deeply marked by reactions to these movements.

Nevertheless, there seems to me something disturbingly accurate about Block's initial premise for *Postindustrial Possibilities*, even if it is skewed by his specific formulation: "In our own period, it is economic ideas—and ironically, pre-Keynesian economic ideas in particular—that have filled the vacuum left by the silences of contemporary social theory. The remarkable revival during the 1980s of classical free-market economics has served to fill people's need for some kind of social understanding to guide their day-to-day actions" (2). Block, that is, would address directly the way in which economics has become a crucial constitutive factor of "everyday" common sense. The problem in his formulation is how the metaphor of "the vacuum" functions to naturalize a politically constructed space whose historical constitution has much less to do with the silences of recent social theory than with the long legacy of Cold War policies, which were dedicated to clearing a space empty of any plausible commonsense alternatives to a capitalist economy. Social theory in any case hasn't been nearly so silent as Block assumes, even if economic thinking was not particularly fore-grounded. It has, however, been ignored—and often silenced—at any point when it might threaten the maintenance of that vacuumlike space to be occupied only by conceptions of capitalist production and markets.

The definitions of capitalism and capitalist change that emerge within each of the three narratives I've described are by no means purely eco-nomic definitions, nor is it useful to assume economic conditions as a kind of material bottom line that grounds their ideological projects as rational-izations. My point is that whatever their ultimate source or ground, the commonsense perception of the absence of alternatives to economic pro-ductivity as capitalist that they share positions economic practices as a crit-ically important field of conflicts over political control. It's no accident that Reaganism's dream of a radical dismantling of the welfare state, together with the devastating increase of poverty in "developing" nations, had to await the "collapse" of communism to be realized. It's not that an expan-sion of the brutal regime of the Soviet Union would have forestalled these developments, but that the disappearance of a communist menace created the freedom to intensify economic exploitation as a weapon within prolif-erating possibilities of direction and the struggles among them to assert po-litical control. In short, an economic "space" empty of alternatives to cap-italism becomes the obvious territory on which to wage battles for political control, at the expense of a vast global population who must live out their lives in the constant physical and material oppression of poverty.

It's true enough that common sense is intricate and conflicted; opera-tive definitions of capitalism are multiple; "capital" measurement itself a fuzzy field, to say the least; both exploitative labor relations and processes of commodification mutate in utterly unexpected ways. There is no one im-mense field of The Economic that can be targeted for "anti-totalizing" cri-tique, disarticulation, and disruption. Political struggle can't be confined to a metaphysician's lonely war with the specter of totalization. At the same time, however, the existence of conflicts and even contradictions within capitalist economic practices and capitalist common sense doesn't consti-tute automatic grounds for hope, that somehow "something different" will necessarily emerge because the dominant is a fissured formation—the utopian accompaniment to a dystopian thematics of capitalism as relent-lessly expansive.

I will argue in subsequent chapters that, contrary to a capitalist common sense, economic resources not only can be but *are* being produced, distributed, and consumed in significantly countercapitalist ways. That is, the image of economic devastation and poverty visited on so many groups in the United States as well as in "developing" nations shouldn't be allowed to obscure a recognition that these populations are not merely passive victims—or, at best, economic victims nevertheless heroically engaged in resistant cultural practices, or whatever. People "survive" because they've been busy constructing economic alternatives that work despite the intense political pressures on their daily lives, and despite how capitalist common sense has made their economic resources seem invisible.

It is doubly important to recognize this multiplicity of everyday economic resources, because capitalist common sense has also located the weapons of political struggles for control within the often conflicted social spaces of economic practices and direction. Thus groups of the population represented as lacking in economic resources and as economically "unproductive" or "marginal" are assumed politically insignificant as well. As a result, whether subsequently imaged as in need of assistance—or simply expendable in some ultimate sense—such groups appear in any case as incapable of exerting influence over political direction. When economic resources are made invisible, political invisibility is not far behind. There's no reason to claim some inherent "material" priority for attention to economic practices. But when you're living in poverty, it means you're likely to have caught on more quickly to why, if such economic determinism remains a kind of epistemological luxury, countercapitalist economics nevertheless becomes a tactical necessity.

TWO

Murder to Go: Transnational Capital and Countercolonial Economics

That cheap capital is the basis for economic expansion is a long-familiar lesson embedded in capitalist common sense. The creation of cheap capital, however, is now often assumed to require an internationalization of both production and markets, and the very process of capital creation appears to be a global rather than a Euro-American phenomenon. Perceptions of this internationalization have occasioned a whole new set of dilemmas for capitalist common sense in the United States, reflected everywhere from debates over NAFTA to the passage of Proposition 187 in California, targeted at the influx of "illegal aliens." A resurgent nationalism, such as Patrick Buchanan's for example, very directly images a zero-sum game in which every kind of investment in teaching skills to workers beyond U.S. borders means a diminished opportunity of access to skilled positions for groups in the United States.

A more positive spin, in contrast, arrives at the proposition that as the industrialization of export processing zones in "developing" nations penetrates more and more of the national economies, the "developed" world can move securely into its postindustrial phase, featuring highly skilled and mobile technicians, the proliferation of what Robert Reich refers to as symbolic analyst services, and the flexible specialization of manufacturing high-quality, high-return niche goods. The dilemmas of internationalization are rewritten into a new and "postcolonial" form of the divide between "developing" and "developed" world that admits a possible resolution in the large-scale coordination of different rates of industrialization in "developing" countries, together with moving the "developed" world toward flexible specialization, much as Piore and Sabel had anticipated in *The*

Second Industrial Divide. In this scenario, internationalization actually works to the benefit of U.S. national interests.

These increasingly familiar commonsense terms of debate in the United States thus seem framed around a question of whether internationalization is opposed to or congruent with U.S. national interests. Needless to say, such framing is often the despair of professional economists, as evidencing little or no real understanding of the economic issues at stake. In another register of attention, however, it's possible to recognize instead how the debates over economic internationalization and U.S. national interest both disguise and express a set of commonsense disturbances around issues of political incorporation.

Thus one reason why a "positive" alignment of internationalization with U.S. interests has so little appeal to a wide range of "nationalist" supporters is that it effectively assigns the labor of industrial production in which they are engaged—or, increasingly, used to be engaged—to the "developing" world. As a result, it disengages them not only from their jobs but also from an economic basis for a claim to political incorporation in the United States. Crudely, economic expansion seems to come at the expense of making them Third World citizens. Conversely, as even Reich willingly admits, it may well seem to symbolic analysts that their economic activities function to incorporate them politically as world citizens first, who owe little if anything to the United States as a nation. Debates over the relation of international to national interests also express these rather different concerns about who is incorporated as a citizen, and where exactly they are incorporated.

The attempt by major corporations to lower labor costs by locating production in so-called developing countries exacerbates internal issues of political incorporation by introducing a new form of economic division in those countries. On the one hand, there is a series of unrelated, very differently constituted local industries and service providers. On the other, there is an extroverted ensemble of relations in major industries where everything from raw material to personnel can both enter and leave the circuit of production and exchange from any number of internationally linked points. Thus the division isn't only between the relative concentrations of capital in domestic enterprises of all kinds and in the internationally affiliated sector, but between very different forms of economic organization. Likewise, it doesn't reflect a previous division between domestically controlled and internationally controlled economic interests. Rather, the specific form that division takes in each nation is itself constituted and maintained through the process distinguishing the external linkages of what are then "major" industries from regionally autonomous local sectors of the domestic.

In principle it's not hard to see the advantages for major industries in an often quite extended and horizontally discrete series of domestic enterprises. Each can be tapped separately only when needed for specific services and workers, while the existence of the series generally both decreases the size of an unemployed work force and maintains at least a subsistence living for a population who might otherwise become a political time bomb. One effect of IMF activity, for example, is to preserve this "delicate balance" between major industries and domestic enterprises. Nevertheless, if in principle the advantages seem to extend well beyond the initial goal of lowering labor costs, the risks are now becoming considerably more apparent as well.

Crudely, the more a domestic sector thus remains undercapitalized the more the capitalization of major industries depends on foreign investment, and the more that capitalization depends on foreign investment the more undercapitalized a domestic sector becomes. This equation often worked well enough for industries that were organized around manufacture and durable goods, but becomes a distinct liability in the circumstances of an international information economy where capital input depends on an elaborate research infrastructure and skilled personnel. In these circumstances, the undercapitalization that preserves a large reserve army of cheap labor and makes locally cheap in-person services available simultaneously prevents the possibility of drawing capital input in its new sense from anywhere in the sectors of the domestic economy. In other words, it makes capital input as figured in terms of "knowledge skills" an invariably very expensive proposition, and consequently one that can be made cost effective only by concentrating on spots designated as precisely as possible in the value-added stream. One effect of this logic as it works itself out is a whole range of political disturbances, depending on where you are situated economically.

Martin Sklar among others has argued persuasively that through much of its history, the United States itself must be understood as a developing nation. His study, *The United States as a Developing Country*, focuses for the most part on the Progressive Era and the 1920s, but in his concluding chapter he emphasizes how current problems of development are by no means limited to the so-called developing world. In this context, it seems to me possible to recognize an organizational contrast in the United States similar to the familiar pattern in "developing" nations, between the vertical integration of major international industries and a horizontal series of discrete domestic enterprises. A recognition of such a disjunction affords a rather simpler way of questioning the thematics of First World capitalist progress than deconstructing the metaphysics of its narrative teleology—namely, the thematics don't work. You can understand more about what's actually happening economically in the United States, and understand it better, by looking to the ostensibly more "primitive," still "developing," "earlier" phases of capitalism in "developing" nations than by trying to foretell what the logic of a high-tech postindustrial future will be. California as a bellwether state certainly furnishes good evidence for such an emergent pattern. The covering metonymic linkage of "illegal alien" and "crime" in California indirectly refers to elaborate "informal" economies in cities like Los Angeles which have a number of parallels to the series of domestic enterprises in São Paulo or Kingston or Mexico City.

By suggesting such parallels, I don't mean to deny profoundly significant differences, between Kingston and Mexico City no less than between either and Los Angeles. The point is that, far from a now-global process of capital creation embracing everyone, a so-called internationalization of capital in fact intensifies the *exclusion* of whole groups of the global population from any capital process whatsoever. In his critique of what he refers to as "the postcolonial aura" of much recent left theorizing about internationalization, Arif Dirlik draws a very different picture, which registers the implications I've been drawing from organizational contrasts: "What the new flexible production has made possible is that it is no longer necessary to utilize explicit coercion against labor at home or in colonies abroad. Those peoples or places that are not responsive to the needs (or demands) of capital, or are too far gone to respond 'efficiently,' simply find themselves out of its pathways. And it is easier even than in the heyday of colonialism or modernization theory to say convincingly: It is their own fault" (351). In Dirlik's argument, this capitalism doesn't really "work" by relentlessly commodifying all forms of social relations worldwide until there's virtually nothing left "outside." It works by "simply" throwing away whatever isn't of value to "its pathways." Much of the time much of what I've referred to as a horizontal series of domestic enterprises of an economy—involving worldwide, as Dirlik dryly comments, four-fifths of the global population—is treated as so much wastage out of the pathways of capital flow.*

---

* Much of my argument in *Throwaways* has to do with how the politics of Reaganism accelerated this process of "removing" people from capital pathways, while at the same time fixing the blame on those removed.

Any sampling of widely available statistics can give some indication of continually worsening economic conditions worldwide. In 1974, for example, Africa's debt-service ratio was 4.6 percent; already by 1987 it had reached 25 percent. In Jamaica, after the defeat of the People's National Party by the foreign-capital-backed Jamaica Labour Party promising economic recovery, the balance-of-payments deficit went from $200 million in 1980 to $600 million in six years. In both Africa and Latin America, per capita incomes dropped significantly between 1980 and 1990. Further, as Anne McClintock points out, worsening conditions have fallen disproportionately on women: "IMF and World Bank policy favoured cash-cropping and capital surplus in the systematic interests of men, and formed a predictable pattern where men were given the training, the international aid, the machinery, the loans and cash. In Africa, women farmers produce 65 percent–80 percent of all agricultural produce, yet do not own the land they work, and are consistently by-passed by aid programs and 'development' projects" (92).* The process McClintock describes was exacerbated by the shift in World Bank policy toward so-called structural adjustment loans in the early eighties.

Economically, this situation seems to me to represent a description less of a globalized postcolonial world than of a mutation of colonialism from a nation-centered concentration and organization of economic resources to a globally structured network of corporate resource management and political control. As Dirlik puts it: "Perhaps the most important consequence of the transnationalization of capital is that, for the first time in the history of capitalism, the capitalist mode of production, divorced from its historically specific origins in Europe, appears as an authentically global abstraction" (350). The result, however, is not a "purer" form of capitalism finally realizing its inherently totalizing global logic. It is, precisely, an "abstraction," the removal of a political network of power from the multiplicity of socioeconomic organizations of people's lives worldwide. Capitalism in this sense is perhaps best understood as involving the political maintenance and control of diverse economic colonies.

Thus I want to suggest, rather than "postcolonial," with its perhaps inevitable temporal implication, some term on the order of "countercolonial" to identify multiple directions and ways of contesting that abstracting political remove of global capitalism. In looking to "developing" nations for a hermeneutic of understanding economic changes in the United

---

* For a persuasive and detailed account of such effects, see, for example, the essays in Mariarosa Dalla Costa and Giovanna F. Dalla Costa, eds., *Paying the Price*.

States, I will argue in this chapter that countercolonialism challenges the logic of capitalist common sense by insisting on the ways in which an abstracting network of transnational capital nevertheless depends on its colonies, on ensembles of local, domestic economies. And despite how transnational capital imposes organizational, market, and productivity constraints on the horizontal series of domestic enterprises in an economy, there exists within such enterprises a continual production of economic resources, often in decidedly noncapitalist terms. Such production is not a residual carryover from some precapitalist past. It involves the continual invention of new practices responsive to the immediate political circumstances of transnational capital.

"Asking what *single* term might adequately replace 'post-colonialism,'" McClintock argues, "begs the question of rethinking the global situation as a *multiplicity* of powers and histories, which cannot be marshaled obediently under the flag of a single theoretical term, be that feminism, Marxism, or post-colonialism" (97; McClintock's emphasis). And I have no intention of nominating "countercolonialism" as such a single term. Countercolonialism as I understand it doesn't really replace postcolonialism or any other conceptual register of the "multiplicity of powers and histories" that shape "the global situation." It does seem to me, however, to be a way of recognizing specifically why the inventiveness of new economic practices becomes necessary to the many political wars of position in which conflicts are fought out. While "internationalization" often appears as a summary description of the stakes of conflict, it is a description that deploys those conflicts around a familiar binary of global and local. Such a division reduces the political dimensions of countercolonial economics to the struggle to preserve an existent local economy against the always encroaching menace of internationalization. Thus, at worst, countercolonial economics would become simply a nostalgia-driven salvage job.

Perhaps equally important, negative critiques directed at internationalization as the Enemy make it very difficult to recognize the itineraries of internal corporate change that produce the mobilities required by a politics of transnational capital. In what follows, then, I begin by borrowing a narrative construction from an unlikely source in order to better understand this process of corporate change and the kind of mobilities it involves. Those mobilities are both structural and organizational. To the extent transnational capital is a matter of abstracting a network of political power from the immediate exigencies of economic production, circulation, and marketing, what's at stake are the politics of incorporation into and exclu-

sion from capital pathways that are political no less than economic. Mobilities not only maintain the terms of division, but also function to construct
new forms altogether.

❋

Much of the plot of *Murder to Go*, one in the series of Emma Lathen detective mysteries featuring Wall Street banker John Putnam Thatcher, turns
on the proposed acquisition of Southeastern Insurance by Chicken Tonight,
a phenomenally successful take-out dinner franchising operation. Begun in
a single neighborhood kitchen by entrepreneur Frank Hedstrom and his
accountant partner Ted Young, Chicken Tonight has grown to over 400
units stretching from the East Coast nationwide. As the story opens at this
point, the partners are contemplating what seem to be two rather different kinds of corporate expansion: the acquisition of the insurance firm, and
also of an immense broiler farm run by Pelham Browne (who, conveniently for the murder plot, also happens to be on the board of directors of
Southeastern Insurance) that had been the primary supplier of chickens for
Chicken Tonight operations. Thus for the financially unsophisticated, the
novel offers still another mystery besides the familiar search in Emma Lathen stories for a murderer in the midst of corporate intrigue. There seems
a certain immediate logic in a take-out chicken dinner operation acquiring
a broiler farm, but what's the point of acquiring an insurance company?

By the end of the sixties, when the mystery was written, such takeovers
had already become so routine that the narrative can afford to be skimpy
on the rationale. So while there's much discussion of the details of stock
splits, the investigative procedures by which each of the two companies assess the other's financials, the role of Robichaux and Devane as the firm
handling the stock offering, and the intuitive business acumen of Hedstrom as he moves from the world of calculating franchise differentials in
delivery truck times to the world of high finance, there's no direct answer
to the question of why buy an insurance company. We're assured that Hedstrom would make money; he always does. But unlike the action and the
motive for the murder itself, which we get to see secondhand at least
through Thatcher's adroitly comprehensive reconstruction, there's nothing
remotely resembling some scene where Hedstrom presumably would have
explained his reasoning to Young, his ever more cautious partner.

It's necessary to infer that Hedstrom somehow must have acquired a
very different form of working knowledge than his familiarity with fran-

chise details that would have led him to his acquisition decision over Young's opposition. "The instinct of the trader," eulogized later in the novel by Tom Robichaux, isn't much help here. Hedstrom isn't just out to acquire a particular firm, an insurance company; he's not simply gone from trading in commodities to trading in potentially lucrative firms. The choice of Southeastern Insurance follows on a far more important process, which has already reorganized Hedstrom's thinking about Chicken Tonight itself. In order to approach the point where he initiates inquiries into Southeastern Insurance's financials, he's had to learn a kind of symbolic logic that allows him to reconfigure the *meaning* of a franchise operation such as his in a way that the available data about its daily balance sheet of profit and loss might be made to register the potential gravitational effects of something beyond the addition of still another orbiting franchise extending Chicken Tonight's territory. What would the system look like if, rather than just putting another planet in orbit that behaved exactly like the others, you introduced a second star in the corporate firmament? The insurance company is picked to fit the part.

It's Hedstrom's having learned this logic, I would suggest, that also divides the partners over the issue of acquiring Pelham Browne's broiler farm. Young thinks of that acquisition in the "literal" terms of vertical integration—would it make better sense to own a chicken supplier or to continue to contract out for chickens?—and questions whether ownership would ultimately improve Chicken Tonight's market position. Hedstrom, in contrast, has arrived at the point of seeing the acquisition of a broiler farm symbolically, in something of the same terms as acquiring an insurance company relative to his newly projected trajectory of corporate motion. Indeed, with the collapse of the Southeastern Insurance takeover due to the complications of the murder plot, we last see his business mind at work focusing on the future acquisition of the broiler farm, in a way that still mystifies Young.

Thatcher's reconstruction of the murder, however, is only the penultimate scene in the mystery. If rather implausibly, the reconstruction has taken place in a New Jersey Chicken Tonight franchise, with Hedstrom, Young, and their spouses together with Thatcher, Robichaux, and the franchise owners happily munching on different versions of Chicken Tonight entrees. Iris Young, Ted's spouse, had been central to one of the novel's complicating subplots. Driven by jealousy at what she sees as her husband's becoming completely overshadowed by Hedstrom in the corporation, she had taken advantage of the public panic occasioned by the murderer's having poisoned a truckload of Chicken Tonight dinners to try to organize a stock proxy fight challenging Hedstrom's control. The attempt got nowhere; the men were simply embarrassed, Joan Hedstrom serenely unconcerned throughout; and all has been forgotten by the reconstruction scene.

The novel actually ends, however, on the following moment of Iris's triumph, as she's been abstractedly murmuring names over and over to herself while the others talk about the murderer and eat away on chicken Mandarin, chicken Creole, and chicken Tarragon: "Suddenly Iris' voice rang out like a clarion. 'Frank! I've got it!' she cried. 'We'll make it with Jaffa oranges.' Frank Hedstrom came to attention immediately. 'Yes, Iris?' he said respectfully. Iris' head was thrown back. 'We'll call it . . .' she said softly, as one who sees truth plain, 'we'll call it chicken Sinai!' There was a reverent silence. It was Robichaux who responded with ready gallantry. He raised his beer can to Iris in a toast. 'To chicken Sinai!' Admiration was succeeded by awe. 'It will make a mint!'" (224)

Unlike Hedstrom's exercise of symbolic logic, only glimpsed here and there as embedded in the details of stock splits and the like, Iris's symbolic naming appears in the full brilliance of this isolated concluding moment, Iris positioned like an oracle while the others wait in silence for her to pronounce. The isolation of the moment thus pays tribute generally to the new and already important role in corporations of initiatives similar to Iris's symbolic "multiculturalism" of food, and anticipates the equation of "woman" and "culture" that would soon begin to function so significantly in corporate recruiting for "diversity." However hopelessly muddled she may be about the economics of stock proxy fights, her contribution in cultural terms to corporate success is unquestionable. For this isolated moment is quite clearly a recurrent phenomenon. Chicken Mandarin, chicken Creole, and so on, must have arrived in very much the same way. That is, Iris's multiculturalism of food has already been as integral to (and as regular in its effects on) the expansion of Chicken Tonight as Hedstrom's "multieconomism" of corporate diversification promises to be in the future. Robichaux the gourmet, admitting that chicken Tarragon actually doesn't taste bad, and Thatcher, always the banker, even with all his sleuthing, stand linked in mutual witness to the miraculous conjunction of Iris Young and Frank Hedstrom. The novel at once invites you to register the similarity at the same time that it positions Iris and Frank on utterly detached, parallel planes from whose accidental vectors of coincidence the mysterious energy emanates that drives the corporation forward: "It will make a mint!"

There's reason that Ted Young's "literal" logic sees what both Iris Young and Frank Hedstrom do as a mystery, since neither's symbolic logic seems to contribute directly to the production of material goods and services visible in Young's accounting. But this distinction between symbolic and material, like the distinction between symbolic and literal, leads into a conceptual trap. The "secret" to how symbolic logic works in this form—which the novel's ending preserves as a mystery—is not that it disguises a literal referent or a material base, but rather that it rewrites one form of economic resource as another. Marx's own analysis of capitalism furnishes at least two paradigmatic examples of such a transcoding, in the way a process of production is represented as a commodity, and in how use value is subsumed by exchange value. What I've been calling symbolic logic in this context affords still another and more recent example.

Iris's naming doesn't really introduce anything new into the "mix" of resources that yield Chicken Tonight dinners as a product. Yet she's done much more than simply invent a new way to market the "same" product. What she has done is to rewrite marketing as production. The metaphor of the name figures how the resources necessary to selling stuff can be "translated" into the resources necessary to making stuff, where the question of what's literal or material and what isn't about this process is irrelevant. Selling stuff is both "symbolic" and "material/literal," just as making stuff is. Iris's logic doesn't oppose symbolic to material/literal in this sense, but functions symbolically insofar as it translates one complex form of economic resource into another.

Likewise, Hedstrom's "business acumen" in proposing the acquisition of Southeastern Insurance would add nothing new to the product; Chicken Tonight wouldn't begin offering take-out insurance any more than Southeastern Insurance would start feeding chicken to its clients. What would happen with the takeover is that Southeastern Insurance profits would begin feeding Chicken Tonight stockholders, as Chicken Tonight would insure the profit margins of Southeastern Insurance. If Iris has rewritten marketing into production, Hedstrom's proposed acquisition in parallel fashion would rewrite production into circulation. For like Iris's product name, Hedstrom's acquisition is a symbolic figure, in this case for how the productivity involved in Chicken Tonight's goods and Southeastern Insurance's services are translated into the economic resources available to stockholders of both from the new motions now possible to *capital* circulation. And here again, the question of what's really literal or material about this process is less immediately important than how it functions to translate one form of economic resource into another.

Iris Young and Frank Hedstrom are thus primary sources of value added to the general economy by Chicken Tonight, even though neither one "adds" anything whatsoever by way of goods or services. Ultimately, the conceptual trap of opposing symbolic to literal or material lies in how such oppositions make it impossible to grasp both halves of this apparent paradox. That is, if in a rather bad caricature of Marx's reasoning you assume that the "real" value of Chicken Tonight has its source in the material labor of producing dinners, then Iris and Frank's symbolic manipulations appear merely exploitative, appropriating the surplus labor of the real producers. The trouble with this picture is that Iris and Frank's work is in fact indispensable to corporate Chicken Tonight, as at least Dottie and Vernon Akers—the franchise owners present at the murder reconstruction, and engaged in turning out dinner after dinner, night after night—have recognized clearly. Conversely, however, it's no less true to say that Iris and Frank's work *is* symbolic; it's everywhere a second-order operation which in itself not only wouldn't yield a single chicken dinner to anyone, but couldn't possibly exist as an "in itself."

By way of Iris's naming, Chicken Tonight consumers can eat where they've never been before. They can do so, of course, because the corporation has arrived before them, mobilized on a symbolic name. Likewise, had Hedstrom's acquisition gone through (but assuredly there will be others), Chicken Tonight stockholders would profit from, of all things, the selling of insurance—once again because the corporation arrived before them. As symbolic converters of forms of economic resource, what Iris and Frank "produce" is first and most importantly a coincidence of corporate change and corporate mobility. Young in contrast knows perfectly well that acquiring Southeastern Insurance would change the corporate organization of Chicken Tonight, and he understands that the acquisition would move the corporation into new and unfamiliar territory. What his literal logic cannot grasp about Hedstrom's project is the reciprocal symbolic equation of change and mobility as itself a source of added value in the eyes of stockholders and investors, much as Iris's symbolic naming is a source of added value for consumers.

In *Global Capitalism: The New Leviathan*, Ross and Trachte argue that the "international division of labor associated with the era of monopoly capitalism becomes altered" (83). Rather than being concentrated in a core of older, well-developed regions of Europe and North America, manufacturing production has shifted significantly to the periphery. Workers in at least certain sectors of the periphery are no longer engaged in the extraction of raw materials but in the production of manufactured goods. The reason for the shift, Ross and Trachte argue, has finally to do with restoring the rate of profit: "By substituting workers in the periphery for workers in the core, manufacturing firms have been able to increase their rates of surplus extraction. Even when this substitution is a *relatively* small fraction of a global firm's *total* employment, it looms large in the strategic relation between employers and employees, lending firms important leverage with remaining employees in the core. Spatial mobility has been the critical instrument used to restore the rate of profit" (84–85; authors' emphasis).

Spatial mobility, however, cannot be assumed as simply an already available "instrument" to be deployed strategically in a process of corporate competition for profit. Like any form of mobility, it requires specific conditions of possibility that have to do with cheap labor, favorable political relations between classes, and so on, assumed to be readily available beyond U.S. borders. Equally important, mobility requires a redefinition of internal corporate structure, new forms of symbolic work in the corporation, and as I've been implying, redefinitions of corporate relations to consumers and stockholders. *Murder to Go* isn't about international business and the internationalization of corporate location. Yet it can be made to yield a remarkably suggestive account of how the necessary conditions for corporate spatial mobility are created. Further, it anticipates a rather different form of an international division of labor than in Ross and Trachte's detailing of a shift of manufacture from core to periphery.

What's important in this division is neither the relative location of raw material extraction and manufacture of finished goods, nor the hierarchy implied between management "conception" and worker "execution" of production processes. The division exists between workers (wherever they are) who produce the conditions of corporate mobility, and workers (wherever they are) who don't. Ted Young as partner and chief accountant for Chicken Tonight is by most classificatory schemes a high-ranking corporate manager. Yet in terms of the division I'm suggesting, his labor belongs with that of Vern Akers the franchise owner, or Clyde Sweeney the murdered delivery truck driver, insofar as it contributes nothing directly to corporate mobilities. There's considerable substance to Iris's perception that despite his pay and his friendship with Hedstrom, he's become a second-class worker in the corporation. Like Clyde on his driver's route or Vern at the

levers of his pressure oven, Ted's accounting also follows the paths of corporate movement constructed by the symbolic logic of Iris Young and
Frank Hedstrom.

Thus in the novel's conclusion, which carefully separates Iris's moment
of triumphal naming from her takeover scheming, the plotting of the novel
also preserves in larger terms the separation between its corporate story and
its murder story. Chicken Tonight in its newly reorganized form will continue to prosper under the twin emblem of Iris and Frank's multisymbolic
direction; the murder from which that reorganization emerged has been
decently swept from view, bodies cleared away. All that remains at the conclusion are the open vistas of new times, the corporation endlessly on the
move.

In the next section, with my version of *Murder to Go* as an early cautionary fable of corporate change and labor recomposition, I want to turn
first to the "transnationalization" of capital made possible by corporate mobilities, and second to the schematic of labor recomposition that Robert
Reich introduces in *The Work of Nations*, built on his understanding of
transnational corporations. In other words, I want to put the mystery's twin
plots back together again. By identifying the work that Iris Young and
Frank Hedstrom do as a kind of symbolic logic, I've anticipated Reich's
emphasis on "symbolic analysts" as the primary corporate players in a global
economy and the primary sources of value added to the economy. By way
of *Murder To Go*, however, I hope also to have anticipated an answer to the
question Reich finds so difficult and confusing: namely, what exactly do
symbolic analysts do?

❖

The distinction Masao Miyoshi draws between *multi*national and *trans*national corporations is crucial to understanding the abstracting remove of a
now highly mobile network of capital relations from local economic conditions. While recognizing that such a distinction can't be absolutely and
cleanly demarcated, Miyoshi argues that in general terms "a multinational
corporation (MNC) is one that is headquartered in a nation, operating in a
number of countries. Its high-echelon personnel largely consists of the na-
tionals of the country of origin, and the corporate loyalty is, though increasingly autonomous, finally tied to the home nation. A truly transnational corporation, on the other hand, might no longer be tied to its nation
of origin but is adrift and mobile, ready to settle anywhere and exploit any

state, including its own, as long as the affiliation serves its own interests" (736).

Unfortunately for my purposes, Miyoshi figures the distinction first in terms of corporate affiliation to national origin, with the result that in contrast to MNCs, transnational corporations appear in his argument as free-floating entities, only incidentally concerned to observe the laws and practices of the specific nations in which they do business. As Peter Dicken has demonstrated in *Global Shift: The Internationalization of Economic Activity*, however, by far the greatest percentage of foreign investment actually circuits among a very small number of nations whose policies largely continue to determine the shape of that circuit. Thus when construed as an issue of relative freedom from national origin, Miyoshi's distinction remains questionable at best. It seems to me possible to recognize a distinction more clearly in terms of a process of recruiting "high-echelon personnel," as Miyoshi puts it, "workers thoroughly familiar with local rules and customs as well as the specific corporate policies for worldwide operation. For that purpose, their workers usually are of various nationalities and ethnicities. . . . In that sense, TNCs are at least officially and superficially trained to be color-blind and multicultural" (741).

The recruitment task Miyoshi describes means that TNCs have potentially very different relations with domestic enterprises of the economy than MNCs. For the latter, domestic enterprises remain primarily an available source of cheap routine labor and in-person services, to be tapped only when needed. And even here, as J. K. Gibson-Graham argues in *The End of Capitalism (As We Knew It)*, following out the implication of Dicken's research, the circuit of actual investment financing suggests "the much publicized orientation of MNCs to areas of low wage costs bears re-examination" (127). TNCs in contrast can be distinguished by how their recruiting process looks to some level of domestic sectors for highly skilled workers who are expected to remain with the corporation and whose loyalties are expected to be to the corporation first. Thus TNCs do more than "obey the laws in every country we operate," as Percy Barnevic, CEO of Asea Brown Bavari asserts in the interview Miyoshi quotes. TNCs also have a powerful—if highly selective—corporate interest in *nationally* constituted and supported educational systems and research infrastructures. They are at once more highly abstracted from and more deeply embedded in relations with domestic economies than MNCs.

The abstraction of MNCs remains a centered abstraction, less in terms of an opposition between national origin and international sites of produc-

tion and marketing, however, than as an antagonistic structural relation of
"headquarters" to "periphery." That is, internal corporate tensions typically
result from a disjunction between the concentration of decision-making
authority at headquarters and the concentration of local knowledges at
whatever specific sites—inside or outside the borders of the country of
corporate origin—that appear as the corporate periphery. Thus the abstraction from local conditions can never really be complete; the corporation is always centered around a headquarters site.

The abstraction of TNCs seems in contrast a radically decentered abstraction, because neither decision-making authority nor capital flow is oriented across a division of headquarters and periphery. Capital and authority always move from somewhere in the corporate structure; this isn't a picture of some endlessly free-floating series of exchange relations. But where
they move from and where they move to isn't determined in advance by a
fixed relation of headquarters and periphery. "Headquarters" can be any
concentration of capital and authority on the occasion, which may well be
somewhere else tomorrow. The contrast in other words is organizational
rather than a matter of a division between national origin and international
activities.

At the same time, however, such concentrations occur at all, in any
given location, only insofar as whatever barriers may separate corporate
activity from "local rules and customs" are systematically reconstituted for
the occasion rather than, as with MNCs, simultaneously maintained and
yet also decomposed indirectly, through the tensions existing between corporate headquarters and periphery. A TNC contemplating opening a regionally autonomous operation will look to seek leverage through the
malleability of tax laws, zoning ordinances, and environmental regulations;
the availability of transportation linkages; the infrastructure of in-person
services and the potential for outsourcing piece work, and so on, as
MNCs do. But TNCs also look to the potential for recruiting a skilled
local work force, as that might involve local commitments to improving
an educational structure and providing research possibilities; the presence
of domestic firms who can be outsourced for highly specific and knowl-
edge-intensive services is also desirable. That is, the question is not what
already exists that might be of use or, in contrast, present insuperable barriers to use. It's a matter of what must be reconstituted to be of use toward the immediate end of enlarging the mobile flexibilities of organizational structure. The decentered abstraction of transnational capital
thereby permits a much greater power of *abstracting from* the local by this

process of reaching much further into and reconstituting the networks of local conditions.

Nevertheless, while the mobilities of capital and decision-making authority indeed make the organization of TNCs look decentered relative to MNCs, that decentered organization everywhere involves complex networks of affiliation that bind personnel first to the corporation, in all its mobilities. TNCs can look decentered from one perspective only because from another they involve a much more intricate network of internal affiliations. Miyoshi suggests that the resulting multiculturalism of TNCs is in fact only "superficial"; its personnel may come from different countries and different ethnicities, but all are corporate players first. In a certain sense, however, that multiculturalism is anything but superficial. What it means to be a corporate player is to work within a network of relations that identifies the corporation itself as, precisely, a multicultural construction through and through, not just on some superficial level. That is, one isn't identified as first a citizen of Sweden and only secondarily as an ABB executive who happens to work alongside citizens of other nations. One is first an executive of ABB as a multicultural enterprise, who happens also to be a citizen of Sweden as a specific nation.

For the "multi-" of this "multiculturalism" doesn't identify Swedish and Senegalese and U.S. and Taiwanese countries of origin for ABB executives (any more than Iris Young's naming of chicken Sinai identified her as a native of the Sinai now contributing to Chicken Tonight's multicultural food offerings). Rather, "multi-" identifies the always mobile, shifting multiplicities of ABB operations in these and other countries. What the "culture" of the "multiculturalism" identifies is of course a construction, but that hardly makes it superficial without some buried assumption of "natural" or "authentic" cultures. As I suggested above, the multicultural construction of TNCs is an abstraction, and one that works by reconstituting elements of local cultures into the multicultural saturation of the TNC corporate organization. TNCs, again, are at once more highly abstracted and more deeply embedded in relations with domestic economies than MNCs.

Just as the multiculturalism of TNCs can be constructed through reconstituting the elements of any culture, their multieconomism, like Hedstrom's, addresses symbolically *any* form of labor. Its symbolics decomposes and recombines labor into always more elaborately distinguishable elements. TNC personnel must know that there are cultural differences between, say, how operations are carried out in Taiwan and how they are carried out in Tennessee. But they must also know that potentially significant differences exist *within* local labor markets, for example, between available in-person messenger service in a Taiwanese city and in-person messenger service in a Tennessee city. Robert Reich's new schematic of labor classification in *The Work of Nations* (discussed in the last chapter), with its fundamental categories of routine production, in-person services, and symbolic analyst services, can be understood in this context as an attempt to generate new categories that might help make sense of how the composition of a labor force has been affected by transnational corporations. His categories, however, are at once far too general and not nearly general enough to account for transnational capital's multieconomism of labor.

They're too general in that the large distinction between routine production and in-person services can't begin to register the enormous multiplicity of specific forms that labor takes in the United States, let alone in other domestic economies worldwide. That is, for all that his model of corporate change acutely recognizes the emergent characteristics of TNCs as they differ from MNCs, his labor categories continue to reflect an MNC vision of a global labor market, for which general categories like routine production and in-person service are perfectly adequate to express the terms of corporate interest in the labor available in any country in which the firm operates. For TNCs, in contrast, any local labor market represents a potentially unlimited multiplicity of work skills, labor organizations, and combinatorial possibilities of linkages among different sectors. Hence, to extend the example above, the skill with languages that may be necessary to a Taiwanese messenger can be recognized as potentially suitable to a completely different position within a transnational corporation—perhaps transcoding e-mail across several regionally autonomous units. The language skills necessary to a Tennessee messenger may not be suitable for such work. In this TNC perspective, to lump the two workers together as Reich's scheme would within a category of in-person service is far too general to be of use, for economic reasons no less than for cultural ones.

At the same time, however, Reich's categories don't reach anything like the level of generality necessary to express the symbolics of labor that articulate the multieconomism of TNCs, even though his thinking about labor classification begins in an impatience with the attempt at specific, empirical accuracy that inspires Census Bureau and Labor Department proliferation of categories. He points out rightly that such thinking is impossible because it is too empirically specific. Jobs and job descriptions in any case change continually, and hence any such empirical classificatory system, no matter how detailed, will inevitably look like an afterimage of yesterday's jobs. Reich proposes instead that we leap to the new conceptual ground of recognizing large, general forms of labor that would make, for example, work on a thirties automobile assembly line and work on data entry in a nineties bank both versions of a category of "routine production." He doesn't mean by that leap to suggest that the work practices of the auto assembly line and of data entry involve precisely the same motions or skills or that the work forces are comparable, but simply that both jobs add value to the economy similarly.

As a result, however, Reich must assume the same grounds of distinction as the classificatory system he challenges. His general categories of routine production, in-person service, and symbolic analysis are distinguishable from each other in exactly the same way as the many more specific categories that appear in Census Bureau schemes: if on a more general and comprehensive level, they still answer the question of what is produced that adds value to the economy. His otherwise lucid account of what routine production and in-person workers do thus stalls out at the top of his scale, in describing the ultimately *symbolic* work of symbolic analysts. Indeed, he comes very close to admitting that the question of "what do you do" is entirely the wrong question to ask of symbolic analysts.

As my version of the Emma Lathen mystery implies, the reason is that symbolic analysts don't "produce" anything in these terms. A TNC analyst isn't even involved in the circulation of messages in either Taiwan or Tennessee, let alone the production of message meaning, or goods and services. The analyst constitutes a symbolically significant difference between the Taiwanese worker's language skills and the Tennessee worker's language skills in relation to an immediate configuration of corporate service needs. In so doing, the analyst then also rewrites one specific aspect of this specific Taiwanese labor skill from "outside" to "inside" the pathways of corporate capital insofar as the labor has been symbolically converted into the form of transcoding e-mail and the laborer into a new TNC employee—without directly affecting the many other ways other Taiwanese workers continue to function in other multiple grids of "outside/inside" and other appropriations of labor. That is, the analyst has first of all "produced" *from* the local the conditions of abstraction beyond embeddedness *in* the local, conditions necessary for capital mobility. TNCs are at once more highly abstracted from and more deeply embedded in relations with domestic economies than MNCs. Reich's categories are neither general enough to express the abstraction, nor specific enough to express the embeddedness, because they can't identify the indispensable resource symbolic analysts

produce for transnational capital. As I've tried to suggest by way of my reconstruction of *Murder to Go*, the spatial mobility implied by internationalization itself depends on a far more fundamental symbolic equation of corporate change with the complexities of corporate mobilities of organization, labor force selection, and forms of political management.

❀

Suppose you imagine yourself as the parent of a child just arrived at school
age. You've been invited to a meeting called by the local public school system for the purpose of explaining to parents like yourself the projected job
prospects that await the district's children on completion of their education. And suppose further that the agenda was framed in terms of Reich's
categorial reclassification of the labor market. During the first part of the
meeting, representatives from each of Reich's three general categories
would be asked to speak to the issues of job qualification, work practices,
pay scales, prospects for advancement, and "quality of life" values that could
be expected from the position they represent. The idea is that you could
then choose at this inaugural point in your child's education the appropriate educational "tracking" path for your child that would guarantee she or
he landed, respectively, in a symbolic analyst position, a routine production
position, or an in-person service position upon graduation. Thus at the conclusion of the general part of the meeting, parents would be invited to
make a tentative declaration of intent and to attend an afternoon session
with job representatives and school board personnel to learn more about
their specific choice.

It's a safe bet that one of the three rooms set aside for afternoon sessions
would be very thickly populated in comparison to the others, and this
looks like a good explanation for why any form of such a meeting would
seem an absurdity in the "real world." It would of course be the "wrong"
room. By far the great majority of the population must learn instead—if
they're lucky—to accept routine production or in-person service jobs, not
the kind of work and prestige that goes with symbolic analyst positions as
Reich describes them.

Facing increasing pressures for accountability to parents and to students,
however, educators at all levels express dismay at how parents especially
seem nevertheless to be acting precisely as if they had attended such a
meeting, gone to the symbolic analyst room for the afternoon, and now
expect the school system to deliver on a guarantee. The reason is that nei-

ther parents nor students are stupid, and even without the benefit of Reich-manual instruction they can read thousands of signs in U.S. culture that emphasize the relation of "good," symbolic analyst jobs to education, and the necessity of choosing, and choosing early, the path you will eventually follow. My hypothesis of a meeting may seem an absurd, schematic model, but the message modeled by my hypothetical symbolic analyst representa-tive at the meeting in fact appears in countless different forms, from ad-vertisements to civic brochures and newspaper classifieds. The immediately relevant question is why such messages appear all over the place if, like my meeting, they would seem to lead inevitably to packing the "wrong room," to expectations that education will lead to high-level employment. It's not quite a sufficient answer to say that public education has always involved a lure of "false promises." It isn't primarily educators after all who dissemi-nate the message. As educators, we spend much of our time instead insist-ing to anyone who will listen that education isn't just about getting a job in any case, it's about—well, getting an education.

Recent studies of colonialism suggest the possibility of a rather different kind of answer, having to do with the dynamics of colonized/colonizer re-lations. Part of being a colonizer is to find ways of making sure colonized populations know that they depend on you, and part of how they're made to know they depend on you is by enforcing a lesson that nothing much can really happen without the intervention of your agency. To some great extent, however, this lesson doesn't require actually making things happen. Rather, it involves a performance of the *desirability* of being the agent for things happening. Likewise, translated from this colonial model, the "mes-sage" parents and children read from innumerable cultural signs can be un-derstood as a message about the desirability of symbolic analyst agency. In terms of my hypothetical "meeting," what could be more desirable than occupying the room everybody wants to get into?

Reich perhaps prefers the metaphor of "boats" rather than "rooms" be-cause of his insistence that symbolic analysts are cutting themselves adrift from the rest of the nation. Reich's narrative of a crisis of national iden-tity in *The Work of Nations* begins with the premise that the symbolic ana-lysts who are the primary source of added value to corporations in a global economy increasingly see themselves as corporate citizens rather than as citizens of a nation. As a result, what's happening in the United States is a gradual process of secession from the union by its most productive mem-bers. While the effects of secession may be politically damaging to a vast majority of the U.S. population who are not symbolic analysis, Reich argues that nevertheless the process of secession has been generally peaceful: "In sum, because in-person servers and routine producers need symbolic analysts much more than symbolic analysts need them, the former have little political leverage over the latter. . . . The politics are relatively peaceful, in other words, because the other side lacks any political artillery" (300).

What shapes Reich's argument generally is thus a commonsense assumption about economic productivity. Economically, "in-person servers and routine producers need symbolic analysts much more than symbolic analysts need them," and as a result in-person servers and routine producers can't afford a sustained politics of opposition to symbolic analysts—however much they may engage in sporadic acts of criminal violence—without simultaneously cutting their own economic lifelines. In other words, his assumption about political power is grounded in the discursive matrix of capitalist common sense I discussed in my introduction: productivity of resources is what capitalism is all about. If capitalism has now mutated into its present form of a globally abstracted transnational network, then that's where productivity of resources now comes from. Given the economic leverage available from their critical positioning in this new form of capitalist productivity, symbolic analysts are politically free to choose secession; or, in Reich's vision, they can choose instead to take ethical responsibility for redefining the very idea of "nation," and thereby ensure that resources become more generally available to more people in the nation.

The many cultural messages that model the desirability of symbolic analyst positions, however, suggest a more intricate picture than the political secession Reich argues has been taking place. The invitation proffered by such signs in the United States pictures less withdrawal and secession from the nation than the possibility of *realizing* yourself as "American." That is, in the room you're invited to enter, symbolic analyst positions are seen as desirably American positions in a global culture, as the "subject" all cultures worldwide are increasingly all about. Thus what makes my hypothetical school district meeting an unreal schematic is not the effect it would have of packing the "wrong" room. It's that I've naively assumed a representative voice at the meeting for routine producers and in-person servers. And if you take recent McDonald's recruiting ads as one familiar example of the cultural message that appears in so many forms today, quite clearly what you don't meet anywhere in the ads is an image of the importance of routine assembly line production of fried hamburgers or of the importance of good service to customers. Rather, young people "just like you" are represented as already branch managers at Mickey D's, already occupying a proto-symbolic-analyst position and on their way to still better positions. *That's* what it means to be American. There's really no other room you could possibly be interested in as an American citizen.

It is an illusion, in a contemporary economy, as Reich ably argues, to try to maintain an image of U.S. competitiveness predicated on the market position of uniquely American corporations. Yet there is a substance to the illusion, once you recognize the construction of an Americanness of American identity linked not to the market position of ostensibly U.S.-based corporations, but to the subject position of a U.S.-identified management of the economic. Reich's exhortation to symbolic analysts to share his nation-based vision isn't a new ethical direction; it's a new spin on an already existent direction. Its basis is a kind of sleight-of-hand that functions to disguise a colonizing logic of dependence applied to large groups of the U.S. population no less than to "foreigners." People already positioned in routine production and in-person service are taught by such "ethical" logic that they must depend on symbolic analysts for their very identity as citizens of the nation no less than for their economic support. "Americans," in this imagery, are not after all engaged in the actual production, marketing, and circulation of economic resources. Real Americans don't fry, or serve, hamburgers (or deliver Chicken Tonight dinners). What "we" do is a second-order process, existing at the level of the control and management of economic resources. What "America" has to offer to a global economy is a symbolic *politics* of management.

While in Reich's account such a politics of management seems to have an exclusively American face, in global terms it expresses more accurately the corporate structure of TNCs as political organizations through-and-through, actively engaged in management politics. TNCs live on the analytic separation of the political from the economic, not in order to preserve economic processes from "political interference" but in order to maintain political control free from the embeddedness in conditions that determine the production, marketing, and circulation of specific economic goods and services. The resurgence of theories of "free market" capitalism over the last three decades should be understood as, precisely, a political ideology of transnational capital. Even if paradoxically, "free market" means politically free *from* embeddedness in the local conditions of any given market organization. As I will argue in Chapter 4, the "market" is neither an extension of classical capitalist principles nor a disguised "production model," as Fredric Jameson suggests. It is a new form of colonial political hegemony with transnational corporations as the primary agents.

The symbolic analysts of transnational capital possess a remarkable armory of "political artillery," in Reich's phrase, because of how they maximize the political freedom of their remove from economic conditions. The "free market" they occupy is a political market freed from the encumbrances of economics that can be left to those in the colonies. Reich's equation might well be rewritten in something like the following way. Routine producers and in-person servers are made to feel they "need" symbolic analysts if their labor is ever to appear as incorporated within the *political* pathways of transnational capital. That is, they seem to have no "political artillery" insofar as, unlike symbolic analysts, they remain embedded within the conditions of the production, marketing, and circulation of economic resources. They appear as condemned to economic colonies by the politics of transnational capital.

Rather than a new mutation of capitalist economics feeding globally on whatever remnants of precapitalist formations still linger, transnational capital thus stands in relation to *already capitalized* local sectors like a ghost from the past. Indeed, given the decentered corporate structure, the regional operating units of a TNC have an autonomy unheard of for decades and decades in corporate organization. So much so that, as I argued in the last chapter, quite careful, sober analysts such as Piore and Sabel no less than enthusiasts for a New Order like Richard Crawford have been led to see the present forms of corporate decentralizing and flattened management hierarchy as a revival of classical capitalism's economic innovation and "entrepreneurial spirit."

In one sense such ostensibly historical retrievals are nothing but a fantasy of displacement. But in another sense the refusal of a neatly linear teleology of steady capitalist growth and progress can be inflected toward a recognition that transnational capital's symbolics of labor nevertheless does mark a certain kind of repetition of a much earlier moment in the history of capital/labor relations. It's worth recalling Dirlik's comment in this context: "What the new flexible production has made possible is that it is no longer necessary to utilize explicit coercion against labor at home or in colonies abroad. Those peoples or places that are not responsive to the needs (or demands) of capital, or are too far gone to respond 'efficiently,' simply find themselves out of its pathways" (351). The history of "explicit coercion against labor" is now so long and intricate that it's easy to excuse Dirlik for not adding the coda that "explicit coercion" was not always a crucial aspect of management control of labor. Like the flexible production Dirlik attends to in the present, early forms of industrialization also left whole groups of the laboring population "out of its pathways" rather than using coercive force against them. At the same time highly skilled craftspeople were rewarded—sometimes extravagantly—for bringing their skills to the factory in a way that "abstracted" them from the local conditions of production and marketing in which they had been embedded. Explicit coercion became a necessity only with the emergence of a sufficiently large and potentially threatening mass of industrial workers.

The difference of this repetition, however, may not narratively lend itself to the dramatic contrast of "tragedy" and "farce" Marx saw in the secondness of the Second Brumaire, even if there is something farcical indeed about the recent discussions of a revival of "the entrepreneurial spirit" and so on. What's different about transnational capital's repetition of this early moment in capitalist management/labor relations is that while industrialization, for better or worse, organized workers to produce new forms of economic resources in sometimes breathtaking quantities, the organization of transnational capital, strictly, does not produce economic resources in this sense at all.

I suggested in my introductory chapter that the central spine of capitalist common sense is that where you find economic resources in abundance, there you'll also find capitalism at work. But contrary to Reich's version of this capitalist common sense that grounds the political power of symbolic analysts in their economic productivity, what you *won't* find in a contemporary global economy is transnational capitalism directly at work producing, marketing, or circulating economic resources. The multiplicity of markets and market relations I will explore in Chapter 4, like the multiple ways to exploit a consumer labor of production that I will focus on in the next chapter, exist in these many and varied forms because in contrast to the process of industrialization, transnational capital doesn't organize production or marketing homogeneously. It does not operate like industrialism at the level of a global "modernization" of economic practices.

Transnational capital is a second-order operation, a process of symbolic conversion of resources, and it is a highly mobile operation because its political pathways must always lead to where economic resources *already* exist. That's where you'll find transnational capital's symbolic conversion at work. MNCs are in this sense a vestigial reminder of industrial capitalism, engaged now in a worldwide search for cheap raw material and cheap labor for processes of production. TNCs in contrast go in search of cheap capital, in the form of already capitalized economic resources. The promise they hold out in return is not only integration into the pathways of a global economy but, more fundamental, incorporation into the political organization of transnational capital.

In "Multinational Corporations and the Internationalization of Production: An Industry Perspective," Julie Graham argues that internationalization and what she calls the "capital flight story" has become a far too pervasive explanation on the left for worsening economic conditions for many. "If we are concerned with job loss, worker dislocation, and community decline"—which seem to me crucial and central concerns to countercolonial economics—she suggests that "it is important to recognize that the internationalization of production is only one contributor to these processes, one that plays a major role only in certain industries and communities" (222). Or as she puts it more bluntly later: "There are many things corporations can do to jobs besides export them" (237). Focusing only on the "capital flight story" thus ignores a great many ways in which corporations "do things" to jobs, and to workers.

I have argued that the mobile organizational structuring of transnational capital is in fact even one more step removed from the "job loss, worker dislocation and community decline" associated with the spatial dispersion and capital flight involved in multinational corporate operations. Unlike MNCs, which directly introduce such dislocations as they go in search of cheap resources of raw material and labor, TNCs, again, go in search of already cheap capital. At the same time, however, the organizational mobilities of TNCs arguably have a much greater effect on the *multiplicity* of factors that lead to worsening economic conditions, to the "many things corporations can do to jobs."

What makes capital "cheap" after all is not internationalization per se, but the intensification of exploitation; the assumed social necessity of "the market" and its competitive marketplace economic relations; the priority of profits over the satisfaction of human needs for economic resources; the national directions of economic policy making; the reconstitution and deployment of race and gender constructions; the internal autonomy of corporate selection practices; the commonsense feat of prestidigitation that links "capitalism" to economic productivity. All contribute in one way or another to the formation of cheap capital, and economic resources in the form of cheap capital are what is most readily available for conversion into the politics of transnational capital.

❖

In contrast to both the "modernization" thesis and more recent variants like Piore and Sabel's macro-coordinated global hybrid of "developing" country industrialization and "developed" country flexible specialization, Hernando de Soto's popular analysis of the "informal sector" in *The Other Path* and elsewhere emphasizes instead the innovative entrepreneurship of small, domestic producers in *developing* countries. His argument is driven by a combination of Hayek-inspired attacks on legal, government-imposed bureaucratic interference with free enterprise, and a romanticism of the "informal" as a sleeping giant of economic growth, the true embodiment of early ideals of capitalist entrepreneurial flexibility. Thus his notion of the state and its legal apparatus as the primary block to economic productivity would have been anachronistic even in the early twentieth century. Likewise, his understanding of informal sector labor conveniently leaves out any recognition of structural connections to the politics of transnational capital and its symbolics of labor. Nevertheless, it is important to recognize, as de Soto does, that economic productivity occurs in many ways throughout the mazy intricacies of an informal sector, and that informal workers are not simply passive victims of circumstances.

Looking to the economic catastrophes that have devastated so many in so-called developing nations over the last three decades should be a reminder—if one were necessary—that leveraging economic practices into effective "political artillery," in Reich's phrase, is a complicated and difficult task. The difficulties are easily compounded, however, by a willingness to see "developing" countries only through the lens of economic devastation. Against the post–Soviet Union crescendo of triumphal hymns about the success of a capitalist "free market" everywhere, the importance of recognizing the actual effects of that "free market" on developing nations should be obvious. Nevertheless, translating that recognition into an imagery of implacable marketplace expansion and its devastating effects can also work to reinforce a sense of inevitable transnational capital power. As J. K. Gibson-Graham succinctly puts it in *The End of Capitalism (As We Knew It)*: "For the left, the question is, how might we challenge the dominant script of globalization and the victim role it ascribes to workers and communities in both 'first' and 'third' worlds?" (126). Left politics cannot simply continue to replay a "rape" story of capitalist violation of worker-victims.*

* Gibson-Graham's challenge to a left positioning of passive worker-victims of international capitalism deliberately parallels Sharon Marcus's challenge to the idea of passive rape victims in "Fighting Bodies, Fighting Words: A Theory and Politics of Rape Prevention."

In "Development Strategies in Latin American: Which Way Now?" José Távara remarks how commonplace it's become to see the eighties especially as a "lost decade" for Third World countries. Certainly economic conditions by any statistical measure worsened significantly. "The term *lost decade* might be misleading, however," Távara adds, "if it is taken to mean that nothing substantial happened in the Latin American region. In fact, one of the most significant features of this period has been the development of new forms of production organization and social institutions as those affected by the crisis have banded together in an effort to survive. Diverse collective initiatives have been organized, such as communal kitchens and primary health-care workshops, along with a wide range of small-scale activities, mostly in commerce and services but also in manufacturing" (391).

Using a distinction between "unembedded" and "embedded" business enterprises first proposed by Karl Polanyi, Conrad Arensberg, and Harry Pearson in 1957, Távara goes on to argue that World Bank policies and the internationalization of the economy during the eighties exacerbated the economic disparities generated by "unembedded" business operations such as multinational subsidiaries. Yet at the same time, the decade also saw the proliferation of a number of very different and "embedded" developments, "'attached' to the localities and regions within which they operate" (398). Villa El Salvador, in metropolitan Lima, affords a good example of such embeddedness. The idea for Távara, however, is not simply to celebrate Villa El Salvador as some kind of utopian countereconomics of the local, an embattled enclave resisting the encroaching menace of internationalization. It was heavily supported by the Velasco government as almost a lab experiment in central economic planning. In fact, as Távara points out, along with the remarkable successes in housing, schools, health care, and food supplies, it's also true that unemployment among the now some 250,000 inhabitants is widespread. As a result, small producers among the many business enterprises remain competitive by paying low wages; monopoly power among producers selling beyond the district is quite common; and family labor for firms has often reinforced rather than reduced gender inequalities.

The reason such disparities exist between collectively organized economic practices successfully yielding material benefits and political practices that in contrast exacerbate inequalities is, precisely, that Villa El Salvador and similar districts are not isolated and strictly local phenomena. They actively challenge both the economic and political power of unembedded enterprises and the complicated ensemble of policy determinants of the state. Thus they represent what Anibal Quijano calls "a type of power within society" (113), one that involves new forms of economic practices, but which also forces conflicted political intersections extending well beyond the district. The population groups of Villa El Salvador are neither simply passive victims of a "lost decade" nor a reason to celebrate some triumph of "the local" preserved against invasively evil forces of internationalization. The tensions and contradictions of their everyday lives are part of an everyday struggle necessary for economic practices to appear as a political force otherwise than within the pathways of transnational capital. They are part of a countercolonial economics that doesn't depend on trying to preserve indigenously local economic practices, but rather engages actively in the conflicts that result from trying to take advantage of the dependence of transnational capital on newly organized forms of economic production and marketing. Challenges to "the dominant script of globalization" begin in recognizing that transnational capital power is neither complete nor self-generated. In large part its vulnerabilities result from its dependence on economic practices outside its pathways.

In revising his own earlier and more optimistic discussion of so-called informal economies, longtime PREALC (Employment Program for Latin America and the Caribbean) director Victor Tokman argues in "The Process of Accumulation and the Weakness of the Protagonists" that while at least some informal enterprises have reached a visible level of capitalization, the result has not been the emergence of an entrepreneurial class willing to invest their newly acquired capital in support of domestic improvements. Such domestic enterprises have not remained "embedded" for long, because in Tokman's analysis the position of these new "protagonists" in the economic scene seems too "weak" to sustain the potential risks. Thus their capital flows elsewhere; as my argument would suggest, it becomes an attractive investment for TNCs in search of cheap capital. Tokman sees the weakness of the protagonists in economic terms, which are compounded by a lack of political "will" to take the risks necessary to sustain domestic growth.

"Necessary" risks, however, are always easier to assess from somewhere else, from a position that purports to know what you obviously ought to be doing politically that you're not. Tokman's position is thus rather like someone at my hypothetical school district meeting who stands above the fray, urging parents not to go to the symbolic analyst room, but to take their children back home to their local in-person service and routine production jobs and work politically to see that those jobs get better in future. And so long as the symbolic analyst room of transnational capital seems to represent the only going game in town, you'd have to be considerably less than "weak-willed" to take that advice. It's often all too true indeed that people's jobs depend on the movements of corporate capital. But this is just another way of saying that the "creation" of jobs is first of all a political praxis. The "choice" Reaganomics offered, for example, between "run-away" inflation and biting the bullet of higher unemployment, wasn't about a "healthy" direction of the economy, but about the politics of who gets to create, or deny, which jobs where.

On a global scale, the mass migration of workers in search of jobs, to-gether with the increasing frequency of refugee populations, has created an apparent dilemma for "receiving" nations: how to distinguish between "economic" and "political" reasons for population movement. United Na-tions directives maintain a distinction in these terms by first assimilating labor migration to a conception of a now global version of a reserve army of labor, and then contrasting the movements of this army to the specific plight of refugee populations condemned to seek political asylum in other nations. In the first case, while migration may seem economically neces-sary, it remains politically voluntary.

The recent theorizing of "nomad" and other similar terms, and the cor-responding critique of a term like "migration," offers one way to point out the multiplicity of often very different conditions utterly ignored by this framing of U.N. policy. But in even simpler terms, the distinction prevents U.N. policymakers from hearing how populations on the move for osten-sibly economic reasons narrate their expectations from "migration." More often than not, economics appears in these narratives as an instrument rather than a goal. The goal is identified as political incorporation, how-ever defined exactly, with the organization of economic practices under-stood as a means to this larger end. The dynamics of migration in this sense are certainly different from the desperate search for political asylum to which so many have been condemned by, among other things, the inter-national politics of the United States and other potential "receiving" na-tions. But the distinction cannot be understood as if it involved a division between economics and politics. Migrating in search of work is as political as seeking asylum. What it responds to are the political conditions imposed by the organizational mobilities of transnational capital.

The "weak protagonists" who are the focus of Tokman's analysis are by no means in the same situation as political refugees or migratory popula-tions leaving their native countries in search of work. Nevertheless, the role of these "protagonists" in the migration of capital from the domestic circumstances of capital formation into transnational circuits is no less a response to the colonizing politics of transnational capital. As a political organization, transnational capital functions through the symbolic conversion of economic resources rather than directly through the production, marketing, and circulation of goods. To the extent that seems the only political game around, those left "out of the pathways" of transnational capital don't have the luxury of simply choosing some other form of politics altogether. People attempt as best they can in their circumstances the politics of a symbolic conversion of economic resources that might lead to new forms of political incorporation. With Tokman's "weak protagonists," expectations for incorporation might well involve the domestic accumulation and then international "leakage" of capital. In other circumstances, however, what happens is the repetition "internally" of "external" economic inequalities, such as in Villa El Salvador, as incorporation imposes the proliferation of relative exclusions in the process. Far more commonly the very movement of the laborer's own body from one nation to another articulates the hope of some eventual political incorporation.

The larger point of considering these multiple forms of response to transnational capital is that countercolonial economics can't be understood as grounded in the utopian gesture of choosing the "embedded" economic enterprise against the "unembedded"; local and specific political organization against the globalization of transnational capital politics; the authentically revolutionary direction against the co-opted; and so on. Such choices, no less than Reich's ethical vision of a national focus for symbolic analyst politics, assume an already existent political agency, an already incorporated transnational player. Countercolonial economics in contrast is about the *formation* of political agency, which throughout economic colonies necessarily occurs in the very midst of colliding political antagonisms. The population groups of economic colonies nevertheless do find ways to entangle transnational capital politics with economic conditions, and to encumber its symbolic conversions of economic resources with the exigencies of multiple types of production, marketing, and circulation of goods and services.

Unlike industrial capital, with its intimate system of linkages between a concentration of political power and a concentration of ownership of economic production, the political power of transnational capital remains tied to economic conditions occurring "outside" capital pathways. Tokman's "weak protagonists," ensembles of domestic production like Villa El Salvador, even the migratory movement of "developing" country populations are essential to transnational capital not simply as labor to be exploited for economic gain, but more fundamentally as the multiple, shifting configurations of economic practices and networks required by transnational capital's politics of symbolic control and management. Control depends on the maintenance of a fragile balance between keeping these populations "outside," and at the same time continually opening new pathways *to* the necessary resources produced by and circulating within their multiple networks of economic practices. "Nomads" and similar categories may theorize an attractive image of free possibility, enviably floating just beyond the reach of transnational capital pathways. In contrast, understood as actual migratory movements in search of political incorporation, the movements of populations identify the spheres of transnational capital dependence on colonies. Thus they also identify points of potential political contestation and leverage.

There is of course an unstated corollary to my premise that an understanding of transnational capital must recognize such vulnerabilities and dependencies and not just the implacable, expansive power so frequently imaged in left critique. Crudely, that corollary suggests the global acceleration of conditions of poverty during the eighties and early nineties cannot continue at the same pace, since conditions of extreme poverty cannot make the necessary producers of economic resources available to transnational capital, let alone make available already capitalized sectors to be managed. The acceleration of poverty jeopardizes the very conditions of production of economic resources, and by extension the possibility of consolidated political control by transnational capital.

Needless to say, I find that corollary attractive, but logic and history rarely coincide. In retrospect it's easy enough to see that the desperate conditions of a working class during the early phases of industrialization had to be altered in order to create markets for the vastly expanded quantity of goods industrialization generated. But it should be equally easy to recognize that my passive-voice construction—"had to be altered"—disguises a terrible and bloody history of change. Working-class populations learned to organize and to exact a political authority for their "necessary" incorporation into markets for industrial goods—at a great cost, to a great many working-class people. A working class didn't thereby win a revolution "once and for all," and for that reason this story remains the despair of left utopian thinking, the Great Co-Optation Tragedy of the twentieth century. But working-class organization and political demands changed the course of capitalist development and made a lot of people's lives better in the process, by taking advantage of what the conditions of industrial production and marketing made available.

Obviously a nostalgic history lesson serves no better than a tragic narrative of working-class co-optation to meet the political exigencies of the moment. The point isn't to attempt some repeat of working-class organization, but to learn similarly how to take advantage of existing conditions, how to exact a political price for the economic dependence of transnational capital politics on production and marketing in the colonies. Thus no matter how "logical" in relation to my picture of transnational capital's vulnerabilities and dependencies, my corollary is simply an indicator of possibility. There will be no "inevitable" amelioration of poverty. Without active interventions, the historical course of the present is much more likely to recapitulate my cautionary fable from *Murder to Go*, where the dead people are simply swept away as the novel's symbolically adroit remaining cast of corporate characters celebrate the mystery's "solution."

I have suggested that the horizontal economies of so-called developing countries offer a hermeneutic of future possibility for political change in the United States as well, and it's with that model in mind that I will focus attention on some diverse sectors in the internal social formation of the United States in the following chapters. In the United States, too, economic practices in these sectors represent far more than the romanticism of "survival" by which they're so frequently imaged. Such practices are tactically designed to yield a political payoff, in circumstances where the alternatives are clear and survival isn't enough. For transnational capital isn't really about a new economics of profiting from a chicken in every pot. It's a politics of murder, to go.

THREE

Done In: Conspiracy and Agency in the Conditions of an Information Economy

The "conspiracy news" now so much a part of Web culture echoes a familiar and repetitive chorus of the nineties. Not long after Oliver Stone's film *JFK* was released on video, for example, Perot supporters, as yet unaware their candidate would withdraw from and then return to the presidential race, charged that representatives of the two major parties were making it difficult to get his name on primary ballots. Meanwhile, still another book was published about the suspect circumstances of Marilyn Monroe's death. The possibility of George Bush's involvement in "Irangate" once more reemerged, including information about a number of secret arms deals with Iraq during its war with Iran. In the wake of the first Rodney King beating verdict, enterprising reporters "discovered" that African American groups in Los Angeles felt that police often arrested black males on trumped-up charges; in the wake of O. J. Simpson's arrest, enterprising reporters were accused of manufacturing the scene in the first place. U.S. automakers, who at the time of Perot's candidacy had been considering a suit against Japanese firms for "dumping" minivans below value on the U.S. market, were themselves represented two years later as deliberately flooding the market with used cars by way of their shortened lease programs. Britain's leaders continue to feel the German government had too much secret influence on establishing ground rules for the negotiation of European currency rates. More new talk shows continue to be launched on U.S. television, leading to speculation that network executives must all in secret employ the same market research analysts.

As reported, each of the stories above represented somebody or another conspiring with somebody else to do something to someone, and my list could be extended almost indefinitely. The news of the nineties so far is that conspiracies are no longer news. Nevertheless, there is something odd about this proliferation of conspiracy theorizing in the circumstances of a postmodern culture that seems to have shattered any familiar idea of a "unified" subject who could be the agent of conspiracy. As Thomas Pynchon's novels, for example, endlessly remind us, the notion of a conspiracy inevitably seems to imply agency, or at the least some specifiable location where agents might exist to control the web of conspiratorial power relations. Long before deconstruction and the like, left theorists, including Marx himself, inveighed against conspiracy thinking as a counterproductive simplification of complex social conditions to the "intentions" of inexplicably evil agents—as if the exploitation of workers in a capitalist system could be eradicated if only one could find and eliminate those who participated in closed-room conspiracies to fleece the vast majority of the population out of their just rewards.

Conspiracy theories, however, are typically about agency *somewhere else*, and hence in one form they begin not with an agent at all, but with a victim, with some dramatic, visible index of effective power having been exercised. When conspiracy is recognized in this form, it is possible to understand why historically such conspiracy theorizing has had a certain utility for exploited groups. No matter how suspect for left theorists, or how often the identification of self as victim has been dismissed as merely paranoia, the location of conspiratorial power elsewhere has had the virtue for these groups of an education in anger. It helps teach you how to avoid, against every kind of cultural incentive that encourages it, the massive and inward turning of anger into self-hate and self-destruction. Conspiracy theorizing thereby keeps you alive in circumstances that insistently solicit your obliging cooperation in plotting your own demise. As any number of critics have tirelessly (and tiresomely) pointed out, conspiracy thinking perhaps can't really fund an effective program for radical social change. But there's not a lot of point to radical social change unless somebody can survive to benefit. Among other things, the recent proliferation of conspiracy theorizing is also the production of an education for survival.

At the same time, no one can fail to recognize that conspiracy theories are by no means the exclusive property of oppressed groups, and in other circumstances they may take very different forms. Totalitarian regimes, for example, are often effective propagandists of conspiracy, where rather than being played out across a radical asymmetry of power between agent and victim, the story becomes an epistemological narrative of appearance and reality. The "elsewhere" of conspiratorial agency is potentially "everywhere," a sinister reality lurking beneath even the most immediately familiar, commonplace, and apparently benign exterior. Likewise, power is understood as everywhere at stake in this epistemological configuration, requiring a totalitarian agent capable of Herculean efforts to reveal the agency of conspiracy and legitimizing the indiscriminate use of force, just in case.

Both forms of conspiracy theorizing I've outlined above depend on some relatively direct image of the "totality" of the social formation. The ultimate goal of conspiratorial agents is understood to be political direction and control. Marx may not have liked the way workers often saw themselves as the victims of a "capitalist conspiracy" centered in some relatively small group of "fat" owners, but no less than his own such theorizing also addressed the issue of controlling social direction. Similarly, the epistemological vision of a society everywhere riddled by sinister conspiratorial plots lurking just beneath the surface exempts no corner of the social field.

Keeping in mind these paradigmatically different versions of conspiracy, with their respective projections of social totality, helps foreground still another confusing element about my list of conspiracy stories in the news throughout the nineties. It's odd indeed to think of a recognizable postmodern landscape as populated everywhere by conspiratorial figures of agency. But what's even more curious is the simultaneous deployment of adjacent discourses of conspiracy from so many otherwise very different positions within the social formation, each with its relatively local image of a field of relevance and drawing its strength from the detail of the local rather than from the penumbra of "larger" implications that surround the representation. Thus however similar they are in form, these discourses, unlike the conspiracy theorizing above, seem to be small representations that become ever more vague and indeterminate as they approach the task of identifying some ultimate form of agency beyond the web of local detail.

Taking these two features together, it's tempting to read what does seem to be a recent proliferation of representations of conspiracy as a version of postmodern *style*. What they express is less a belief in controlling powers actually able to affect the historical direction of an entire social formation than something like a pastiche of agency whose emblematic form might well be the video game, with its immensely powerful "enemy" hidden behind one screen after another of obstacles. At once pervaded by that familiar nostalgia for an earlier and "simpler" time when History might be understood as driven by a few powerful agents, and yet also suffused with the video screen's blank emptiness of any such general historical signification conspiracy theories, like Oedipa Maas in Pynchon's fable, circulate amphibiously across a contemporary landscape. They absorb a new atmosphere of burgeoning paranoias in a culture, as Fredric Jameson puts it, that has forgotten how to think historically.

In the aftermath of successive waves of poststructuralism, "agency" still remains a hot topic in criticism—can agency be theorized in some way that doesn't simply "return" us to one version or another of that infamous unified subject poststructuralism had made the target of so many and such devastating critiques? Is there any alternative to something like Jameson's blankly postmodern culture locked in the "windless closure" of a perpetual present? Posed in these limited terms, however, it is the question itself that lives in a rather rarefied air, not unlike all those interminable post-Hegelian debates Marx had so much fun satirizing in his early work. The image is worth recalling, because in common with most satirists Marx had a serious point in mind. His impatience with the debates didn't really have its source in their endless fussiness over "technical" terms of expression, or even their frequent banality, which he satirized so effectively. It was their inflated importance that concerned him, as if no one else anywhere else had even got to the point of being able to think about such matters, and hence as if the issues at stake had to await a correct resolution of the debates before anything happened.

To locate issues of agency through this poststructuralist frame seems to me to risk a similar inflation of the importance of current critical debates. It may not have been Derrida or Althusser who, Darth Vader–like, asthmatically haunted the nightmares of General Motors boardroom discussants worrying how in the world to rethink The Force of agency and to regain (market) "presence" for the troubled corporation. But throughout the recent turmoil of naming a new CEO and launching wave after wave of new automobiles, it seems a safe assumption that "theorizing agency" in relation to a profoundly different set of volatile marketplace conditions occupied everybody's attention who was involved. Not to recognize certain continuities across the very different languages of "theorizing" in university departments and in corporate boardrooms is a conceptual mistake. A failure to understand that *how* General Motors management theorizes agency will have enormous and immediate effects is a political mistake that can't be rectified by re-combing the texts of Althusser, et al., to see if just maybe there isn't some chink somewhere that would permit a still viable notion of oppositional political agency for the future.

I will take up the issue of agency in what follows, but I want to do so by looking to what seems to me a now pervasively familiar context of conspiracy theorizing within which representations of agency occur across any number of sectors of the contemporary social formation in the United States. That is, I take the insistence with which questions of agency are posed in critical theory as involving only one of many sites where figures of agency are projected. The context of conspiracy theorizing thereby alters the question from "What form of agency might be possible after post-structuralism?" to a broader complex of concerns: What forms of agency are *already* projected as social possibilities? From where? What are their conditions of possibility? What are their effects?

These questions suggest a third feature of my attenuated list of conspiracy stories which can serve as a connecting link across its otherwise disparate terms and representations of conspiracy discourse. Whether directly expressed as the mapping of power relations that identify agent and victim, or as the epistemological detective work required for the revelation of what is "hidden"; whether exercised at some relatively local level or implying some more general level, conspiracy theorizing on my list is invariably represented as trafficking in the currency of information. Thus the most immediate condition of possibility for any power of agency is assumed to be an economy of information, a process of information production, circulation, distribution, and use. And with this recognition, it becomes possible to bring into sight another field of recent discourse, the no less familiar ensemble of theorizing that takes as its subject the emergence of an "information economy" from an older and goods-based system of industrial relations. At the conjunction of such urgent, liminal descriptions of a new economic order with the proliferating representations of conspiracy stand the "mysteries" of information as a commodity.

It shouldn't come as any surprise that the vocabulary of conspiracy, with its positioning of agents and victims, obligingly lends itself in turn to ostensibly economic accounts of the flow of information. Thus while widely circulated cultural representations of conspiracy assume the importance of an information-based economy, the economics of information flow is more often than not represented as occurring in conspiratorial configurations. The proposed suit by U.S. automakers against Japanese firms located giant corporations like General Motors as the victim of unfair trade practices centered in a Japanese conspiracy to block information flow. And it recommended enlisting the U.S. government in the practice of protective trade barriers involving goods, to enable these corporate "victims" to compete successfully in an economy increasingly driven by and dependent on information rather than goods.

By an extension of this peculiar conspiratorial logic of agents and victims, conservative social commentators have been able to popularize the notion of a "society of victims" in highly selective terms. They target "minority" social groups as abusing the "rights" of victimage in their protests, while exempting from attack corporations and their publicity machines filling headlines with stories of being victimized by unfair foreign competition. The latter are assumed to "make sense" in the emergent conditions of an information economy. That is, they are grounded in epistemologically justifiable premises, unlike the former, which are "really" just so many claims for "special rights" drawn from a now hopelessly outdated image of a rigidly hierarchical society of inequality. Thus by a remarkable feat of prestidigitation, this linkage of conspiracy theorizing and information economy theorizing manages to fuel the agency of corporate power from the *reversal* of a terminology of victimage. In these circumstances corporations learn that they can best renew their power not by directly representing themselves as "good" agents, but instead as victims of "bad" agents elsewhere, conspiring against them.

Such deployments of conspiracy theorizing can't really be conceptualized as postmodern style. Rather, the reversals of social position, from agent to victim and back again, become resources for new forms of determining political direction. In "'1968': Periodizing Postmodern Politics and Identity," Kobena Mercer notes how any number of terms that at one time might have seemed securely identified with the left reemerge within the very different discourse of politicians like Enoch Powell, as he "explained" the threat of a "racial conspiracy" in Britain. Powell didn't steal or co-opt these terms. For Mercer, what Guy Debord's conception of a "reversible connecting factor" implies instead is that Powell's conspiracy theorizing "encoded a racist version of English cultural identity, not in the illegitimate language of biologizing racism, but through literary and rhetorical moves" (436), thereby reversing the positional political relations of "cultural construction" and "racism" altogether. Likewise, the term "victim" in a new conspiratorial configuration of discourse cannot be assumed to be reserved solely for the purposes of left politics. At his confirmation hearing, Clarence Thomas, for example, made remarkable use of positioning himself rather than Anita Hill as a victim, in ways that demonstrated just how fluid the movement of the term "victim" has become in political discourse. Like Powell in his context Thomas drove home his reverse by implying a conspiracy at work, this time in control of the "high-tech" apparatus of a "lynching."

Such reversals seem to me now a familiar feature of the media representations of conspiracy in my initial list. Recognizing the political stakes in the status of information, representation foregrounds a whole range of epistemological issues, from what counts as "information" to "confusions" about exactly who is agent and who is victim in an alleged conspiratorial plot. Within a two-year span, U.S. automakers and Japanese automakers exchanged positions in conspiracy charges. Likewise, the media reporting conspiracies are just as frequently charged with acting conspiratorially themselves to manufacture events.

Marx began his massive project of revolutionary economic analysis in *Capital* by looking at the "mysteries" of commodity form, but what he was out to understand was the exploitation of workers. For reasons I'll describe in a moment, "information" is a mysterious commodity indeed. I intend my examples, however, to suggest that the political discourses of reversibility that emerge at the conjunction of conspiracy theorizing and information economy theorizing radically extend, enlarge, and differentiate the social field of exploitation. Thus while the focus on commodity form in Marx's account leads inevitably to the exploitation of workers, analysis must now instead recognize how exploitation in an information economy not only takes a number of different and specific forms, but also targets multiple "victim positions."

Looking through my list of representations of conspiracy, however, should also imply a reminder that conspiracy theorizing in the present, no less than across the histories of exploited groups, has continued to function pedagogically as well as epistemologically. The epistemologically driven discourses of conspiracy I've been describing by no means saturate the fields of conspiracy theorizing. Despite how their stories were represented, for African American men arrested on "trumped-up" charges it seems to me altogether unlikely that theorizing a conspiracy at work either accords much priority to the "confusions" detailed in the media or devotes much energy to elaborate epistemologies of how you know that you know you've been fucked over. Conspiracy theorizing serves a rather different and pedagogical purpose.

General Motors might hope to influence favorable trade legislation by fashioning a discourse of conspiracy to secure for itself the position of being victimized by unfair trade practices in the pricing of minivans. Unlike General Motors, however, for anyone already caught in the proliferating effects of multiple forms of exploitation in an information economy, conspiracy theorizing is an education in the conspiratorial power *of effects*. It's not about how to secure recognition as victim, as conservative commentators imagine, but how to make use of what resources are available to make sure you don't disappear as victimized. Conspiracy theorizing as pedagogical in this sense may finally be unable to tell you how to change the social relations of exploitation, but it is an invaluable education for constituting agents who can survive long enough to develop and realize altogether unexpected tactics for change.

Like Marx, I want to understand exploitation through beginning with an analysis of commodities, in this case the specific form of the information commodity. My analysis, however, is projected everywhere through a double lens of conspiracy and conspiracy theorizing: as epistemological discourse, with its reversals of agent and victim that figure a multiple process of exploitation in an information economy of human capital; and as pedagogical discourse with its educational formation of political agency for oppressed groups. I don't intend to leave the field of conspiracy, to find some "higher ground" of argument, because the effects of conspiracy theorizing seem to me anything but a form of nostalgia or ahistorical pastiche. Conspiracy discourses are located at particularly crucial junctures of cultural practices and economic practices. They help focus social relations of both exploitation and struggle in the present, and they are involved in very different processes of agent formation at work.

❧

In a fully developed capitalist marketplace, Marx argued, use value is subordinated to exchange value. The only exceptions are goods produced strictly for self-consumption, in the home, for example, or on a farm where the food is consumed by the farm family rather than sold on the market. The exceptions are important to recognize because they clarify a constitutive boundary between use value and exchange value in this Marxian lens: exchange value presupposes conditions where the labor of production results in a product that is not consumed by those involved in the labor. It presupposes a division of labor. Use value in contrast does not depend on a division of labor. Products may be produced and consumed by the same worker.

It has become a truism that information is a primary commodity in a contemporary global market, but information is a curious commodity in relation to this boundary line between use value and exchange value. Information of course can be used and exchanged, but its exchange value as a commodity depends less on already existent conditions of a division of labor than on the conceptualization of use in the circumstances of exchange. Information *is* information only if and when some conditions of use are made conceptually visible. Unlike other commodities, the very identity of information depends on conceptualizations of use. "Useless information" is an oxymoron. Corn, for example, has a myriad of uses which may presuppose a certain commonsense concept of the identity of corn, yet that identity can be discursively represented and understood quite apart from understanding the uses of corn. Information, in contrast, has no identity as information except as represented in relation to conceptualizations of its uses. Thus even when produced strictly for exchange—that is, when the labor of production is nowhere engaged in the consumption of what is produced—the exchange value of information is nevertheless directly dependent on conceptualizations of use that determine something is indeed "there" to be exchanged at all.

At the same time, however, exchange value does not necessarily depend on the use-identity constructed by those who produce information. "Use" in this context has no intrinsic connection to any metaphysics of "primary" labor. Thus the exchange value of information may depend instead on a use-constructed identity by those who purchase information from others. In the process of such an exchange, information changes identities. That is, the exchange between producer and consumer not only involves money (or whatever) for information; it can also involve identity for identity. Information A is exchanged for money and in the process becomes something different, information B. The division in this case *produces* a division of labor, between producers and consumers who are themselves producers. The latter no less than the former are involved in the labor of conceptualizing the identity of information as information. Unlike commodities such as corn, the discursive conditions that locate information as information entail no referential possibility of separable identity apart from conceptualizations of use. While corn no more possesses a "metaphysical" identity than information, corn as commodity permits discursive representations of identity in ways information as commodity does not.

Further, while the identity of information is dependent on conceptualizations of use, it is not identical with any specific uses. Even when the "material" aspects of information A that when exchanged becomes information B remain exactly the same, its identity as information can be radically altered. The same table of data on the same computer disk may be identified as information under one construct of identity (A) and identified as information under a completely different construct (B) because it has no identity at all—it's not even a table of *data*—except under the sign of (A) or (B). Still another division of labor thus can emerge between those who produce the material form of information (the table of data and the computer disk in this case) and those who conceptualize the use-identification (A or B) of that material form as information. The exchange of information in this register of exchange likewise produces a division of labor rather than being dependent on a prior division.

All this may seem an abstract play of conceptual possibilities, but the play is important to understand before turning to apparently more concrete discussions of an "information economy" now so familiar in recent discourse. To take an early example, Marc Porat's massive nine-volume study of an information economy, undertaken for the Commerce Department and published in 1977, has often been criticized for lumping together as "information workers" those who assemble computer hardware, for example, and those engaged in scientific research by means of that hardware. But the critique remains at the level of comparing work practices, worker autonomy, wages, and so on, where differences are so obvious as to make Porat's aggregation seem at best farfetched, and at worst the result of a polemical intention to buttress perceptions of a growing information economy with a mass of statistical detail. What the critique overlooks is how the peculiar conditions of information as a commodity can produce as well as rely on specific divisions of labor. The workplace and work practice differences are certainly real enough, but they derive from conditions of an information economy. Both hardware assemblers and scientific researchers are "information workers," and the differences between them no less than their aggregation as information workers have everything to do with the peculiarities of the information commodity.

In *In the Era of Human Capital*, his unabashedly enthusiastic hymn to the wonders of an emergent new economic order, Richard Crawford would distinguish "mere" information from knowledge: "Information is the raw material of knowledge just as wood is the raw material of a table. . . . When you distinguish between information and knowledge, it is important to recognize that information can be found in a variety of inanimate objects from a book to a computer disk but that knowledge can only be found in human beings. . . . Information is useless without a knowledgeable human being to apply it to a productive purpose" (10).

Yet "raw material" is not the same as a commodity, and information as I suggested is neither commodity nor even recognizable raw material apart from the conceptualization of use Crawford would identify as "knowledge." The distinction Crawford draws between information and knowledge is simply a way of referring to the two sides of information as commodity. By extension, however, Crawford succinctly—if inadvertently—draws attention to the peculiar mode of production characteristic of information. This is not a matter of transforming "raw material" into a "commodity." That is, human agency is not applied to raw material in order to produce a commodity available for use or exchange. Agency itself is produced in terms of the power of conceptualizing use, the "productive purpose" in Crawford's language, which constitutes one side of the form of the information commodity. Thus rather than the commodification of an existent human agency now embodied in the information available for exchange, Crawford's "knowledgeable human being" names the constitution of human agency as already in the commodity form of information, without which information isn't "useless," as Crawford suggests, but nonexistent. The mode of information production thereby generates divisions of labor that are simultaneously divisions in the constitution of powers of agency. Or perhaps more exactly, the specificity of information as a commodity inheres in its necessary linkage to the production of human agency. Information, unlike corn, seems a productive commodity, producing human agency as a constitutive component of its commodity form.

In *Post-Industrial Lives*, business sociologists Jerald Hage and Charles Powers are considerably more attentive than Crawford to the new conditions of agency in the information economy of a "postindustrial" world. Their focus, however, is in fact a double one. Explicitly, they are concerned to shift the emphasis from individual to collective forms of agency: "In the past," they argue, "agency has been viewed as a question of choice. Can individuals choose, or do they lack choice? Our analysis suggests that this conceptualization is inappropriate for our times. . . . Choices must be made, more than ever before. But these choices are increasingly made by people acting collectively, rather than by individuals acting unilaterally as if they were autonomous." Yet as the passage continues, the larger context of this shift in emphasis is framed in terms of the conditions for the production of knowledge: "We demonstrate that knowledge growth, and more specifically the ways in which new knowledge is implanted in minds, in machines, and in patterns of social organization, determines the structural need for the exercise of agency as a functional prerequisite to flexible adaptation in the face of uncertain and changing conditions" (210–11).

More specifically, "knowledge growth," with all it implies for them about collective forms of agency, has an impact on the work of *professionals*, those assumed to be most directly involved in the production of knowledge. Thus in an earlier chapter, with a familiar technological echo of religious stories of rebirth and regeneration, Hage and Powers had explained what exactly "flexible adaptation" involves by way of example from their own professional field of sociology: "Rapid growth in knowledge not only makes products obsolete, but also means that human capital depreciates quickly. . . . As a personal example, in sociology, the authors have had to retool their methodological skills about every 5 years" (39), moving from the bivariate correlation analysis of the late fifties to the simulation strategies of the nineties. It is not only the disappearance of an older religious language of rebirth into the technological language of "retooling," however, that characterizes this example. In contrast to religious stories, this narrative of agency, like one of Donna Haraway's "cyborgs," yields no thematics of origin, no "birth" of agency somewhere else which then enters the field of knowledge. There is only the blank sequence of "rebirths," with no original emergence anywhere in view.

As a professional engaged in the production of knowledge, you know *when* you must "retool" at a point when rather than being constituted as agent in the field, you find yourself instead constituted as victim. You face the sudden realization that you've become a victim of the "march of knowledge" controlled and capitalized from somewhere else. In the equation of "human" and "capital" ("human capital depreciates quickly," as Hage and Powers point out), capital names not only what you have, what you use, or what you want, but what you *are*. Thus it comes to seem that the "surplus labor" of retooling, realized in the surplus value that accumulates as human capital, must be extorted from yourself—or more exactly, multiple versions of yourself as victim endlessly being "reborn/retooled" as agent across the labors required by the formation of human capital. Like some grotesque Hegelian nightmare, you must learn to see yourself in the "other" of the victim so that it becomes "your" labor to overcome your self-as-victim that is realized in the capital of your human agency, endlessly retooled in the interstices of the information commodity.

Like all commodities, information circulates. And Marx was careful to point out that in a capitalist marketplace, commodities may be traded—that is, move within a specific process of circulation—in ways by no means identical to the movement of material goods. A futures market in corn exists well before any produce is harvested and taken to distribution points. Nevertheless, there remains a definite relation between the patterns of circulation established through the process of futures trading and the movement of material goods. Control over the latter can be achieved through control over the former. With information, in contrast, the circumstances are considerably more complicated. There are ways to institute controls over the production of information, albeit in a computer age the difficulties of maintaining control are often considerable. Given a process of exchange that can involve the transformation of the identity of information as information, however, control over circulation is not only difficult, but often becomes impossible altogether. In such a process, the very identity of what circulates is up for grabs, as giant corporations like IBM have had to learn to their considerable financial embarrassment.

Thus I have every political sympathy with critiques like Herbert Schiller's in *Who Knows*: a critique of what he thinks should be more accurately labeled a *mis*information society, and a vision of an immense and capital-driven suppression of "real" information together with the controlled dissemination of misinformation. But this seems to me at best a premature theorizing of power relations in this new economy. The military's obsession with secrecy, like corporate attempts to "protect" their products and advertising practices from competitors and from consumer knowledge, are not simply part of some vast apparatus of control over information flow. They're more often than not rather desperate attempts to exert a control that seems always to be receding into some already vanishing past. "Official" concern about Tom Clancy's knowledge of nuclear submarines, for example, were gainsaid by Clancy's admission that in researching *The Hunt for Red October* he picked up all this "secret stuff" from newspaper reports. The obsessiveness and the secrecy, that is, are less the expression of possessive control than an acknowledgment of its impossibility. Understanding power relations that involve the commodity of information must begin by recognizing a certain "genuineness" to the constant corporate, and military, profession of powerlessness to control a flow of information, despite the intensive efforts to control both information production and the movement of information's material forms.

None of this means that "real" power isn't exercised in the interstices of information exchange, or that anybody at any time can have access to any information she or he pleases. Obviously neither is the case. The information commodity isn't just a "signifier" floating happily in an endless sea of exchange relations. It isn't anything at all without a "signified" of conceptualizations of use, for which people pay dearly, in all kinds of ways. At the same time, however, control over the *circulation* of information can't be possessed at any single—or even multiple—site of power. With respect to information circulation at least, Foucault's often rather nebulous theorizing of the simultaneous "everywhere and nowhere" of power can be taken with some considerable degree of literal accuracy. A commodity that can obligingly change its very identity in a process of exchange "grounds" the power of control over circulation everywhere and nowhere indeed. The insecurity of such grounding helps explain why it is that radical critics like Schiller, no less than General Motors corporate management and Pentagon officials, so routinely construct some version or another of "conspiracy" to identify the possession of control—a possession, however, that like the agent of conspiracy always appears *somewhere else.*

The now familiar corporate obsession with the symbolics of "human capital" reflects these "mysteries" of the information commodity, supplying the full measure of "metaphysical subtleties and theological niceties" Marx would require us to recognize in the commodity when "looked at closely." Thus what at one time may have seemed to capitalist economists relatively secure indices for the measurement of "capital" and "capital input" in any given instance have dissolved into near anarchy when suddenly confronted with a recognition that a firm's primary capital assets actually lie in the "knowledge" possessed by its research personnel. Knowledge in this sense, as I have suggested, is one side of the information commodity form. Human capital is the immense Imaginary of the information commodity.

Despite the many attempts, capital measurement indices in such circumstances can no longer be registered in quantitative norms.* Measurement becomes epistemology, and conspiracy theorizing has become an indispensable epistemological instrument for the "science" of human capital, for how it is that the information commodity in the form of human capital wealth is employed for the purposes of producing still more wealth. A notion of "conspiracy" takes this ultimate mystery of the information commodity—a wealth of knowledge that miraculously produces more wealth out of itself—at face value, assigning the motivation of agency to the miracle, the "human" to the "capital." Conspiracy theories have become the privileged epistemology of an information society, so many attempts to "read" the process of information flow as somehow intelligibly related to an agency in control.

❀

In retrospect, given such evidence as the near-collapse of the California economy, the burden of national debt inherited, the transfer of countless

* As Fred Block, for example, argues persuasively in *Postindustrial Possibilities*, 120–28.

jobs from the relatively well-paid manufacturing sector to the much lower wages of the service sector, the corporate liabilities occasioned by the frenzy of leveraged buyouts, the scandals in financial institutions, the sanctioned abuses of civil rights, and the now very visible schisms in the Republican party that obviously weren't resolved in the 1994 off-year election sweep, it is becoming even easier than before to characterize the rapidly receding Reagan years as having been merely a triumph of image over substance. The Gipper's ability to hold together the diverse constituencies of a conservative coalition while simultaneously convincing so many to "feel good again" about being Americans looks like a mirage, a trick that only momentarily allowed people to forget the encroaching desert landscape with which we're now surrounded.

The greeting chorus of "I told you so" from the desert's liberal hermits, however, ignores how for all the spectacle produced by its "feel good" signs, the Reagan image was never just a matter of the light and promise of a "reborn" America. Its constitutive terms were drawn from a vocabulary of conspiracy, with the implied menace of secret, threatening forces at work everywhere: communists, welfare "cheats," blacks, feminists, corporate raiders, the Japanese, the "media elite," the Trilateral Commission, government, lobbyists, lawyers, doctors, labor union leadership, humanists in the university, gays, pornographers, rock stars, people with AIDS, drug cartels, the National Education Association, the ACLU, environmentalists, serial killers, and so on. The list of conspiratorial agents flourishing in the interstices of the Reagan image suggests that what in retrospect appears the desert vision of a mirage might be better understood by way of borrowing from one of those television nature show accounts of primeval marshland nutrient soup. It was a marshland image, positively teeming with new and potentially menacing life forms.

Juxtaposing this list with my initial reiteration of perceived problems inherited from the Reagan years affords a convenient way to dramatize what only seems a paradox: the affective investments in an epistemology of information flow have continued to expand long after Reagan left office. Even as the Reaganite vocabulary of "hot" menace and proliferating conspiracies turns into the nineties' "cold" statistical data pointing to "real" problems, the latter preserve the affective charge that backlit the scene of conspiracy. Thus the data that register corporate liabilities incurred by a raider buyout earlier, for example, function to exacerbate rather than relieve the emotional tensions generated by the pressures to correctly read the movements of continually shifting indices of information. It's as if you walked out of the flashing circuitry and suspended animation of a video game only to discover its geography of movement had been imposed on your trip home from the arcade while you weren't looking. So, far from disappearing, the vocabulary of conspiracy generated during the Reagan years has become a commonplace everywhere, part of the familiar scenery of the nineties.

Conspiracy theories are not all the same, however, and one distinguishing characteristic of a vocabulary of conspiracy inherited from the eighties is that it focuses attention on the epistemological detective work of revealing the motivations of putative agents rather than on an inventory of effects. That is, rather than reasoning backwards from a constellation of perceived social effects to locate their cause in the collusive activity of conspiratorial agents, such theorizing instead concentrates on establishing plausible motivational grounds for the existence of a conspiracy. Proving a conspiracy means "exposing" the potential for a congruent pattern of motivation among agents occupying otherwise different positions in the social field. Thus Reaganism typically supplied a portrait gallery of "social villains"—communists, welfare cheats, blacks, feminists, and so on—whose sinister "motivations" could plausibly find expression in the formation of conspiracies among them. Effects, when considered at all, appear as a second-order confirmation of what has been established by this epistemological detective work uncovering hidden motivation.

To take a familiar example, the so-called welfare bureaucracy, with its complicated and overlapping offices, programs, indices of benefit calculation, and so on, was assumed to have a vested interest in the continued presence of a welfare constituency. No constituency, no relatively well-paid and secure jobs in the government bureaucracy dispensing welfare benefits. That vested interest then drove the funding of university research producing information about the magnitude of a constituency requiring welfare benefits to survive, where in turn university researchers acquired a supposedly powerful interest in controlling not only the production of the information but its circulation. With so much assumed at stake, a conspiracy among government and academic investors in the market of welfare *information* was made to seem not only plausible but likely.

By thus framing attention through a question of the plausible motivations of conspiratorial agents, it wasn't necessary to claim that certain groups of the population lived on welfare because conspirators existed who made a living off dispensing welfare aid. By only implying such a direct cause-and-effect claim against its foregrounding of plausible conspiratorial motivations, this discourse of conspiracy also conveniently avoided the whole issue of why great economic disparities persisted at all in an affluent country like the United States. The issue simply disappeared into the terms of a debate about the reliability of information. That is, debate centered on an epistemology of information rather than on an assessment of the effects of income distribution. If a conspiracy of information producers is plausible, then there are reasons to doubt the basis for any requirement to maintain the present levels of welfare benefits that assume the reliability of the data supplied by information producers. More important, there are reasons to "relieve" corporate and high-income individuals of the tax "burden" occasioned by those present levels. Welfare "reform" targeted toward the ultimate end of eliminating all welfare programs could then appear as a point of "nonpartisan cooperation" between a Republican Congress and a Democratic president.

In other words, what this epistemology of conspiratorial motivation accomplishes in its mystification of effects is what I described earlier as a "reversal" of victimage. The reversal depends on the mystification of effects. Rather than people on welfare, who might to the untrained eye seem to be the victims affected by unequal income distribution, it's those who can afford to *pay for* welfare who become the visible victims not of welfare recipients, but of a conspiracy controlling the circulation of welfare information. Welfare recipients thus disappear from view as victims, because this conspiracy theorizing functions to repeat, by reconstituting, powers of agency through locating their "origin" in the position of a victim forced to pay for welfare benefits to others. That position is secured by defining the plausibility of a conspiracy at work somewhere else. If plausibly conspiratorial agents exist elsewhere, then one has available for oneself the position of victim. It doesn't really matter that the effects of such conspiracies aren't documentable, or even capable of being identified exactly. The point, again, is how being in a victim position then justifies newly reconstituted powers of agency.

Human capital, however, as Hage and Powers remind us, depreciates quickly. The agency of human capital accumulation must continually "retool" itself or risk the obsolescence that comes with the fatally quick rapidity of change in the production and circulation of information. The conditions of retooling thus require the continual possibility of reversing agent and victim positions; it is not self-as-agent but only self-as-victim that can become available to be retooled as newly empowered agent. As I've argued, the economics of human capital (like the economics of capital generally) hypostatize this mysterious wealth as "self"-generating. Human capital endlessly generates human capital across the continual retooling required by agent becoming victim becoming agent again. But human capital, too, is a *political* economy. What it exploits is the labor of others, in the divisions of labor produced across variable powers of agency. Equally important, what is also exploited is the victimage of others, as welfare recipients, for example, disappear as victims in a social landscape now populated by the "victims" who pay for welfare benefits. The means of exploitation—and hence the politics of human capital—is embodied in the epistemology of conspiracy, which creates the conditions for the necessary reversibilities of agent and victim.

Statistics that attempt to measure the production of information in the United States, and the rate of investment in education for production, are staggering indeed. *The 1988 Economic Report of the President* prepared by Reagan's economic advisors arrived at a figure of over $610 billion expenditure in 1987 on all forms of education and training. Academic scientific journals alone publish new articles at a rate of roughly two per minute. The humanities traditionally lag well behind scientific fields in quantity of publications, but anyone who has been on hiring committees for junior appointments or even admissions committees for incoming graduate students is likely to be blown away by the number of publications now typically appearing on vitas and applications. At the same time, undergraduate classrooms even at relatively "prestigious" universities are likely to have a large percentage of students who in their instructors' eyes are incapable of producing a coherent sentence, let alone a "publishable article" of any sort. At community colleges and secondary schools, that percentage of course rises exponentially. Such attempts at quantifying measures of human capital make the extremes of "knowledge" wealth and poverty in the United States look at least as dramatic as extremes of economic disparities.

The disparities in human capital have been the subject not only of radical critics of an "information society" like Herbert Schiller and Noam Chomsky, but also corporate human resources analysts and economic sociologists. For it isn't necessary to assume a strict correlation between the possession of human capital and of economic wealth to recognize that the absence of human capital resources in a huge mass of the population creates a "problem" as fraught with potential for social disruption as the absence of economic wealth for a "mass" of the population. Different positions obviously see the "problem"—and, correspondingly, optimal solutions—in very different terms, but nobody imagines it will simply disappear.

In these circumstances, however, some form of conspiracy theorizing becomes an immensely attractive explanatory tool for left theorists no less than for the political directions inherited from Reaganism. Indeed, to the extent human capital is assumed to emerge from a process of information circulation and exchange, it lends itself rather more easily than financial capital to a vision of a very small number of conspiratorial agents plotting together to control the movement of vast quantities of information. Films like Tim Robbins's *Bob Roberts*, with its summary playing of the Woodie Guthrie hymn to the importance of "knowing" as the credits roll, serve to dramatize a "left" perception of "right-wing" conspiracies at work to prevent our "knowing." Likewise, the web of connections among corporate, military, and academic producers of information, exhaustively documented by critics like Schiller and Chomsky, and the funds made available for investment in production, seem to make possible an apparatus likewise able to control where the information does and doesn't go. The procedures implemented during Reagan's presidency for classifying documents under the banner of national security, for example, which permit single agents acting without review to identify such documents, appears as a particularly telling instance of control. Thus I'm not at all intent on challenging the documentation, available in Schiller and others, of practices of information control. Assessing the *effects* of these practices, however, is another matter.

I've played familiar left narratives about corporate, military, and academic collusion in deliberate parallel to typical conservative conspiracy stories about welfare, and so on. The "content" of these conspiracy discourses is hardly similar, and certainly the political ends, as with *Bob Roberts*, are very different indeed. In both cases, however—and specific examples could be multiplied at great length—the discursive frame of attention is fixed epistemologically around the plausibility of an existent conspiracy rather than focused on the means of assessing what effects result from conspiratorial agents at work.

Once framed epistemologically, however, in terms of plausible motivation, it soon becomes very difficult to know *how* you would know an effect if you see one. You might be able to show why specific agents have reasons for conspiring to keep documents "secret," but how would you know what the effects are of X number of documents having been classified as secret? In that form, the question is an impossible one; you could only *know* if the documents were unclassified and something different happened. Or you might well be driven to speculate, because nothing much seemed to happen with declassification, that "real" secrets were still preserved—as, for example, in the circumstances of the promise in the wake of Stone's *JFK* for a full disclosure of the FBI file on Kennedy's assassination. In other words, in terms of effects at least, there is a certain epistemological redundancy in the capacity of conspiracy theories to "read" the process of information flow and blockage. What seems plausibly conspiratorial motivation might even be "proven," but frames of plausibility become ultimately self-referential at the point where they must also supply indices that permit the identification of specific effects.

The reversibility of agent and victim inherited from the politics of Reaganism, however, requires precisely this epistemological self-referentiality. The reason to identify conspiracies "elsewhere" is not finally in order to document the effects of conspiratorial power exercised from "there," but to reconstitute—"retool"—powers of agency "here," by exploiting the possibilities of a new "origin" in the position of victim. The epistemological emphasis on plausible motivation, that is, serves Reaganite politics and its contemporary extensions well; left politics in contrast has little if anything to gain from becoming tangled in such epistemologies, with their mystifications of effects. If you already know you're exploited as victim, with relatively little power of agency to produce social change, you can't have a lot of use for a form of conspiracy theory that not only can't tell you anything more about being a victim, but which also—in contemporary circumstances—puts you in an inevitably losing competition with a great many other discourses of conspiracy likewise claiming an "origin" in the position of victim.

Marx of course was always suspicious of the value of conspiracy theories as support for revolutionary social change. His suspicions were grounded in an analysis of political economy that looked to its structural organization rather than to the motivations of agents as the source of exploitative powers. Thus exploitation has a specific, "technical" meaning in Marx's analysis. It names the extortion of surplus labor from workers who have only their labor power to sell on the market in return for a wage, and the primary economic narrative of *Capital* is the (albeit very complicated) process whereby surplus labor is eventually realized as capital in the hands of only a few. Conspiracy theories short-circuit this complex structural analysis by immediately assigning to capitalist owners the motivation of exploiting workers rather than of accumulating capital. As an instrument of social change such theorizing could only project two hopelessly utopian solutions for Marx: a "romance" version involving armed revolution to eliminate the "bad guys" and replace them with "good guys"; and a "realist" version of reform that, through education and the inculcation of ethical ideals, would turn us all into "good guys" whose sense of ethical responsibility would compensate for any nasty effects of an economic system. In Marx's analysis, neither version could address the structural conditions of exploitation.

Baudrillard's often reiterated critique of Marx extends Marx's own emphasis on structural description of exploitation by challenging what for Baudrillard remains implicated in a certain metaphysics of the "human" in Marx. In this reading, the affective charge carried by "exploitation" derives ultimately from Marx's assumption of labor as an essential quality of the human; workers are not only exploited, but denatured in effect. And for Baudrillard, the survival of that assumption in a contemporary information economy of signs condemns any Marxian account of exploitation to an as yet incomplete level of structural description.

Despite how the concept of human capital suggests an analogy to economic capital, it does seem to me impossible directly to transfer Marx's analysis of the former into a similar structural analysis of the latter. In contrast to Baudrillard, however, I want to preserve the appropriateness of exploitation as a term of analysis. The difficulty of transferring Marx's argument to an analysis of human capital is less a matter of "essentialist" assumptions that limit the completeness of his structural description of the system than of the limitations of structural description itself, evident in Baudrillard's account of an economy of signs no less than in Marx.

Unlike economic capital, human capital articulates agency as a determination of capital accumulation. *Human* capital, again, names not only what you have but what you are as agent. Further, as I argued, it accumulates across the mobilities of reversal: self-as-agent becoming self-as-victim becoming self-as-agent once more. Clearly the dynamics of this "self" are not occasioned by some radically autonomous "subject" forever acting in unpredictable ways that would frustrate any attempt at systematic description. Nevertheless, no structural account of human capital accumulation can plot with any degree of accuracy anything like Marx's identification of exploited workers as the ultimate source of economic capital. There is no inherent "logic" in the mobilities of reversal that could tell you exactly when, where, and which victims will be displaced and made invisible in the repositionings of self-as-agent into self-as-victim.

Unlike exploitation as Marx uses it, which in his analysis of economic capital accumulation inevitably will lead to workers in any workplace any time organized in capitalist terms, the exploitation of victims that drives the mobilities of reversal in human capital accumulation can lead in a thousand very different directions at once. As a group, African Americans are victims of a white supremacist social formation in the United States. But which African Americans will be exploited when, under what conditions, in what ways, and through what specific process of reversal of victimage remains impossible to anticipate by way of a structural account of human capital. Thus "racial discrimination" in the workplace, in the purchasing of homes, in the possibilities of school "choice," and so on, has become difficult to prove in any specific case, and charges of "reverse discrimination" as a particular instance of the reversal of agent and victim have become quite common.

In these circumstances, I want to argue that conspiracy theorizing nevertheless can have effective uses, despite Marx's fear that it short-circuits systematic analysis. What it must address is the limitations of such systematic analysis, the point where structural description becomes incapable of revealing the multiple effects of exploitation at work. I understand the organization of conspiracy discourses in this form as pedagogical, rather than epistemological. Where structural analysis might work to reveal the disparities of human capital, the positionalities of those who are the real victims of an information economy and its valorization of human capital, pedagogical conspiracy theorizes the *effects* of specific forms of exploitation. It walks around the epistemological issue of the reliability of information about "real victims" (are African Americans "really" the victims of a white supremacist society?) and emphasizes instead the education of agents in the midst of fields of effect. While it won't, like structural description, yield a determinate analytics of change, I will argue in the next section that it is an indispensable pedagogy for constituting agents of change.

❧

Rates for advertising spots on network television typically are set in relation to projected audience size and demographics. The data for such projections are supplied by rating services like Nielsen, who thus trade in a market of information, offering data simultaneously to advertisers and to network management as "of use"—and hence identified as "information"—in determining rates per spot. These two potential consumers, however, have very different interests in the information Nielsen markets.

If advertisers feel information about audience size might be skewed toward a result that inflates percentages of viewers or desirable age demographics among viewers, they will also feel victimized by network negotiators' demands for high rates per spot. Conversely, network negotiators will feel victimized by advertisers offering low payment if audience size seems small or demographically undesirable.

Nielsen's interest in this complicated process of exchange depends on a double positioning. Nielsen must have no use whatsoever for the information generated by audience measurement; information is produced solely for exchange. At the same time, Nielsen must also conceptualize the use of the information as absolutely necessary to advertiser-network negotiations over rates. Should it seem instead that Nielsen is not only conceptualizing use but *making use of* information (by, say, "conspiring" with advertisers to profit from projections of low audience size), the realization of exchange value is jeopardized. The exchange value of information as a commodity depends on conceptualizations of use. But exchange value can be realized quite independently from the realization of use value.

In these circumstances, the "objectivity" of the ratings has nothing to do with being disinterested—Nielsen is very interested indeed—and little to do immediately with the methodological coherence, technological apparatuses, and control procedures for ensuring "accuracy" of audience measurement. Purchasers may demand accurate information, but the first test of accuracy is the objectivity that results from splitting conceptualization of use from the realization of use value. This doesn't mean Nielsen workers don't try in every way to be accurate, or that the information generated is somehow "unreal," merely a simulation that is constructed rather than a description of what is actually "out there." It simply means such questions are irrelevant to the initial process whereby information becomes objectively available to be exchanged. Conceptualizing use identifies information as information. The division between conceptualizing use and realizing use value objectifies what is identified as information to enter into the circuit of exchange.

Purchasers of information, in contrast, can of course make use of the information to secure specific effects. An advertiser in possession of data indicating a relatively low percentage of viewers for a given show will use the information as a lever to negotiate lower rates with the network. But as a user of information, the advertiser is in no position to guarantee the objectivity of the information. What the advertiser must also purchase from Nielsen is thus metainformation, as it were, a guarantee of objectivity that permits realizing the use value of what has been purchased, or, conversely, raising questions about its accuracy.

In other words, information can't be purchased from just anybody at any time. A "smart" consumer knows the difference between, for example, purchasing a copy of *Motor Trend* and a copy of *Consumer Reports* for information about new cars on the market, even though in both magazines one will find carefully controlled tests of car performance, data about size and features, and so on. *Motor Trend* accepts advertising copy—and cars—from manufacturers of the cars it tests; *Consumer Reports* does not. No matter what information is available in each, the metainformational guarantee is different because the objective position of the producer of information differs.

As I've implied, specific charges of conspiracy for those who have a role in a circuit of information directly address the terms of metainformational guarantee rather than the accuracy of information. That is, it is objectivity rather than accuracy which is immediately at issue in conspiracy charges, and objectivity is constituted by a division between conceptualization and realization of use. Information, however, can affect a great many people who are not directly involved in its production and exchange. New car purchasers who never read either *Motor Trend* or *Consumer Reports* nevertheless are affected by what such magazines publish and how automobile manufacturers respond to test reports and the like—as television viewers who have no active role in the negotiations among Nielsen, advertisers, and networks are affected by the information at stake in those negotiations, and people who draw welfare benefits are affected by the status of information that circulates in the debates about welfare.

For those outside a circuit of information, however, with no immediate stake in the metainformational guarantee of objectivity, the plausible motivations of conspiratorial agents at work become considerably more difficult to establish. If you look to the motivations of agents who might have reason for conspiring to control your television viewing, for example, you're blind-alleyed immediately. Nielsen can argue rightly enough that it has a powerful interest in learning what "you" collectively as a viewing audience actually watch. Advertisers—again quite rightly—can argue a double interest in a means of access to projections of the largest, demographically desirable audience for their products on the one hand, and low rates for their commercials on the other, with as a result lower product cost to pass on to "you" as audience. Network representatives can plead an interest in putting on programming "you" will want to watch and collecting large advertising fees to fund a higher quality of programming without "you" necessarily having to pay anything for the privilege if "you" don't want to purchase the products advertised. Even if a conspiracy could exist, it would be for the best of motives and ultimately work for "your" benefit. Given such blind alleys, it's little wonder critique is driven either to push conspiracy theorizing to the epistemological limits—trying to reveal some still more deeply hidden motivations behind the obvious—or to abandon it altogether in favor of a structural description of the system that can identify the lines of power at work and measure their field strength through terms other than the motivations of agents.

What Marxist description yields is a recognition of the structural priority of objectivity in the information circuit, or, in other words, how in this specific circumstance exchange value dominates use value. The objectivity necessary for exchange must come before any realization of use value. Thus agents with a role in the circuit of information will act first to ensure the objectivity of information as a commodity, rather than moving to control your viewing choices or habits, whatever interests they might have in what you see or don't see. The structural "problem" with the system lies in how you are excluded from participation in that circuit of information production, circulation, and exchange. You are positioned instead as the *subject* of information, and are subjected to the effects of the objective status of information as a commodity.

What structural description in this Marxian sense can't tell you much about, however, is what it's like to occupy this position as subject of information. Nor can it explain much about the effects of an information circuit to which you're subjected; the only "effect" that really matters is your exclusion from a role in the circuit. Yet in the situation, those effects are multiple. In my television example, you're faced with a range of different programming, not simply with a program you must watch; a constellation of different advertising spots, not just a single commercial; repetitions of all of the above in a great many different contexts, not just while viewing television. Likewise, the configuration of possibilities continually changes, affording different possibilities of response and engaging different levels of interest, even "resistances" to specifically coded ideological messages in the programming. At the same time, however, neither the multiplicity nor the changes appear random. Patterns can be traced across the available field and its changes, and there does seem to be a recognizable field of effects, not simply an endless sequence of endless "differences" among effects.

A pedagogical discourse of conspiracy has its uses in this field of effects, and takes the form of what might then be understood as theorizing a "conspiracy of effects." The emphasis on plural "effects" registers the sense of multiplicity and change involved, and precludes an attempt to isolate each effect and line it up directly with some causal agency, "motivated" to produce the effect. "Conspiracy," however, implies not only a certain coherence of effects, but a collusive coherence as it were, a "center" around which effects cohere. In the circumstances of the circuit of television information, that "center" is not an agent—Nielsen, advertisers, the networks—causing the effects. It is, precisely, the *subject* of the effects that emerges at the center. A discourse identifying a conspiracy of effects is a narrative told from this position of a victimized subject. And while it may seem epistemologically fantastic to think the oxymoron of "effects conspiring," or a psychologically treacherous paranoia to see yourself at the "center" of a conspiracy, pedagogically there's much to learn from such a focus on the subject of information as caught in a conspiracy of effects.

In contrast to versions of Freudian structural description, however, which if applied to television viewing would at this point focus attention on how the subject's needs and desires are externally mediated and constrained, the theorizing of a conspiracy of effects preserves a Marxian emphasis on the *position* of the subject relative to the information circuit. Thus rather than immediately looking to the possibility of some radical "excess" of desire, exogenous to the terms of structural mediation and control that Freudian analytics could describe, a conspiracy theorizing of effects poses the question of why your subject position is of interest at all to a circuit of information that nevertheless excludes you from that circuit. The answer is that while advertising and television programming may indeed solicit your pleasures, simulate your desires, manufacture your needs, or whatever, advertisers and networks profit from trading in information. The conspiratorial collusion of effects has as its subject "you" as a body of information rather than "you" as a body subject to pleasures or desires, excessive or not.

Donna Haraway's marvelously resonant phrase "an informatics of domination" anticipates this sense of a subject as body of information, as well as any number of effects produced across the rapid expansion and mutation of scientific fields of discourse. Yet it also slides rather too quickly into a familiar vocabulary of "domination," as if the goal were the constitution and control of subjugated bodies. But the immediate terms of profit involve the capitalization of information, not the domination of subjects, or bodies. And information, as I have argued, involves the interconnections of human and economic capital. Economic profit in information thus refers everywhere to human capital, and depends on the variable, specific means of exploitation by which human capital accumulates. In theorizing a conspiracy of effects, you learn what you "want" by first learning how effects are configured not to exploit your desires, but to exploit what your informational body yields "of interest" elsewhere to the accumulation of human capital.

What it yields first and foremost is replaceability. In my television example, the condition of your being a subject of information is that you become available to be replaced by the information produced by Nielsen as a commodity available for exchange. Which is not quite the same as "being commodified."* It's not your desires, your interests, your habits, your "person"—or whatever—that become an information commodity in the circuit of exchange. Nielsen doesn't sell "you" the audience in a market for information; Nielsen sells itself. Nielsen can thereby realize the economic capital from the exchange of information that you can't, by becoming the human capital agent that you aren't. Nielsen replaces you as subject of the configuration of effects that makes up available programming, advertising spots, and so on, by offering itself as now occupying that newly "retooled" position. Nielsen "embodies" the information for sale in its exchanges with both networks and advertisers. That is, Nielsen's mechanism of replacement depends on reversing the position of agent and victim, for human capital must always be made to seem a matter of *self*-exploitation. Nielsen sells itself, not you. What disappears in this process of information production is thus the subject position that has been replaced. In these circumstances exploitation is a matter of replacement rather than of commodifying your desires or extorting a profit from you as excluded from the circuit of information. You can't be excluded from what you were never part of.

What a pedagogy of conspiracy has to offer in contrast is a narrative in which you are irreplaceable. However multiple and multidirectional effects may be, they are focused around you. Thus theorizing a conspiracy of effects doesn't involve a narrative about your "identity" as subjected to effects, but about the irreplaceability of your subject position as the guarantee of what will count as information for you. Nothing counts that isn't linked to that irreplaceable positionality. The metainformational guarantee, in other words, is subjectively positioned within a field of effects. Information such as Nielsen's is suspect—whether accurate or not—because it is objective, a function of the human capital circuit of information exchange.

* The commodification of the audience is the argument made by Eileen Meehan, for example, in "Why We Don't Count: The Commodity Audience."

It is not driven by what you need to know—a need that begins, as a conspiracy of effects teaches, in the awareness of the irreplaceability of subject positions. Theorizing a conspiracy of effects keeps you at the center of the narrative of conspiracy in and through the pedagogical formation of agency that identifies the "you" as what's at the center of effects. Unlike the familiar figure of the "nomad" in Deleuze and Guattari or in more recent accounts, such as Rosi Braidotti's, pedagogies of conspiracy theorizing in this sense are not an attempt to keep ahead of the game, just beyond the mechanisms of replaceability that produce a subject to be replaced. Conspiracy pedagogy refuses to leave, even when it's on the move. It's about the formation of political agency that everywhere contests the power of replacing subject positions.

Economic exploitation in Marx's definition depends on a process whereby large masses of the population must arrive at a workplace with nothing to sell but their labor power, no matter how many itineraries they follow, no matter what specific experiences they bring with them. Exploitation in this account is indifferent to victims; it makes no difference *whose* individual labor power is made available to exploit or in what other configurations of social position that labor power might exist. Thus the great revolutionary narrative Marx's work has to tell is a story of mass collectively organized action whose agent—despite all the metaphysical encumbrances it has often been forced to carry—is *class* consciousness. That is, the immediately strategic importance of class consciousness has little to do with an ontology of "consciousness," and everything to do with how effectively to take advantage of the indifference of exploitation. "Workers of the world" not only can "unite," but already are united by the indifferent identifications imposed by exploitation. The task lies in turning that indifference to advantage by "consciously" directing its class-united force toward the end of revolutionary challenge to the system of exploitation.

Human capital exploitation, in contrast, requires specific, finely differentiated, and multiply positioned victims of exploitation. Human capital exploitation succeeds only to the extent that the "same" victims can be represented as victims over and over, each time "differently," each time in new circumstances, each time victimized by continually shifting constellations of forces, each time newly available to the reversible replaceabilities of victim and agent positions.

The first crucial point about Nielsen projections of a viewing audience of 12 million, for example, is less the "indiscriminate mass" of 12 million than the discrimination of positionality *as viewer* from all the other subject positions individual viewers might also occupy. This isolation as viewer thus functions as a qualitatively different index than identification as worker. "Worker" is unidirectional. Very different subjects may arrive in many different ways at many different workplaces, but in arriving at a workplace with only their own labor power to sell, the itineraries involved all fold into the identification as worker. Informationally, however, the position of viewer affords a means of access for those interested in the many different subject positions occupied by viewers. These interests might involve anything from network demographics working out the competitive scheduling of programs for particular time slots, or advertising profiles of "lifestyle" indices in calculating how to target marketing for a particular product, to political opinion polling, number of "hits" at a Web site, and so on. Each of these interests carves up the 12 million informational bodies very differently, as information is used differently. "Viewer," unlike "worker," leads into rather than away from a multiplicity of other positions.

Thus, unlike in Marx's account, there is nothing inherent in the logic of human capital exploitation that "unites" victims. Victim positions are instead disarticulated into always more finely differentiated circumstances— circumstances that are now often endlessly played and replayed in the proliferation of television talk shows. In response to human capital exploitation in these terms, recognizing a *conspiracy* of effects creates the possibility for a pedagogy of agent formation across the intersections of multiple, specific practices of exploitation. Against the divisibility of victim positions, pedagogical conspiracy narratives function as a reminder that from whatever directions they come, effects always "conspire" in the instance toward the replaceability of a specific subject position, one that will change again tomorrow. Resistances to exploitation may of necessity require multiple forms of knowledge and often complicated exchanges of informational resources among different and proliferating subject positions. But the agency of resistance begins at the conspiratorial, intersecting dynamics of replacement.

Agency can't emerge as a subject position *in* the field, a position occupied "in common with" others, or "as equivalent to" the positions of other victims of exploitation in the kind of "democratic imaginary" projected by Laclau and Mouffe's logic of equivalence. If the nightmare of the economic exploitation Marx describes is an oppositionally directed class consciousness of union, the nightmare of human capital exploitation is the formation of a political agency dedicated to preserving the irreplaceability of subject positions. Agency works to make impossible the capitalization of replacement of victim positions on which human capital depends. A conspiracy theorizing of effects is also a pedagogy of agent formation.

❀

The creation of cheap capital is a long and continuing story. What makes specifically *human* capital cheap is the proliferation and exploitation of subject positions in and through the mechanisms of replacement. What makes information a primary commodity in a global market is what it promises by way of the cheap availability of human capital. An epistemological structure of conspiracy theories functions to plot the formation of human capital across the movement of information as it circulates. "Conspiracy" in this sense doesn't have as its field of reference some vanishingly small picture of a now remote and "simpler" past. It expresses a political logic required by *current* narratives of the historical emergence of an information-based economy.

Within these narratives, human capital thus becomes a metonymic name for the agency of political control exercised by transnational capital. For the "wealth" of transnational corporations depends less on the convertibility of human to economic capital than on how the formation of economic colonies "there" makes possible the realization of political agency "here," within the corporation, in the form of human capital. The formation of economic colonies depends in turn on exploitation as replacement: labor producing economic resources is replaced by the symbolics of labor that produces the organizational mobilities of transnational capital; subject positions are replaced by bodies of information available for exchange. Transnational capital is a "conspiracy" that *produces* political agency as human capital from the formation of economic colonies.

In contrast to an account of the colonizing powers of transnational capital, such as my own in the preceding chapter, for instance, pedagogical conspiracy discourses seem to project only a kind of twilight zone of intersecting market effects. That is, conspiracy theorizing yields little by way of an analysis of transcapital political organization. Thus "capital" appears within these discourses as an ontological cyborg—part myth, part monster, part gossip, each part filling the spaces of the whole, with no way of telling for sure whether myth, monster, or gossip points "outward" to limn a structure of implacably imposed political control or "inward" to express what Pynchon recalls us to as "the orbiting ecstasy of a true paranoia" (137). It's no wonder that serious political analysts from Marx to Gramsci often suc-

cumbed to a kind of blank fury at the persistence of conspiratorial thinking in the groups they addressed, as if it bypassed altogether the primary
structural coordinates of economic power relations.

Yet as a pedagogy of agency formation, conspiracy discourse might better be understood as a form of cultural practice necessarily adjacent to the
field of countercolonial economics. For while in strictly economic terms
the production and circulation of resources seem condemned by transnational colonialization to often ad hoc and frequently extralegal forms of organization, a pedagogy of conspiracy functions at the borderlines of these
economic practices, pointing to the configurations of effects that push the
presence of transnational politics into local sectors. As I will argue in the
next chapter, markets trading in economic resources may seem to exist as
parallel worlds in a great many different forms, some recognizably capitalist in organization and some not. But conspiracy theorizing is a reminder
that none exist completely independent of the political imaginary of the
market as a vast, labyrinthine ensemble of effects where parallel lines inevitably intersect. Thus however nebulous it is as a structural economic
analysis of transnational capital, pedagogically, conspiracy discourses invite
a continual recognition of the forces within which revolutionary political
agency must be developed. They recognize the continually shifting web of
knowledges tuned to the mechanisms of replacement that would obliterate
subject positions from any purchase in social fields.

From the other side, as it were, romanticizing the persistence of conspiracy pedagogies is perhaps no less tempting than a kind of Marxian
anger at its fantasies. Such romanticizing of conspiracy discourse assumes
that a careful analysis of the many, many conspiracy stories that circulate
among exploited groups would somehow yield an immediate and embattled knowledge of political resistances. Analysis in this sense, however, is
itself a fantasy of displacement that even at best produces "knowledge" of
resistances only by obscuring the pedagogical *work* of conspiracy discourses. Thus I've avoided any extended discussion of so many available
conspiracy narratives because the point isn't to "read" conspiracy stories in
a new way. In this pedagogical context, conspiracy is only a figure of
change, a field of education for the formation of political agents who learn
to conspire together against the exploitative powers of information.

Someone is always done in by a conspiracy, and there are a lot of some-
ones done in by a lot of conspiracies day in and day out in the formation of
human capital that drives an information economy. While information is
exchangeable, however, learning can be shared. Effective alliance politics

depend on the shared learning that begins in the connections of counter-colonial economics to a politics of struggle. Conspiracy pedagogy is not itself resistance, but it borders on politics. It's the border sign of something happening in the colonies, the cultural recognition of disruptive market economic practices that enables the formation of agency necessary to challenge the political dominance of transnational capital.

FOUR

Your Dog's Just a Dog: Literary Scholarship and Market Politics

Neoclassical market theory has always lined its attention to rates, volume, growth projections, capital input, and statistical data generally with an insistent rhetoric linking "freedom" and images of individual growth. Thus if you can ignore all these massively foregrounded numbers for a moment, neoclassical theory looks like nothing so much as a triumphalist version of Freud's Oedipal narrative. It's the successful story of a little boy growing up free to follow his interests and initiative in his own way, in open competition with others intent on the same ends. In this imagery, such "rational agents" who populate smoothly functioning markets are paradigmatically adults and masculine; national economies are characterized as "adult" or "mature"; terms like "developing" and "developed" are so frequent it's easy to forget the adjectives are applied in almost the same way to adolescence and adulthood as to nations. Conversely, the economic equivalent of Freud's psychopathology of everyday life is traced to the actions of "irrational" market agents who, like women, fail to recognize the necessity imposed by the marketplace Law of the Father: somebody's always going to have a bigger one. Thus Politics is born, the fatal pathology of penis envy that forever threatens to interfere with the equilibrium of market conditions.

Isolated in this way from its mathematical exoskeleton, what's striking about the rhetoric of neoclassical economics is that for all its congruities with familiar pop versions of Freud, nevertheless it offers no theory of the unconscious. Whatever is "unconscious" in the behavior of adult, rational agents is immediately factored without remainder into the stabilizing properties of the market, which obligingly compensates for any irregularities. Yet Keynes, after all, had introduced an explanation for the dynamic of economic growth that occurs, like Freud's castration anxiety, in the midst of a contradiction, the fact that supply and demand never line up neatly. Thus marketplace "laws" always involve trauma and generate "unconscious" anxieties. Correlatively, so far from a failure to grow up, politics in its Keynesian version becomes the socialization of repression, necessary therapy, and the identifying mark of true adulthood: what it is, for example, that really distinguishes "developed" from as yet adolescent and "underdeveloped" economies.

Keynes, however, is not exactly a favorite of neoclassical theorists, for Keynes knew well enough that the assumption of markets populated by rational agents is only a convenient tautology in any case. The desired equilibrium of market conditions depends on the behavior of people whose rationality consists in having acted in ways that preserve the equilibrium of market conditions. The mirroring between the market and its rational agents is so complete that it's little wonder neoclassical theory has always come with warning labels not to "personify" the market, rather like beer commercials that urge responsible drinking. Yet Keynes remained a good modernist who managed to preserve the universalizing of market theory even while questioning the ostensibly self-regulating mechanisms that restore systemic equilibrium if left alone.

The assumed existence of "the market" as a recognizably separate entity can thereby remain in place as a justification for an enormous range of decisions about social organization. As economic sociologist Fred Block points out, what he calls the "intravenous model" of capital as the "life blood" of a personified capitalist marketplace "serves as a justification for some of the most basic features of the existing political economy. A steady and strong flow of profits to capital holders is necessary to compensate them for their willingness to sacrifice immediate consumption in favor of investment. This necessity justifies the huge inequalities of income and wealth in the United States and provides a powerful argument against redistributive tax policies" (152–53). Likewise, the necessity of capital flow justifies the division between "public spending" and "private investment," as well as the designation of the former as inherently wasteful, drying up the flow of capital. "The market" with its pulsating tumescence of capital blood is universalized as the largest defining form of what ultimately counts as the *necessary*. Whatever else goes on—socially, culturally, politically—must at some level observe the Law of the Market.

Even neoclassical theorizing, however, recognizes that so-called exogenous factors operate on the individual level, "interfering" with purely rational economic decisions. Recent attention to the motivations of economic agents has attempted to supply means of calculating their effects. The analysis of exogenous factors, however, becomes both an indispensable and a dangerous adjunct to the "necessities" imposed by the market: indispensable to the extent that, perhaps in contemporary political circumstances especially, it seems almost impossible not to recognize other claims beyond the market for what counts as the socially necessary; dangerous because recognition in this context amounts to an acknowledgment that decisions weighing various claims on what counts as the necessary can't be adjudicated automatically on market grounds, whatever "rational expectations" may be imputed to agents. You must prove not only that the market enforces certain necessary conditions, but also that those conditions afford the *best* means of maximizing the realization of everyone's "necessary" equitably.

In a Reaganite politics of the economy, a "safety net" for the unemployed, for example, was acknowledged, if often reluctantly, as a necessity; risking the return of high inflation by striving for a full-employment economy, in contrast, was something "we" couldn't afford. The work of maintaining such divisions between social necessities and social luxuries helps explain why neoclassical economic theorizing is "classical" as well as "neo." What it derives from classical economics is less a set of still-useful descriptive terms that can be extended into the present than a resource of propaganda on behalf of the market, whatever its shortcomings in practice, as the best field available to ground policy decisions about social organization generally.

Postmodern economics, however, has meant that even little boys grow up with "unconscious" anxieties. Recently familiar corporate buzzwords like flattened management hierarchy, diversity, flexible specialization, corporate reengineering, and the like also always register as a symptomatic vocabulary of stress, for the mirror stage of "market" and "agent" so dear to neoclassical theory has turned into endless metonymic substitutions. Rather than the consummation of Desire as the Berlin Wall collapses on a virgin East, you encounter first one, then two, then three, then four, and who knows how many more "Asian Tigers" yet to come bursting from the Unconscious of market presence "everywhere." A neoclassical economics unable to project a theory of the unconscious finds itself forced into the increasingly uncomfortable position of inventing an increasingly baroque vocabulary for always more alien marketplace agents and marketplace behaviors. Thus as corporate motivational guru Tom Peters's rescripting of growing up succinctly emphasizes, before trying to market anything you've got to learn to ask yourself, "Is it weird enough?" (quoted in Newfield, "Corporate Pleasures," 41). At least Peters is funnier than Lacan, and like Pynchon's mythical Pierce Inverarity, knows how to keep it bouncing on stage.

Given its barely subcutaneous psychological story of maturation and adulthood, what interests me particularly about the renewals of neoclassical economics in the present, however, is another kind of metonymic slippage involving a figure of field, as it were. Market theory continues to represent itself—often to an absurdity of mathematical detail—as if addressing, precisely, the field of marketplace practices of exchange. From the "outside," this can easily look reductionist, as if a vast economic metaphor of "the marketplace" afforded the only means for a consideration of general social organization. Fredric Jameson takes market theory seriously in these terms, applauding Gary Becker for at least having made explicit the totalizing social implications of market as metaphor. But it is more exactly a metonymy at work, where "the market" stands in for some larger and otherwise unrepresentable value that can only be imaged in the displaced adjectival form of "free" and narrativized in the borrowed psychological language of growing up. The question is why economic practices are metaphorized at all, why "the market" is used particularly as the field location of metonymic power for these otherwise undefinable values. Fictions of historical continuity are especially treacherous here; "free market" as a metonymic signifier also signifies the immense gap separating Adam Smith from someone like Milton Friedman and his followers. The resurgence of free market theories in the present owes little to a tradition of economic thinking.

Neoclassical theory persistently ignores the diversity of actual markets in the present, or at best indexes them in relation to the assumed self-regulating mechanisms of an ideal market form. As a spot market involving rapid transactions among countless buyers and sellers seemingly linked by little more than their trading activities, a stock exchange seems closest to the ideal. Yet even this perception comes at the expense of downplaying what Wayne Baker refers to as the "social structure" that organizes and makes possible trading in securities, for example. And for most people, everyday images of "markets" bear little relation to a stock exchange. There is a market in familiar commodities like washing machines, but consumer purchasers at Sears aren't making economic choices in anything like the same way as traders on Wall Street. This isn't because they operate less "rationally" (or like obligingly congruent monads achieve the desired effect anyway so long as they walk away with a good deal), but because they are involved in a particular contractual relationship that presupposes a complex and very different network of established social relations.

Still further afield, admitted generalizations about a free "capitalist" marketplace appear suspect even in their generality. There's no real reason to assume that goods marketed in capitalist terms can't have been produced by a very different and decidedly noncapitalist organization of production, and no internal logic that inevitably links goods produced through a capitalist organization of labor to a capitalist marketplace. For all its "illegality," the production of crystal meth, for example, can often observe the most advanced practices of high-tech flexibly specialized flattened management organization. But anyone who thinks it is sold under the "laws" of a capitalist marketplace has never tried to buy some in alien territory. While production may often be postindustrial high tech, the marketing of crystal is feudal. The work of producing any number of so-called craft goods, in contrast, is typically organized through a kind of "primitive" guild system. No privileged group is positioned to appropriate any surplus labor of the work. There is none; this isn't a capitalist organization of labor. These goods, however, are often marketed in such remarkably sophisticated ways that IBM could learn a great deal from them about how to survive in a postindustrial economy.

It is important to understand that markets are different, and equally important not to fall into a kind of reverse confirmation of neoclassical theorizing by way of warnings like Laclau and Mouffe's in *Hegemony and Socialist Strategy*, where they can see "practically no domain of individual or collective life" (161) safe from the relentless market commodification of all social relations. But the point is not simply to pursue a deconstruction of fictions of the market that emphasizes, like Piore and Sabel for example, the multiplicity and diversity of market organizations. As I argued in Chapter 2, the mobilities of transnational capital require different forms of markets, forms that set up conditions for competing avenues of possibility for the creation of cheap capital. At the same time, however, it is the proximities of such economic colonies, with all they carry as signs of social disintegration and disorder, that impose a kind of magnetic distortion, such that the vision of a political "true north" must find expression in the now displaced metonymic imagery of "the market." In these circumstances, "market" is not about the actual economic practices organizing markets, nor even an ideal descriptor of how such markets ought to behave. "Market" is a metonymy of field: as if, could the politics of transnational capital be exhaustively elaborated and accounted for under the economic sign of "the market," the dependence of transnational capital on the economic productivity of the colonies could be erased from view and their colonized populations finally dismissed as simply "outside" the pathways of capital flow.

In what follows I want to look at some specific details of market organization within the United States itself by focusing on two perfectly familiar if incongruously paired commodities in the contemporary social formation: show dogs and literary scholarship. This deliberately odd pairing affords a convenient way to emphasize the differences among markets and market organizations. At the same time, however, disturbing parallels exist in the complex ensembles of social relations that constitute the markets in these commodities. Similarities between such disparate markets as show dogs and literary scholarship make possible a recognition of the effects of multiple forms of market discourse on both the organization of markets and the behaviors of marketplace agents. Neoclassical theorizing doesn't offer much descriptive help in understanding the economic practices of either market, because there's no inherent tendency of marketplace organization to conform to any model of the market. Nevertheless, the pervasiveness of a neoclassical psychological narrative can explain a great deal about the rhetorics of legitimization deployed by marketplace agents, no matter how different the markets in which they operate. Thus the parallels between such diverse markets as show dogs and literary scholarship point immediately to the pressures of ideological constraints, rather than to some projected uniformity among economic practices.

Markets are complex ensembles of economic, political, and cultural practices, very much a part of everyday life. They're neither self-regulating entities nor alien impositions that frustrate ordinary pleasures. Commodities, Marx reminds us, are bearers of social relations, and it is the specificities of the show dog commodity and the commodity of literary scholarship that yield perhaps the best angle of entry for understanding the tensions of market organization in each case. No market is a purely local ensemble, uncontaminated by the realities of global politics that drive the field metonymy of the market. Even in the midst of the most affluent country on the planet, however, market organizations afford multiple opportunities for constructing linkages of economic resourcefulness and political initiatives that can take advantage of how "market" metonymies nevertheless ultimately depend on actual markets, no matter how well they're disguised.

❊

Commodities, Marx acknowledged, seem mysterious when examined closely, and show dogs even at a distance are a strange commodity indeed. If what you know of dog shows comes via the distant televised image of Westminster, the most prestigious dog show in the United States, the strangeness can only be accentuated by what you see on-screen—all tuxes, jewels, furs, hushed whispers, and canine hagiography. Neoclassical market theories, however, claim a way to cut across the confusing commodity borderlands occupied by show dogs on the simple premise that like any commodity—no matter how "weird" its characteristics or what its "use value"—the relevant market features of a show dog will appear ultimately in the form of *price*. Fading memories of Ch. Salilyn's Condor's sweep to best in show at the 1993 Westminster may still seem priceless, but his worth as a commodity is what his owners now command in stud fees as a result of his win.

"More than . . . " is always a tempting rhetoric to challenge this "crude" bottom line of price: more than a price, more than a commodity, more than economics involved, and so on. But no neoclassical market theorist in her or his right mind would deny that "more than" price is at issue—just like more than price is at issue in a corporate decision about the location of test marketing a new product or a consumer decision about purchasing a new washing machine. The rhetoric of "more than" in any case is easy to reverse. After all, more than a love of Victorian literature or of Lhasa Apsos is at stake in a decision to write a thesis on the former or breed the latter. At some level there's also money, and price. The market theory claim is not that price alone determines even economic value, but that price will function as a visible register of whatever values may be at stake in commodity transactions.

Price is assumed to function best as a register, however, under the conditions of a relatively high degree of market autonomy. Thus ideally in neoclassical theory "marketplace laws" should operate freely, unconstrained by government regulation, for example. The market must always appear as a recognizably distinct economic field, rather than as deeply embedded in complicated networks of social relations whose structure reflects nonmarket considerations. Yet from very different political directions indeed, theorists like Mark Granovetter, Amitai Etzioni, and Fred Block have questioned whether any index of market autonomy can be adequate to account for what Granovetter sees as the inevitable embeddedness of agents in these exogenous (relative to the marketplace) networks of social relations, and for what Etzioni would aggregate together as "moral" determinants of value.* So-called exogenous factors, in these arguments, are so omnipresent in the behavior of agents in any specific market that Block is led to argue that the assumption of a distinct market field of behavior is nearly useless even as an "ideal" normative concept, let alone as a descriptive term.

The market in show dogs, or literary scholarship, is certainly embedded in complicated networks of social relations. I want to argue that in both cases, however, the emergence of a "commodity" is a matter of specifically determined social structures. That is, commodities themselves no less than the behavior of agents engaged in commodity transactions are bearers of social relations, for which price supplies at best a sketchily visible register, and at worst a completely misleading index. Marx anticipated this direction of argument, which is why, after acknowledging that commodities are full of "metaphysical subtleties and theological niceties," he turns almost immediately to the social organization of production rather than amusing himself with the subtleties and niceties. And it's why the detail of his onslaught on price and "marketplace laws" is largely reserved for the third volume of *Capital*.

In looking at a commodity like show dogs, however, it's worth reversing Marx's order of argument, even while preserving his crucial insight that commodities are determined within the conditions of specific forms of social relations. The "production" of show dogs affords a striking illustration of the dangers encountered in assuming an immediate congruity between "the realm of production" and "the realm of the market." A kennel owner may purchase food and other materials in a capitalist market, but the organization of the work of running a kennel where show dogs are produced nevertheless may not yield any surplus value. Production isn't necessarily organized in capitalist terms. Arguably, however, the commodification of show dogs has as much to do with the structurally peculiar conditions of the market in buying and selling show dogs as with conditions of production. Thus rather than turning immediately to production, as Marx does, I want to explore the commodity market of show dogs. Needless to say, I'm not really interested in the "subtleties" and "niceties" of the show dog commodity—"oh yes, Wiener knows when he's won a show"—any more than in the analogous subtleties and niceties of "great insight into Charles Dickens," or whatever, in the commodity of literary scholarship. I am very interested, however, in how the minute discriminations that identify a champion animal function in a show dog market. Like literary texts, and

* See Amitai Etzioni, *The Moral Dimension: Toward a New Economics*, and Granovetter, "Economic Action and Social Structure."

for that matter like students in a classroom, show dogs are the subjects of a remarkable apparatus of fine-tuned distinction. The process at work on show dogs—and literary texts, and students—has everything to do with shaping the specificities of a market in commodities.

Competition is a concept that lives a remarkably amphibious existence across the boundaries of "sport" and "business." There are of course good reasons to question those boundaries, but not simply toward the end of conflating sport and business entirely. Competition does lead a double life, with relatively flexible breathing apparatuses sensitive to environmental differences. Breeding and showing dogs is a business and a sport, and as good a place as any to observe the functional mobilities of competition in the determinations of a market structure.

At this writing the American Kennel Club (AKC) recognizes 93 different breeds eligible for conformation competition, although it's likely others will soon be added by the time you read this. Like the *Norton Anthology*'s version of a literary canon, the AKC's breed register always seems to be selectively expanding. And in rough parallel to Norton's grouping of texts by genre, the AKC also groups breeds by generic categories: Working, Non-Sporting, Terrier, Herding, Hound, Sporting, and Toy breeds. Each breed has a published "standard" describing the breed in ideal perfection; it is against this standard that each animal entered in a show is judged. "Championship points" are awarded for "best dog" and "best bitch" within a breed, according to a complex formula that varies depending upon the breed and the number of entries in a particular show. (Thus even at this level economics is already linked up with "exogenous" gender conceptions through that familiar slippage from generic "dog" into the division between "dog" and "bitch"; a champion "dog" yields stud fees, a champion "bitch" money from the sale of puppies.) Winners then compete for "best of breed"; bests of breed compete for "best in group"; and finally, bests in group compete for "best in show." In each case, however, decisions are still made in terms of breed standards. A miniature poodle doesn't compete directly against a St. Bernard for best in show; the decision is a matter of whether a designated judge thinks the poodle or the St. Bernard best conforms to their respective breed standards.

The televisual attention at Westminster focuses on the latter rounds of the judging—the best in group and best in show competitions. At the much less prestigious and local club-sanctioned shows, in contrast, these are likely to seem almost afterthoughts for most of the people in attendance. Attention is concentrated on the intrabreed competition instead, for *only* "best dog" and "best bitch" within a breed can earn championship points. There are no points awarded for best in group or show. Whereas at Westminster entries are already champions, competing against other champions, local shows are populated by owners, breeders, and agents working to earn the 15 points required (which must include two "majors"—at least 3 point wins—from two different judges to qualify) to be designated with the "CH" that among other things can bring in money for the sale of puppies and for stud fees.

Historically, dogs worked and were bred for specific tasks; dogs were used for sport of various kinds; dogs played multiple roles as pets and as religious icons in different cultures; dogs were used in scientific research; and so on. Like the notion of a "literary" text, the "show dog" is a palimpsest of many histories and historical uses. AKC breed standards often reproduce elements of these histories, but in more formalized or less formalized ways. For while standards exist for each breed, and are the basis for the judging, there is no uniform standard of standards, as it were, no set of requirements each standard must meet beyond approval by the national breed club AKC affiliate. Thus the standard for Portuguese water dogs, for example, permits a wide variation of weight (42–60 pounds) relative to standards for a number of even very large breeds that specify weight within a few pounds. The variation reflects the club's perception that current breeding lines must preserve a history of the breed's working heritage on fishing boats, where larger dogs worked on the larger boats, smaller dogs on smaller boats. In contrast, while the Sealyham terrier has a no less important breeding history, as a game dog for otter, badger, and rats, the standard reflects little of that heritage so directly.

For the uninitiated, however, one of the curiosities of watching Westminster is how rarely you see an owner or breeder, those presumably most identified with a particular breed, its history, and standard. If you do, it's likely a celebrity in the audience picked out by the camera. (Bill Cosby, for example, shares ownership of a number of championship dogs that have shown at Westminster.) What you see on-screen, in the ring with the dog, are "handlers"—or "agents," in official AKC catalogue language. Getting a dog to show well in the ring is a complex skill. It involves obedience expertise with the dog, and the delicate grooming touch calculated to make this specific dog best conform to standard. But it also involves the accumulated knowledge of individual judges and their preferences, and the largely intangible ability to elicit from the dog on the occasion the "spirit" of the breed—the "look" that will catch the judge's eye and make your dog stand out. Handlers of winning dogs routinely comment that the dog was "on" that night, meaning that it performed to the occasion, exhibited the "spirit" breed standards attempt to anatomize in their categories of desirable and undesirable physical characteristics. Top handlers command top fees for their work; at a show like Westminster, where every dog is a champion, winner of countless local shows, the right handler can make all the difference. There are even magazines (like *The Canine Chronicle*) largely devoted to handlers advertising their big "wins" with various breeds, as well as a proliferation of Internet Web sites where breeders can find information about specific handlers.

While hiring a handler to show your dog may be a sign of seriousness for those who show at local club events, it's often an undesirable step to take, as well as a prohibitive expense even when the handler is not a nationally prominent figure. Thus those you see in the ring with the dogs at local shows are for the most part people who own or have bred the dog. They may be professional breeders but not necessarily professional handlers. As a result, in the ring they are as likely to call attention to themselves as to the dog. At a local show you watch not only dogs, but the people who show them. And so does the judge. Officially, her or his eyes are focused only on the terms of comparison between each animal and the standard; unofficially, of course, a whole host of factors enter in.

It's not uncommon for two clubs in an area to book the same show space on back-to-back days, the first club on a Saturday, for example, and the second on a Sunday. Judges, like external referees for promotions in English departments, must be brought in from outside the area of club jurisdiction, and an entirely different crew of judges will work each of the two shows. A win on Saturday, however, by no means guarantees a win on Sunday. As students discover in taking different courses, and as junior faculty know quite well in shopping essays around to different journals, whatever standards may exist in all these competitive rings, the judging itself is always a subjective practice. But grand epistemological pronouncements of this sort are of little interest or use to those entered in a show, whose work depends on making rather better sense of the situation. If you can't afford or don't want a professional handler, you must learn to handle the dog in the ring. And that includes learning *how* to focus a judge's attention— whether "subjective" or "objective" is a matter of indifference—where you want it, when you want it. After all, a show dog in the ring is hardly a "natural" creature, and much of what you see is created by the handler.

Although what I've described may seem a lot of detail about show dog competition, in reality the process is far more complicated than my sketch covers. I simply want enough of the detail in place to suggest a recognition that the competition, as is very often the case in sports, is structured by a striking combination of intricate, specific, rule-bound, and strictly hierarchical organization on the one hand, and an only vaguely visible congeries of intangibles on the other. Rather like the movements of an insect, the progress of any given local show carries along a mushy inside within the exoskeletal precision of direction toward the final rounds and the one animal that emerges as "best in show." The comparison to other sporting events is clear in any case. One has only to think, for example, of the complexities of scoring in an ice skating competition, and of the elaborate electronic technology that computes scores across successive rounds of the competition, together with the impassive faces of the judges behind which "something"—mushy enough no doubt—is going on that nevertheless supplies those scores. Or for an equally sinister example, there's the relentless apparatus of quantification covering so many details of a professional football game, which then becomes the occasion for sports commentary to valorize an invisible "will to win" that, beyond statistics, supplies the vital difference between playoff contenders and also-rans.

In contrast, the image of competition that appears in neoclassical theories of optimum market conditions is all light and visible space, albeit flanked on either side by intensities of effort, brilliant lightning flashes of intuition, and unspeakable disasters awaiting failure. Whatever terrors surround it, however, marketplace competition in its ideal state is described with a beautiful simplicity: sell the most desirable product at the lowest price, and you win. No formalized breed standard is imposed on decisions about what is "the best" product; there's no AKC to determine that only 93 specific types can count as a "product" in the first place; "judges" are not AKC certified officials, but may be recruited from absolutely anywhere in the population of potential consumers; you can look at your competitors's prices at any point and set yours where you will, pursuing whatever long-term, short-term, or intermediate-term gamble may seem realizable. "Competition," as it inhabits both this marketplace and the dog show ring, leads an amphibious life indeed.

As I've suggested, however, there are good reasons to think the gap between competition's living spaces is not really as wide as it might seem. Walking into your broker's office armed only with an idea of the beautiful simplicity of marketplace competition (and lots of money to invest in cocoa futures, say) is about as bright as a small appliance bulb, facing the

imminent power outage of a margin call. But before collapsing boundaries too quickly, it's good to think a little more carefully about the behavior of commodities (not quite the same as the behavior of show dogs) in
these instances. Unlike cocoa futures—or labor contracts, for that matter—any show dog in a commodity market is a body traced into being
by the elaborate procedures of ring competition. The specificity of breed
standards, for example, produces area after area of an animal's body as
open not only to detailed examination in the ring by a judge, but to a long
history of examining eyes and fingers beginning well before birth and
proceeding through temperament testing as puppies, sperm counts and
fertility scans, obedience training, grooming sessions, and so on—all in-
terspersed, for the animal, with endless, inactive hours in crates traveling
to and from shows.

Show dogs are commodities, no matter that they smell like every mutt.
But their status as commodity is inseparable from the rules of competition
that structure a humanly invested space of finely differentiated animal bodies. The peculiarity of differentiation in show dog competition is that it
functions within the terms of a breed standard. Dogs of the same breed
are sorted out by relative proximity to the image of perfection supplied by
the standard, and even as the competition moves to best-in-group and best-
in-show rounds, judging decisions must still claim a basis in each animal's
differential proximity to its own breed standard. What this means in marketplace terms is that in contrast to the commodities that typically occupy
the attention of market theorists, *no animal has a precise exchange equivalent in
the market for show dogs*. By the end of the first round of judging, every animal entered within a breed has a different judged relation to the standard,
and by the end of the competition the winning animal has been individuated in relation to every other entry.

As a result, the fact that this particular champion flat-coated retriever
may command the same stud fee as this champion Gordon setter, or this
champion lineage and "show quality" smooth collie puppy the same price
as this "pet quality" Belgian Tervuren, is virtually meaningless until read
through the indices of competitive organization, with all its "mushy" in-
sides as well. For what in these instances price has asserted as equivalence,
competition has sorted out into differentiated indices of "value." Thus
price becomes an opacity rather than a visible register of value; it is something you must walk around in order to see the vast range of activities going on and understand the value determinations at stake. At the same time,
however, it's necessary to remember that no matter how opaque it is, price

nevertheless has multiple effects across the whole range of activities carried out during a show.

Another way of making this double point is to recognize that dog show competition, like other sports, has as its immediate end the progressive elimination of competitors. It is "a process of elimination," as the AKC's *Complete Dog Book* explains, "that ultimately results in one dog being selected" (22), with the financial reward consequent on the final elimination. In contrast, while the ideal form of the market imaged in neoclassical theory may involve the elimination of competitors, both price and profit are assumed to be integral at every step of the competition, registering the movement of "values" along the way and determining who gets eliminated. To see the difference in these terms helps explain the absence of exchange equivalencies in show dog commodities: unlike the market competition of neoclassical imagination, the structure of show competition minutely individuates *commodities* rather than simply rewarding the best producer/trader of commodities.

Within the rules of the game, the owner of the best show dog is also the owner of the best commodity, whatever equivalents price may establish after the fact. In contrast, even in the ideal neoclassical marketplace, the "best" producer/trader of commodities is not necessarily by any means the producer/trader of the "best" commodities; it is price, not the rules of competition, that tells all. Yet however opaque price may be as a register of the values at play in show dog competition, it has potentially wide-ranging effects. One of these is on what neoclassical theorists would identify as the "incentive" to become economic agents in a show dog market in the first place, and to compete successfully.

The "paradox" here is that it's the intricately controlled and regulated process of show dog competition that would seem to preserve the "purity" of that economic incentive far better than the free, autonomous market of neoclassical theorizing. To compete successfully you have to have a winning animal, but in the markets that attract the attention of neoclassical theorists there are in fact lots of ways to win profits without the best product. Thus while in theory you can also cheat at dog shows, and certainly fudge a lot, in practice it's hard to cheat in major ways, far more difficult than in most other sports. Those who have been caught cheating are disgraced rather than being toasted at covert Michael Milkin testimonial lunches. Whatever economic incentive exists in a dog show market is everywhere tied to a competition that isolates and determines "the best" commodity on the market.

None of this is meant to imply that the dog show world is some squeaky clean field in an otherwise nasty market arena. Any number of things—from the gendering of "dog" and "bitch" and its economic effects to the disciplining of the animal's body with obsessive, fetishistic attention to every detail—immediately suggest otherwise. The "paradox," however, only appears a paradox, and the incentive to enter the show dog market a matter of purely rational economic interest, through the lens of neoclassical market theory. Once you step outside neoclassical assumptions, it becomes possible to recognize that incentives to become a breeder of show dogs, on the local level especially, are not only a mixed, "impure" complex but incentives that look to a market in show dog commodities *because* of, and not despite, that hybrid impurity. That is, it's not simply that nonmarket factors—and often rather curious exogenous ones—might override economic self-interest in marketplace transactions, as Granovetter and Etzioni argue. The behavior of people in the show dog market, and their attraction to marketplace competition, also function to constitute different and often competing meanings of "market."

Before pursuing any further the terms of those definitions, however, it's crucial to recognize that precisely this point of categorical definition of a market is where the typically double characterization of show dog breeding as a business *and* a sport minds its force. There are good reasons to question an assumed gap between "business" and "sport," but not at the expense of forgetting how the distinction has profound effects. The "and a sport" clause imposes a set of limits on how the marketplace business of dog shows "should" be understood. Those limits function to maintain the social priority accorded a strictly economic "necessary" by neoclassical theorizing of "the market." Thus "and a sport" means that while some people may find dog breeding a desirable and (for whatever good or bad incentives) a socially necessary way of spending their time, the peculiar organization and constraints imposed on a market in show dogs should by no means be allowed to spread beyond the confines of the "sport" designation to contaminate the larger context of the whole social field within which the "real"—that is, strictly economic—market operates. Money may often change hands in the sale of dogs, and there may exist all sorts of business activity engaged in supplying products for dog owners and breeders. But dog breeding, shows, and sales are only "sort of" a market, limited by the imperative to remain also a "sport."

Just as breed standards preserve a narrative heritage of breeding history, the "and a sport" clause also preserves a specific narrative history. This is a narrative that invokes aristocratic *breeders* who enter a market only from above, not under the compulsion of "making money." That is, the narrative history "as a sport" imputes a class position to successful breeders that distinguishes the organization of a market in show dogs from "pure" markets defined solely through economic exchange. Thus as also a "sport," the market in show dogs has a limited social relevance. Certain elements may carry over to other fields—the "spirit of competition," for example, or the desire for "excellence"—but their application must be monitored carefully. The spirit of competition may be fine; in a "real" market, however, it certainly wouldn't involve any organization like the AKC, charged with determining something comparable to breed standards for products on the market. "And a sport" means the specific and peculiar organization of a market in show dogs must ultimately be subordinated to the social necessities of the real market. AKC rhetoric reinforces this injunction from the other side, as it were, routinely admonishing anyone who will listen that "making money" is never a good reason to enter into the breeding of dogs. The narrative of an aristocratic history of dog breeders is assumed to supply considerably better incentives.

Much of this reasoning, however, would likely be news to a great many people deeply invested at the local level (if perhaps not to those at Westminster) in breeding and showing dogs, who tend to understand themselves as participating in a market, not a "sort-of" market, and who would find the notion of descending from some elevated "aristocratic" position to play at the market in dogs an odd one indeed. More specifically, it would be news to the relatively large percentage of working-class and lower-middle-class women who make up that local level—as owners, breeders, trainers, and handlers. In my own experience, four of the five elected officers of the more than fifty-member Bouvier breed club in the Northwest, every obedience course instructor and roughly 75 percent of those enrolled in the classes I've been in, each of the people who does puppy temperament testing, and the entire list of local Bouvier breeders were women. (Although there are a number of women ring judges, as might be expected, the percentage isn't nearly as large as it is in my other examples.) To my knowledge the AKC doesn't keep gender statistics on who breeds dogs, but from as much conversation and networking as I've been able to engage in, that experience is hardly atypical. And perhaps it shouldn't be surprising, for something assumed to be a "sort-of" market one does sort of as a sport sort of on the side. Gender determinations have a far more immediate relevance to the demographics of dog shows than ideas of an aristocracy of breeders.

Given this gender composition, it might perhaps be tempting to rush a number of doubly valenced clichés into the argument as explanatory terms. It is true, as I will argue later, that for all the fierce competitiveness, the individualizing of competition in the ring, and the immense apparatus of animal discipline that differentiates commodity bodies, raising and showing dogs remains nevertheless in many respects a deeply cooperative activity. And it is true that many of those involved—men and women— also extend the most careful, loving, "motherly" affection to their commodity-differentiated possessions. But even if one were to acknowledge some generalizing virtue to clichés, there are of course numerous exceptions. More important, this explanatory direction, no matter how refined beyond generality, would ignore the active inventiveness of what people make of the specific conditions of a show dog market. Thus rather than pursuing immediately the complex of "incentives" that brings people into this market, and the gender composition of its population, I think it worth a more direct focus first on the structural intricacies of how "market" and "economic" are defined, in terms of the values that organize a market *in* show dogs, but *for* those who breed and show them.

Value, Marx explained, appears in the commodity form as exchange value or use value. If an individual show dog commodity has no exchange equivalent, even when price marks an equilibrium of exchange, then by this reasoning the value of the show dog must lie first of all in its use value. Marx doesn't talk a lot about use value, however, and perhaps for that reason it's been relatively easy to subsume his discussion into a nostalgia-driven narrative of a lamentable disappearance. That is, the primacy of exchange value in capitalist market relations condemns use value to the realm of a residual survival from precapitalist economies. The more globally pervasive capitalism becomes, the more markets become a matter of pure exchange relations. Thus, where it manages to survive at all, use value seems an inherently good thing, standing in lonely—if morally desirable— contrast to the relentless, global commodification of all exchange relations.

Breed standards for show dogs very often reference a history of working use in their determination of canine physical characteristics. And no televising of Westminster would be complete without the obligatory "history of use" explanation for what usually appears to the uninitiated as the utterly bizarre way in which poodles are clipped. These accounts cohere nicely with a narrative emphasizing the residual survival of use value. It is true enough that certain breeds exhibited in shows lead useful working lives in the present. Nevertheless, while the same breed may be involved, it's unlikely the same dog will sniff out drugs at the airport on one day and enter the conformation show ring the next. Show dogs, again, are animal bodies elaborately disciplined into individuated commodities, and neither a history of use embodied in standards nor a breed's participation in useful work in the present explain much about the current commodity value of any given show dog.

Marx says little about use value, but it seems possible to infer from his discussion the very different perception that, rather than use value disappearing into a now remote past, the dynamics of capitalist commodity relations might well generate new forms and new meanings of use value. Thus so far from being an inherently desirable—if rapidly disappearing— counter to "pure" exchange, these new forms of use value could function instead to maintain and elaborate complex ensembles of marketplace social relations. Current market theories don't often address use value either, but one notable exception involves the idea of a market in so-called positional goods.* As I will argue later, value expressed in terms of positional goods is by no means the only use value that emerges in the marketing of show dogs. But it has a fundamental importance for understanding both the hierarchical organization of AKC sanctioned shows and the legitimation of connecting links between the specific market in show dogs and general, neoclassically influenced theories of "the market."

The value of positional goods lies first of all in their scarcity; if lots of people could have them, they wouldn't be positionally valuable. Their value, that is, is established less by exchange or exchange equivalents than by the *use* available from the possession of scarce goods to leverage distinguished social position. Exchangeability of any sort in the circumstances might then diminish their value. Thus the "scarcity" at issue depends on a high degree of elaborated individuation which isn't always registered very accurately by price-established equivalents alone. Positional goods aren't the same as luxury goods. Just-harvested Kyomoto oysters from the coast may be scarce in Kansas, for example, and are likely to cost a lot. They're a luxury item. But within a certain range one Kyomoto is pretty much like another. The positional good in Kansas is less this or that Kyomoto oyster—however expensive—to serve your friends than the necessarily very individuated packing/flight itinerary that would get them to you from the

---

* For a good exposition of "positional goods," see Fred Hirsch, *Social Limits to Growth*.

coast in time to qualify as "just harvested." That itinerary is likely to involve any number of factors that don't appear in terms of price. Even if you had the money, you couldn't necessarily buy the itinerary.

Champion show dogs are scarce, and unlike Kyomotos each is an individuated commodity; on these grounds, they can qualify superbly as positional goods. Thinking of show dogs as a positional good commodity thus helps explain how the aristocratic history of dog shows as "sport" gets rewritten into contemporary marketplace terms. What makes a champion show dog is the process of sport competition individuating the commodity, and as commodity that animal has no precise exchange equivalent. It does have a positional use value, however, identifying its owner as belonging by extension to a *contemporary* aristocracy of breeders in a market of show dogs.

Yet whatever may have been the case in the past, belonging to an aristocracy of dog breeders today is not quite the same as belonging to an acknowledged social elite. The dog as fashion accessory, and often as visible sign—like Lycra and other more exotic fabrics—of a prestigious involvement in "fitness" as a leisure activity, has indeed become a marker of status. Nevertheless, relatively few people outside the show dog world seem to recognize a champion show dog as positionally useful because its owner has established herself or himself as belonging to a social elite composed of dog breeders. Outside, it's just the neighbor's mutt that's likely to "position" its crap on your property—no matter how much acreage the owner has—make noise at all hours of the night, disturb your visitors, and quite possibly lower property values.

Outside the world of show dogs there may seem little positional good use value to be had from becoming deeply involved in the process of breeding championship dogs. But it's always possible to act as if there were, or more important, as if in a "better" world, there *should* be. The positional value, in other words, is also a moral value. Understood in these terms, the market in show dogs appears as a specific kind of market that among other things trades in the moral linkages of positional distinction and competitive "fairness." Distinction is privilege, but privilege is fairly realized in this moral market. The show dog becomes the individuated commodity bearer of social relations as they should be.

As a result, the complexities of this morally defined market depend on an obsessively driven apparatus for disciplining animal bodies. But just as in the larger (and in principle not nearly so moral) "outside" world, the realization of positional use value depends even more crucially on the subordination of large groups of people in the market, in this case less than successful owners and breeders. You can't have an aristocracy of breeders without peasant breeders. And peasants must be visibly identified not only in economic terms, but also through the hurt and humiliation visited on them as their dogs lose. It's here that the moral component of market definition becomes indispensable. Without the foregrounded specificities of moral definition, it might simply look like you *wanted* to exercise positional distinction and power by imposing hurt and humiliation on the "losers."

Further, a morality based in competitive "fairness" conveniently disguises still another function of moral terms of market definition. The moralizing of the market justifies not only internal competitive rankings as "fair," but also the disjunction between the positional good value of show dog commodities within the show dog world and the lack of value outside that world. That is, the gap between inside and outside the show dog world is made to represent, for would-be breeders, the terms of a moral choice. You voluntarily sacrifice the distinction that might well be yours in a general social field marked by positional values in return for participation in an admittedly more limited and risky field of "open" competition to establish position. (Anyone in an English department who discounts the general appeal of such a rhetoric of moral sacrifice should pay closer attention to the language of graduate school applicants explaining why English rather than law or medicine, say.) Unlike the social field generally, position can be legitimized by the legislated "fairness" of a show dog market. Positional distinction in the dog show world claims a moral justification lacking elsewhere. Unlike other markets, where morality may seem tacked on after the fact if at all, the economy of a show dog market is defined through its constitutive internal moralities.

Within this moral definition of a market, the containment implied by the tag phrase "and a sport" can be detached from its aristocratic history and likewise turned into a moral imperative. "And a sport" names a form of containment that can simultaneously function as a moral exemplary. The televising of the Westminster show everywhere observes the propinquities that compose the exemplary status. "The market" on display is rigorously represented as a moral copula: "a business [is] a sport." The use value of the show dog is to sustain this specifically moral form of a market.

The internally functional defining power of morality means that on one level at least the complex of social relations organized by a show dog market often collide with imperatives that are grounded in assumptions about the market in general as the largest defining form of the socially necessary.

A market in show dogs never simply reflects "The Market"; it isn't understood as just one more specific instance of a much larger "free market" economy whose "laws" govern the sale and exchange of show dogs every bit as surely as the bidding on pork belly futures. For all that its practices may involve exchange relations, investment decisions, financing, entrepreneurial capitalization, and a whole host of other factors as well as behavior patterns that link a show dog market to the larger capitalist market, its internal moralities constitute this instance of "The Market" as a special and exemplary instance. Your investments in this specific market simultaneously bind you to and yet also morally distinguish you from others whose investments locate them within the general field of the larger idea of the market.

The immediate "price" for the exemplary status of the show dog market remains nevertheless a matter of hurt and humiliation. Something must visibly index the subordination required by positional good value. Even if it is never put on view at Westminster, it is visible all too often in all too many people at all too many local shows. The use value of positional good scarcity always translates into a necessary scarcity of morally aristocratic breeders, a scarcity made possible by how the organization of shows must produce far more peasant breeders than aristocratic breeders. These moral terms ensure that most shows most of the time are about the production of peasants. Indeed, given the AKC formula to determine championship points, the more peasant losers in any given competition, the more points you might accrue for your "win." Thus, by the back door, the effects of the morality that would distinguish this market from the general economic "laws" of the larger capitalist market simultaneously determine its congruity with the *politics* of the larger market. The imagery of "aristocrats" and "peasants," after all, is just a moral retro language for that most familiar of divisions produced by market politics.

The identification of morality and economics in the definition of a show dog market in positional goods explains a great deal about the organization and hierarchy of AKC-sponsored shows. Nevertheless, positional good use value is not the only form of use value that can constitute and define a show dog market. Against the image of ring competition that individuates both commodities and owner/breeders, the far less visible process of staging a relatively "minor" local show involves in contrast collectively organized labor. Without shows there is no market in show dogs, and a show requires not only AKC "sanction from above," but also the lateral adjacencies of a great deal of work by those in the local sponsoring club and its affiliate organizations. Labor appears in the commodity market of show dogs directly in relation to the organization of a market as well as in relation to the "production" of show dogs, and it appears in specific, collective, often volunteer forms.

An emphasis on the characteristics of labor required for the market's very existence thus turns attention from the moralizing individuation of ring competition to the construction of a market where it is possible to recognize another and very different use value of show dog commodities. They are the occasion that sustains the specific configurations of pleasure, uses, and socializing values to be derived from collectively organized labor. The organization of work necessary to sponsor a show can value everyone's labor who participates. Rather than an individuated positional good commodity, show dogs in this very different sense are defined as a site of collective activity.

Further, this collective organization of labor suggests a different model for understanding the process of ring competition itself, as no less dependent on a cooperative set of practices than the process of staging the show. Grooming, for example, is crucial to show ring success, but grooming also requires shared knowledges. It begins in an attention to genetics, how to arrive at a breeding match with an animal from someone else's kennel that might yield a litter with just the right "hardness" of coat specified by the standard, and it continues right to the point of knowing where to trim this particular dog's back line for a show with judge X who favors "long backs" relative to other judges, and so on. Although grooming individuates the specific show dog commodity, at the same time, in order to be shared at all, grooming knowledges locate the animal in a field of affiliations identified at the level of the breed. That is, at some point the very possibility of sharing grooming knowledges depends on features that link this particular dog to others of the same breed. Thus in showing your dog you can *for the same reasons* compete against others showing the same breed of dog and share grooming knowledges with those you compete against, just as in the process of organizing a show you work with those whom you'll later be competing against.

Multiplied across any number of fields of knowledge, this form of use value helps explain why local breeders are often so enthusiastically supportive of their breed no less than their particular dogs, and supportive of others owning and showing the same breed, against whom they compete in the ring. It may still be true enough in our culture that women—who make up by far the greatest percentage of owners and breeders at the local level—are socialized to cooperate rather than to compete viciously. But to think only in terms of some such general socialization ignores the inventiveness of practices that take advantage of specific circumstances to align rather than oppose competition and cooperation. Further, it ignores how the alignment of competition and cooperation functions to define a kind of use value specific to the show dog commodity, and to define a specific form of market organization for the predominantly lower-middle-class and working-class women involved who are often trying to scrape extra income from the sale of dogs to support a family. The complex of social relations in the alignment isn't brought "from the outside" to the market, as if it were an exogenous variable whose effects may "interfere" with the smooth operation of "marketplace laws." Every bit as much as the moralizing hierarchies of business-sport, that complex can function internally, in the very definition and existence of a market.

It would be a mistake to imagine this complex of social relations as preserved from some remote past where cooperative labor and use values used to matter. The cooperative organization of labor is no more a residual survival than it is an organization imposed by a prior gender socialization. The specific social relations are invented on the occasion, and they are born in the collision of conflicting pressures in the organization of a show dog market. That is, it's impossible to celebrate these social relations as if the triumph of a somehow still isolated local sector preserved them against an implacable, totalizing marketplace power. They exist instead in a collision zone where they are everywhere intricated with—and hence often appear "contaminated" by—the larger forces at work shaping the social field. The cooperative labor of organizing a show depends on a relentless disciplining of animal bodies, resulting in individuated commodities. People's behaviors are instructive here, not because they represent a heroically pure effort to maintain democratically organized labor relations, but because they live an ultimately political struggle in a marketplace collision zone, with much more than purely local relations at stake.

Animal rights activists, for good and obvious reasons, have often targeted the AKC as the sanctioning organization for one of the most obsessively sanctimonious apparatuses of control over animals' lives. As these arguments recognize, what gets "remoralized" by the AKC is not only the gap between a show dog market and "The Market," but also the very process of disciplining the animals' bodies, as if somehow it were "good" for the animals. In these circumstances, however, it's important that critique not get caught in the opposite half of an AKC defense of its practices, expressed in that familiar binary of "human" rights and "animal" rights. The moralizing definition of a market in show dogs already links people subordinated as market losers to animals as elaborately individuated commodity bodies, and it's impossible to change the effects of those practices on animals without also changing their effects on people, and vice versa. That is, the issue is not a matter of whether to "extend" human rights to animals, or whatever; in this particular market organization animals and people are already indissolubly linked. Cropping the puppy ears of future show Bouviers and other breeds may seem a "barbaric" practice, at odds with any notion of "animal rights" or what's "good for" the animals. But ear cropping also functions to reward breeders able to afford the best medical service to do the best job on the ears, and hence gain an edge in ring competition. The practice of ear cropping thus produces people as marketplace losers right along with producing mutilated animals, and extending the "rights" of peasant losers to their animals won't help the animals at all. Realizing genuine alternatives involves both people and animals at every level in a complex ensemble of marketplace political practices.

❋

Yvor Winters bred and exhibited Airedales, and a resemblance of this to his work as a literary critic must have occurred to a number of people. Ranking poems by a standard of literary excellence, as he claimed to do, can't seem all that different from ranking Airedales by the points of a consensual standard of canine perfection. The often curious and emotionally charged investments in literary texts and in the animal-commodities of show dogs, no less than the role of "standards," suggest a number of parallels between the fields of Winters's interests. To my knowledge, however, he never really considered at length—in print at least—the similarities between his interests in literature and his interests in dogs, even though he knew perfectly well that neither the judging of dog shows nor the training of critical judgment about literature were socially central activities.* Thus while there's little doubt that he felt informed judgments about literature ought to be more highly valued socially than they were, I don't know if he was equally tenacious on behalf of dog shows, or Airedales.

Like his friend and fellow critic R. P. Blackmur, however, he eventually came to consider with alarm the fate of students of New Criticism in the

---

* Joseph Buttigieg pointed out to me, however, that Winters did occasionally write about his Airedales. See, for example, his poem, "Elegy on a Young Airedale Bitch Lost Some Years Since in the Salt-Marsh," and a story entitled "The Brink of Darkness."

university, as more and more people were educated to produce "close read-
ings" of literary texts with no place to go with their skills except into the
teaching of literature, if they were lucky. It was an education, as Blackmur
would put it, that "is producing a larger and larger class of intellectually
trained men and women the world over who cannot make a living in
terms of their training and who cannot, because of their training, make a
living otherwise with any satisfaction" (8). It's in these terms that dog
shows might have been an instructive as well as a parallel world for Winters, had he stopped to consider the marketing of literary scholars and the
marketing of the skills of breeding and handling dogs. Like a literary training in close reading, the latter, too, pay off largely within the same market
organization in which the skills are learned. You sell "show quality" dogs to
other people interested in, or already showing, dogs.

My "Winters" is admittedly a fortuitous conjunction of these two
worlds, what a postmodern novelist like Thomas Pynchon would note as
the linking feature of a "coincidence," driven by the repetition—if hardly
on the same scale—of how, like Winters, I also write and teach literary
criticism and own a show quality dog. There is no "Market" that can function as some invisibly central economic presence identifying the coinci-
dental fields of show dogs and of literary scholarship. In the non-Euclidean
spaces of contemporary culture in the United States, however, parallel
power lines not only can but often do intersect, with disturbing surges as a
result. My figure of "Winters" is thus a convenient shorthand for my "description" of a commodity market of show dogs that has implied, without
much subtlety, a whole series of roughly parallel lines between a show dog
market and a market in literary scholarship.

Not everything is parallel, but you can, for example, slide "culture" right
alongside and paralleling "sport." The production of literary scholarship is a
business *and* it's culture, where, like dog show sport, the culture of literary
scholarship can look backward to a largely aristocratic history for its notions of "standards" and the importance of standards. The moralizing operations I have described that make a market in show dogs both like and
unlike a projected ideal of "the market" parallel the operations by which
literary scholarship moralizes its elaborate hierarchies of positional distinction and constitutes itself as similarly like and unlike "the market." Literary
scholarship, too, has positional good use value, and the field is full of aristocrats and peasants, stars and wanna-bes.

Long ago rewritten out of an aristocratic history and into marketplace
terms, literary scholarship's intersections of business and culture parallel the

intersections of business and sport in dog breeding and showing, insofar as in both cases what stands at the intersection is a "profession." There has been a great deal of recent discussion of literary study as a profession, similar to professional fields like medicine, law, social work, and so on. Literary study requires a long process of specialized training, for example. In whatever specific form, however, the relations that link professions to a market are everywhere mediated by conceptions of "the public"; professionals sell services to specific clients in a process of marketplace exchange, but professional services are also imagined as having a certain general, "public" value.

In this context of the assumed public value of professionally defined skills and expertise, Winters (the original) worried about a double process in which, to his mind, the "general public" was becoming less and less able to make informed distinctions of value among literary texts, at the same time that literary scholarship was becoming more and more formidably "technical" and inaccessible to a general public. Discussions of the profession of literary study continue to be framed in much the same terms. But suppose you translate Winters's worries into something like the following parallel: there is a double process at work where the general public is becoming less and less able to make informed distinctions of value among dogs, at the same time that the intricacies of conformation competition are becoming more and more formidably "technical" and inaccessible to a general public. From within literary study, it might not be clear exactly who would "worry" about such a state of affairs. But in fact a great many people engaged in the breeding and showing of dogs worry a great deal about it. Local breed club members worry about it in specific terms. When I left Washington State, the Bouvier club to which I had belonged was in the midst of a crisis of direction over the issue of whether club resources should be devoted primarily to those who actively show Bouviers, or to those members of "the general public" who are more interested in just getting together for picnics and fun activities with others who may want to learn more about dogs and who value the companionship of dogs.

The difference between these ensembles of worry might seem to be a matter of the level of their metaphysical artillery. Those who worry over the dissociation between a general public's competence and interest in literature and the technological bristle of professionalized literary scholarship frequently escalate the meaning of the dissociation—sometimes in the course of a single sentence—to The Crisis of Western Civilization, or at the very least to implacably sinister powers. Most members of the Bouvier club, in contrast, seem more irritated at the way club meetings and newsletters spend an inordinate amount of time on how to clip the muzzle for a show and not nearly enough time on the best way to remove foxtails after a run through the park. But any department meeting of professionals engaged in literary study will supply endless equivalents to the foxtail issue, and conversely, if perhaps not quite at the level of Western Civilization Crises, AKC officials nevertheless possess formidable rhetorics locating the care, ownership, and scrupulous professional breeding of dogs as one of the better indicators of a high degree of civilization. Such rhetoric does double duty, at once establishing a sense of general public value and recruiting a specific population into the profession of dog breeding.

Literary study, too, must find ways of recruiting a population into the study of literature. Not only a public perception of the value of the profession, but economic support for its members seem everywhere to involve recruiting powers. Since literary study occurs within a complex field of educational institutions (unlike dog shows), recruiting for it might appear much simpler than the process of recruiting dog people: require all students to take courses in literature, and get enough of the Western Civilization Crisis artillery in place at the front to be sure such requirements are generally enforced. In practice, of course, it's not really quite so simple. Recent directions of scholarship have enlarged the parameters of what counts as "literature" and multiplied the possibilities of related subjects to study. These directions also function as effective recruiting in part because the more things people have to get interested in, the more people might get interested. Thus correlatively, as this happens, different people find very different reasons to engage in the process of study—often reasons that stand in dramatic contrast to anything like the Western Civilization Crisis stuff. The organization of the discipline changes, just as the organization of producing and showing dogs has been changed by how the gender- and class-marked composition of those in the field has been enlarged.

I'm of course schematically retelling a familiar political story of change in the disciplines of literary study, and mean nothing cynical whatsoever by linking it to a notion of "recruiting." It's only a cynical version if your ideas of radical politics are so high-minded that they can't be contaminated by a recognition that in whatever different ways it may be carried out, literary study in the university is a profession that does recruit people and is economically invested in the recruitment process. And I certainly don't mean to imply that hierarchical organization has disappeared with these recent changes. Literary scholarship, too, continues to have its Westminsters and its "minor" local clubs (and to some extent at least the population of women is increasing at its local levels especially), and it's a fun enough game with letters to derive MLA from AKC, as it is with "standards" to parallel designated new literary fields with designated canine breeds newly approved by the AKC once they reach a certain level of "legitimacy."

What interests me are the contradictory pressures that exist in both literary and canine fields. On the one hand, there is an imperative to enlarge the field of breeds/texts and incorporate more people, thereby reinforcing a sense of general public value. (Think of how often new hires in new fields are justified by claiming potential leaps in student enrollment.) On the other hand, however, there is also an imperative to preserve the individuated commodity scarcity on which positional good use value depends—hence the endlessly expressed worries over "declining standards" and failures to "discriminate carefully" among different levels of student (and faculty) work. Although still generally regarded as an alien force in the profession of literary scholarship, economics often makes a convenient and dramatic *deus ex machina* appearance at precisely this point of contradiction. The diminished job market for English Ph.D.'s, we tell ourselves over and over, means that it's "unethical" to continue to support high-volume graduate programs, educating people who will never be able to find jobs in the field. It's the economic "realities" of the market that put a cap on how many literary scholars we can "turn out," and hence on how many we should be recruiting. So we have to pay considerably more attention to standards, make our selection processes tighter, accept the need to put more energy into general undergraduate rather than specialized graduate training—and be sure to tell those undergraduates most "successfully" trained that they'd better not even think of grad school in English. All of which makes for an interesting notion of "ethical."

Markets, however, define economic practices, not the other way around. Markets are complex ensembles of social relations in which the resources produced by specific forms of organization can be designated as exchangeable within conditions thereby identified as economic. Thus, in general terms, an ethics of markets deals with the process of establishing "public value" as well as setting limits on what resources are appropriate to market-produced and -defined economic practices. Corn is a market-appropriate resource; edible human flesh isn't supposed to be; show dogs and literary scholarship, as I've suggested, are sort of appropriate, so long as you don't make too big a deal over the fact that you might get money in exchange for either.

In dramatic contrast to such an ethics of limits, Tom Peters's motivational question addressed to entrepreneurial sellers of goods and services implies that potentially anything is marketable, the "weirder" the better. That is, against the limits imposed by moralizing, which tend to reinforce an imperative to preserve positional scarcity, Peters's postmodern economics of selling seems inclined toward indiscriminately enlarging any given field whatsoever. Lost somewhere in between the moralizing of limits and Peters's ecstatic dance of postmodern freedom, however, is the necessary recognition that markets are not only "volatile" but explosive. Thus whether market volatility is a bad thing (as moralizing implies) or a good thing (as Peters claims), markets can always explode into conflict because the designation of conditions of exchangeability as economic is a primary *political* question. It also affects the distribution of resources throughout the social formation.

Winters had imagined a literary education as a resource of great cultural value, potentially, to every citizen. Even though most would never become professional literary scholars, the education had value to the citizens of a democratic political state. Increasingly, however, students who get enough of a literary education, in whatever terms, to construct a sense of its value do so in ways that already link that value to the possibilities of becoming a professional literary teacher and scholar. As this happens, the long process of intellectual training begins to include an education in the multiple practices of what you do from day to day making a living as a professional literary scholar and teacher. Thus the "job" that may or may not appear just beyond the horizon of the "training" period no longer looks like the beginning of "making a living," after having been trained, but rather a *political* guarantee of social position and authority to extend the complex of intellectual and economic practices at another level. Intellectual training in these terms is also and everywhere part of the formation of a specific market in professional services to a "public," a subject I will return to at length in my concluding chapter. The immediate point is that "economic realities" don't intrude from the outside to set a limit on how many Ph.D.'s we should "ethically" produce; economic practices are part of the training from the beginning. Limits are a matter of the politics of markets.

In these circumstances the parallels between a market in show dogs and a market in literary scholarship serve a double function. The peculiarities of the show dog commodity, as I have argued, suggest a great deal about the peculiarities of literary scholarship as a commodity. Linking dog breeders as professionals to literary scholars as professionals, however, enlarges the social field of positional reference for discussions of literary scholarship as a profession. Such a linkage functions much like Antonio Gramsci's redefinition of "intellectual," which made possible a way of understanding how even a "traditional" figure like Benedetto Croce was inserted into a complex ensemble of social relations of intellectual work and political authority. I will argue in the next chapter that rather than thinking literary scholarship as aligned with traditionally prestigious professional fields such as law or medicine, understanding literary scholarship as inserted into the multiple, diverse market fields of professional service providers suggests how literary study reflects the effects of greater diversity in the population groups entering the field.

Here in any case is where the fun stops in drawing parallels between such disparate markets as show dogs and literary scholarship. Across the numerous possible parallels you also find in one dog show ring after literary classroom after another of both the intersections of discipline with discipline, humiliation with humiliation, hurt with hurt, and exclusion with exclusion. Competition's amphibious life across business-culture no less than business-sport is legitimized by imperatives to preserve the scarcity of the goods and hence increase the production of losers in the marketplace game. The apparent contradiction between preserving scarcity and recruiting more people, that is, is "solved" by how the "more" become "more losers" in the field. The immense proliferation of so-called part-time or temporary positions in the academic world should be read in these terms. It's never simply a "cost-cutting" measure, dictated by economic "realities" existing outside the profession; it's part of the politics of this particular market and its definitions.

An awareness of parallels between show dogs and literary scholarship may actually make it more difficult to find terms of representation that don't reek of "literary sentiment" for those who have experienced hurt and humiliation at dog shows. That is, from a parallel and "literary" lens, the sentiment of such representations seems inevitably to invite a jerk of ironic correction: "So let me see if I've got this, the whole problem is that your dog lost, right?" But this jerk of irony is dangerous in the circumstances, for it gives the game away. If nothing is really lost, then nothing's gained either. Whatever those massive remoralizing operations may try to tell you about the inestimable value of owning a champion animal, your dog's still just a dog. It shits like any mutt. The interesting thing about parallels, however, is not only that they can intersect, but that they also supply reversible lenses at the intersection. Why, exactly, is it so important to preserve existing conditions in a market in literary scholarship, whose market relations and positional good values continually visit so much hurt and humiliation on so many, and continue to exclude so many from participation? Your dog, too, is just a dog.

Whatever qualities of affective investments exist in maintaining standards and the positional authorities they underwrite, the process that preserves the scarcity of positional goods functions simultaneously as a general social operator. It contributes powerfully to the management of political incorporation and the changes it can bring. There's no "public value" at all in keeping positional goods scarce. What's at stake is a politics of incorporation. At this level the moralizing of literary scholarship and professional standards, like the moralizing of dog shows, rejoins the politics of "the market" as the broadest field of the socially "necessary." The politics of the market function to ensure that markets as specific ensembles of cultural and economic practices remain politically subordinate colonies, hostage to "the market" not as an economic fiction, but as a politics of colonizing control expelling the "losers" from its pathways.

Irony, Gramsci remarked somewhere, is produced by distance, sarcasm by commitment. Paralleling dog shows and literary scholarship can yield a wealth of distanced irony; commitments are harder, especially given that they must occur in a collision zone of market organization rather than in some autonomously cultural local space of resistances. The use values that appear in the many such zones worldwide aren't produced by getting rid of markets, as if economics were a natural contaminant or some residual reminder of a now vanishing industrial world. Consequences rest on how markets are defined and organized, for and by whom (people and animals), who is recruited into them, what skills and educational structures they involve, what kinds of labor produce them and what networks of social relations they produce, how they function in the distribution of resources. Dog shows may seem merely an ironic means of commentary on the cultural pretensions of literary scholarship. But as I've suggested, the market in show dogs can also offer models for alternative forms of behavioral values, shared skills, and organization of work. Show dog markets can model the constitution of mutually supportive social relationships, realized against a great many intense pressures. Likewise, the possibility of sustaining markets and market relations that depend on inclusive rather than exclusive competition represents one way of beginning to rethink the very operations of markets.

Markets are different; marketplace agents function within ensembles of relation and affiliation that organize specific practices very differently and respond in often unexpected ways to structural changes. In my concluding chapter, I want to consider recent changes in literary study by focusing attention on another and much larger kind of market complex, one that links these changes to the growth of corporate human resources management. Within any such marketplace collision zone, however, even in these expanded terms, "your dog's just a dog" can become an effective principle of sarcasm, with no distance at all from the investments that thereby make your dog everywhere of use. Whatever you call your dog, it's fortunate that it does shit like any mutt. For then it can be a functional way to eliminate a colonizing market politics imposed from the top down, with all its exclusions, and all its hurt and humiliation for so many.

FIVE

Educational Economics and Human Resources Management

Although identified in many different ways, intellectuals in humanities departments in the university haven't typically been seen as economic agents. Christopher Newfield reminds us of the importance of university structure in establishing a rather different role: "Dominick LaCapra once remarked that the research university is structured like a nuclear family: the scientists are the dads, and they go out and make the money, and the humanists are the moms, and they stay home and take care of the kids" ("What Was Political Correctness?" 341). Men aren't usually socialized to take care of the kids, and the men who set the agendas and terms of value for the humanities during the first half of the century certainly didn't see their intellectual work in these terms. Despite the perception of a great divide between "the two cultures," nevertheless they borrowed liberally from a prestigious scientific vocabulary to describe their work practices. Perhaps more important, they also inscribed the morality of arduous effort and the masculine heroism of discovery into the tasks. Registering the exact measure of ambiguous force to a verse fragment, or the precise field of reference for a historical document, was above all *difficult*; not just anyone at any time could do it. Payday, however, was a reminder that no matter how rigorous, the economic value of their efforts was not exactly commensurate with the value of their colleagues' work in the sciences and in the professional schools.

As Bruce Robbins has argued in *Secular Vocations*, one compensation for this relative economic marginalization in the university was the equation of "genuinely" critical positions with independence from the marketplace. Humanities intellectuals could never expect the financial support extended to colleagues in other fields, but conversely their scholarly work could claim to represent the best interests of a general public, uncontaminated by allegiances to financial interests. In this paradoxical configuration of simultaneous unfortunate and fortunate distance from "the economic," it's little wonder that a "professional" position as academic appeared an ambivalent privilege. To be sure, professional status could function to legitimate the knowledge produced. Yet as registered in the many versions of a "fall narrative" describing the descent into professionalism that Robbins analyzes, professional status was also suspect. Professionals are assumed to represent only their own narrow areas of specialized expertise rather than the best interests of the general public. Still worse, the work objectives of professionals are to some necessary extent market driven. Particularly in English, "service" and "service courses" thus became dirty words, reminders of the marketplace side of professionalism, to be displaced whenever possible onto composition specialists, graduate students, and "junior" faculty, as something quite distinct from the real work of the discipline. English became a high-volume field, but most of the volume of student circulation through the discipline was handled by these lower-level workers.

The now familiar model of economic "development"—from high-volume, mass-produced, standardized goods to high-value, flexibly specialized goods and services immediately responsive to shifts in specifically targeted markets—can't be applied directly to the organization of work in English departments. Nevertheless, there are enough similarities between that model and the assumptions that inform recent educational reform proposals to suggest a range of serious issues. A great many of these proposals imply that the educational "value" of departments like English will no longer lie in high volume, in terms of sheer numbers of faculty, courses taught, and student credit hours produced. Rather, educational value will appear in relation to a wide array of relatively specialized services to very different audiences, and the potential effects of such a shift are considerable. Financial and institutional support, for example, may well begin to be directed not at "English," to be allocated (and often fought over in overtly political terms) within the department, but at specific programs within English dependent on currently perceived demands for services. In such circumstances, programs would be tied first of all to their immediate source of support rather than to English as the general disciplinary field through which all support is funneled. It is already evident that the disciplinary hierarchy that had consigned an indiscriminate collection of service courses and instructors to the bottom of the discipline is changing in any number of ways, as new forms of those services are often in demand. Composition and composition theory, for example, stand out as the one relatively bright spot in an otherwise deeply depressed market for English Ph.D.'s.

For all its apparent recent success, there are good reasons to think cultural studies may not fare well in the midst of these ongoing changes. As many critics have argued, the much celebrated "arrival of theory" emerged most visibly and powerfully in the upper reaches of literary study. Cultural studies made a considerable contribution to the process by which such "theory" has been altered—almost beyond recognition in the eyes of many literary scholars. But it's no less true that the academic success of cultural studies in the United States was piggybacked on the prestige of theory, which is to say on the disciplinary hierarchy that had functioned to visibly identify certain discourses rather than others as theory. Thus, if perhaps perversely, the ways in which cultural studies work challenged that hierarchy also undermined one important ground for its "success."

In his attempt to preserve the significance of Gramsci's term "organic intellectual" for the politics of cultural studies, Stuart Hall acknowledged nevertheless that in the historical development of cultural studies in Britain "[w]e were organic intellectuals without any organic point of reference; organic intellectuals with a nostalgia or will or hope . . . that at some point we would be prepared in intellectual work for that kind of relationship, if such a conjuncture ever appeared" (281). Nor does Hall see that situation to have changed appreciably in the present. Another and rather different way to make Hall's point, however, is to acknowledge that within the shifting configurations of university change in the United States, it's not quite clear what clientele cultural studies serves. The language of my "translation" of Hall may seem demeaning, but it's worth remembering that in Gramsci's definition "organic intellectual" didn't automatically signify good guys fighting for proletarian revolution. Accountants and middle management bureaucrats are also "organic intellectuals," with very specific affiliations. Whether you turn this Gramscian lens or Hall's version of change on cultural studies in the university, "success" looks increasingly precarious. It is possible to try to maintain some critical stance outside the marketplace of academic services and clienteles, alien and unfurrowed by the "success" of cultural studies, refusing at every level to traffic with "compromising" reforms, continuing to publish always more radical critiques. But for whom exactly? Who could benefit, and how?

If for these reasons cultural studies may appear precarious, there are also reasons to think it may instead function importantly in new ways. Before jumping to conclusions about whether that's good or bad, it seems to me necessary first to recognize how the defining importance of "culture" and "cultural discourses" extends well beyond the academic disciplines intersected in the practices of cultural studies. In the midst of recent and variously theorized economic changes, corporations discovered culture. Or perhaps more exactly, corporate managers realized that what had seemed an obvious organizational structure, determined in the immediate as well as the "last" instance by the economic exigencies of market presence, production capacity, and aggregate demand, and so on, was in fact a rather complex construction. Corporate organization also depended on a delicately balanced form of "corporate culture." The discovery of culture in this sense was neither a function of the growing importance of marketing relative to production, nor an awareness of the market potential for new cultural goods of all kinds. It involved the enforced recognition that the very bone structure of corporate organization involved a constitutively specific cultural field of practices.

One of the effects of this realization has been that corporate human resources analysts have broadened the scope of their field, from the interpersonal dynamics of management skills to a larger process of education. To whatever extent corporate success depends on an intricate internal organization of corporate culture, then an informed education in the practices of corporate culture becomes a functional necessity. And to the extent changes in the composition of a corporate work force alter the dynamics of corporate culture, that process of education begins to engage political issues of "multiculturalism" and "diversity" every bit as intensely as the so-called culture wars in the university. "If we ignore the statistics about workforce composition and education," management consultants John Fernandez and Jacqueline Dubois argue, "we will have a severe shortage of qualified workers and a country that continues to have large pockets of extremely disadvantaged people of color" (208). Earlier, however, they had emphasized the point that while educating "qualified workers" and eliminating the "disadvantages" faced by those "large pockets" of people of color may seem radical political goals, they are by no means incompatible with corporate economic objectives: "We must emphasize that companies that are willing to accommodate diversity will reap rewards in traditional dollars-and-cents terms as they listen to their most valuable resource: people" (206). Fernandez and Dubois see no necessary contradiction at all between a politics of "empowerment" for a large, diverse, multicultural population on the one hand, and corporations who expect to "reap rewards in traditional dollars-and-cents terms" on the other.

Further, in whatever ways they might disagree over specifics, consultants like Fernandez are unanimous in their recognition that effective human resources management involves more than internal corporate organization and policy. It requires changes in the orientation of *public* policy generally, and it must begin not in the corporate workplace, but far earlier, in the classrooms of a public educational system. In this vision, a recognition like Piore and Sabel's of increasingly blurred boundary lines between "society" and "economic organization" resolves itself into an integrated ensemble of political education produced across an immense network of locations that includes the corporation itself. Business writer Richard Crawford points out that "IBM can correctly boast that it runs the largest educational system in the country" (29), and much of that education has to do with the "traditional" subjects of the humanities: literacy skills, methodologies of critical thinking and problem solving, historical awareness, the dilemmas of how to read cultural representations, the power of narrative construction, the dynamics of interpersonal relationships—the list of similarities is a long one. Corporations have "discovered" culture, at length.

It doesn't seem to me a great leap of logic to assume that the general emphasis on knowledge growth and knowledge workers that shapes corporate direction will also affect public policy with regard to educational institutions. More concretely, I think it entirely plausible that the corporate educational role of human resources management will be extended to those of us who teach in the humanities in the university. That is, one specific application of general proposals for educational reform targeted to the new needs of corporations will involve a positioning of humanities teachers to carry out work practices similar to the educational work of human resources professionals.

On the one hand, such positional congruity would mean that humanities instructors might well acquire a new status as economic agents. Rather than simply "taking care of the kids" while the scientists did productive stuff, humanities instruction, like human resources management, would make a significant contribution to an economic productivity understood as dependent on human resources. For "the kids" now appear a potential and vitally necessary pool of well-trained and flexibly skilled adults. On the other hand, however, the attention to "Culture" on the right and to "cultures" on the left would have to be altered to include a recognition of how such attention functions educationally as an economic no less than a cultural process. These self-definitions of cultural work could no longer be arrested at some imagined boundary line between "culture" and "economics."

Cultural studies is strategically positioned in the complex of academic disciplinary fields relative to a corporate emphasis on human resources and "diversity." Through a resources management lens, cultural studies can look like a flexible skill-based form of training in critical thinking rather than a discipline grounded in a very specialized field of knowledge. Its interdisciplinary mobility and its attention to the indigenous specificities of "other" cultures seem to link that skill training to a cosmopolitan multiculturalism. Its "radical" politics, no longer inherently threatening, promises innovative ways to tap marketing potential in new areas and augment corporate recruiting efforts among diverse population groups. Thus cultural studies faculty could be "outsourced" to do resource management work with little expenditure of either corporate financing or social prestige, and without even the need to negotiate the often quite complex formal arrangements that characterize how corporations "hire" academic work in other fields. In the reconfigurations of university organization, cultural studies faculty would simply be positioned as "doing" human resources management work regardless of whether it was understood in such terms by those involved.

I realize of course that some such vision of cultural studies as a kind of outsourced junior-level corporate human resources management would seem to justify the punch line of every "co-optation" narrative about the academic "success" of cultural studies. But in any case my interest here is not to theorize how cultural studies, antennae to the wind, might modify itself to "survive" whatever exactly will result from the complex of corporate change and public policy direction I've been sketching very quickly. In focusing attention on the figure of the intellectual as corporate human resources analyst in this chapter, I have two immediate aims in mind.

The first involves a relatively pragmatic recognition that as corporations and universities construct new and different alliances across shifting forms of internal organization, it's necessary to understand a great deal more than most of us do about corporate organization and direction. Clearly it's impossible to remain in that all too familiar state of semiconscious certainty that nasty stuff goes on over there. Knowledge, however, isn't always easy to come by. The pressures on the university from new adaptations of a conservative "social issues" agenda are considerable and scary, and in claims like those advanced by William Bennett or Roger Kimball, for example, that agenda often finds expression, in some version or another, within humanities departments. As I argued in Chapter 1, however, business-oriented proposals for educational reform are not necessarily congruent with new conservative social issues politics, and such proposals are much less likely in any case to have faculty representatives within the humanities. Hence unlike new conservative social issues, the effects of such directions can't be anticipated or challenged in familiar ways, particularly when, as with the recent emphasis of human resources analysis, they arrive in the form of valuing diversity and multiculturalism rather than as an insistence on "crude" marketplace indices or as a nostalgia for the wonders of Western Civilization.

My second and much larger aim involves the proposal of a conceptual frame for understanding both the new forms of corporate pressure on the university and the emergent linkages between corporate and university work practices of human resources management. Far from being obsolete, it seems to me that the complex networks of affiliation Gramsci named by his use of the term "organic intellectual" still exist in recognizable ways, and in fact have expanded to organize much of the fields of intellectual work in a corporate world. It's surely easy enough to recognize that what human resources analysts such as John Fernandez and R. Roosevelt Thomas describe in terms of a "natural" corporate culture (see, for example, Thomas, 28) that rewards diversity and multiculturalism involves a process of ideological construction and direction. But it's also possible to gloss "natural" as something very close to Gramsci's recognition of how organic intellectuals explicitly represent the connections among their political, economic, and group-based intellectual work. That is, human resources analysts see themselves as the "organic" links between often radically diverse population groups and the goals of the corporation. This link functions in a way that alters both the work and "lifestyle" expectations of such groups *and* the very organization and direction of the corporate enterprise; such changes are often profoundly political. Thus rather than—once again—"discovering" ideology at work in an ostensibly natural process, Gramsci's idea of "organic intellectual" can be used to understand the complicated ensemble of pressures affecting the expectations and itineraries of the population groups who inhabit our university classrooms.

Further, if my projection holds that corporate human resources management is being extended to include humanities intellectuals in the university, then this understanding has some serious implications for a concern, like Hall's, for the lack of "any organic point of reference" for would-be organic intellectuals doing cultural studies work. Contrary to Hall's perception of disjunction, cultural studies would indeed find its "organic" reference, if perhaps not quite in the terms of Hall's vocabulary of desire. The connections occur within a politics of incorporation that marks the reshaping of corporate culture as it attempts to "manage diversity." My frame suggests, rather than that familiar and forbidding symmetry between maintaining a critical distance or succumbing to co-optation, that those of us working in cultural studies already have a stake in how the possibilities of political incorporation are played out in practice.

The process by which one might, for example, intervene in the organization of a curriculum by introducing new texts and new thematics representing socially oppressed groups, on the one hand, and the process of acquiring a tenured incorporation into the university, on the other, are not exactly separate and distinct. The effects of this complicated and ongoing double process can't be separated into cleanly divisible units to be catalogued under the covering judgments of radical change or co-optation. Such judgments are far less important than an understanding of the "organic" ensemble of connections that organizes an often-bewildering multiplicity of contested everyday practices, and that also create conditions of possibility for new formations of political direction. The ways in which universities have come to resemble corporations in both organizational structure and management "style" means that humanities instructors, like corporate human resources analysts and managers, begin to function as economic agents. That's not, in itself, either a radical or an already co-opted position to occupy. But what you can do with it depends on at least some understanding of where you are and how you got there.

It's also true, however, that corporations have become, like universities, educational institutions. Thus if, for new conservative social agendas, the relative autonomy of the university poses an ideological threat, in corporate eyes that relative autonomy may begin to seem instead an economic redundancy. For as "human resources" assume primary economic importance for corporations, the university's separate process of "developing" human resources may come to seem unnecessary, redundant. That is, to the extent a separation between universities and corporations as educational institutions imposes a double itinerary of incorporation on the development of human resources in a student population, then in corporate eyes that university process might potentially be eliminated in its separate and distinct form. Such a perception of redundancy, however, would depend finally on a political metaphor that, beyond the wordplay, points to a surplus of incorporation which human resources analysts must learn to manage. Thus it's not hard to imagine why the current emphasis of corporate human resources analysts on an efficient management of diversity might very soon lead to specific reform proposals directed at university educational practices. For unless university training programs can be more finely tuned to the complex intersections of economics and politics within the corporation as itself an educational institution, the "diverse" products of the university might well become considerably more difficult to "manage."

Human resources management in a corporation involves more than training workers for the new technologies of the workplace and educating workers in flexible adaptation to new forms of corporate culture. Perhaps more fundamentally, it links education in this double sense to the *social* technologies of demographics and corporate selection practices that identify a work force. Toward the end of better understanding the work practices of human resources management, I want to turn first to this complex of demographics and selection. That is, rather than immediately questioning the "genuineness" of economic betterment promised by the reshaping of corporate culture under the banner of multiculturalism and diversity, it seems to me necessary to isolate for attention the process by which a "literal" incorporation, the recruitment and hiring of corporate citizens, has come to both model and manage the larger process of political incorporation of citizens of the State. For the process by which this incorporation takes place also rewrites in new and significant ways the boundary lines between "private sector" economics and "public" policy, between the development of "human resources" in the corporation and in the public university.

❖

A now familiar corporate vocabulary like flexible specialization, flattened management hierarchy, and so on, projects often very different narratives and mechanisms of change, but there is at least a certain range of agreement in the recognition that "the new economy," however defined, requires new workplace skills and foregrounds new workers. The expanded role of human resources management owes a great deal to the corporate recognition of the importance of a culture that will encourage development of a different kind of worker. In other words, the "information" in the phrase "information economy" points not only to the specific commodity form that I discussed in Chapter 4, but also to the education of workers. Business sociologists Jerald Hage and Charles Powers title their recent book *Post-Industrial Lives*—rather than, say, "postindustrial economics" or "postindustrial society"—in large part because they want to focus particular attention on these new workers occupying center stage in a still unfolding scene of change.

"Long-term change," they argue, "can be viewed as a composite of two contending forces that shape the way in which knowledge is embedded in activity. For want of better terms, we call these forces the processes of (a) rationalization and (b) complexification. Both processes influence the way social life is constructed. And a shift in the relative importance of these forces recently occurred" (43). Rationalization, as Weber, for example, described it, dominated the development of industrial society; for Hage and Powers, complexification has emerged as the dominant force in a postindustrial society. As in other accounts of economic change, Hage and Powers assume the development of new technologies as crucial: "What is important to recognize in order to understand this process [of industrial deskilling] is that it was predicated on embedding increasing levels of knowledge in machines precisely so that workers could function effectively without much knowledge or experience" (44). In contrast, the recent "impact of complexification on occupational roles is the exact opposite of that of rationalization, for machines don't always simplify or replace roles. Their introduction can also be associated with the creation of new occupational specialties and the addition of new activities to existing roles" (50).

New machines were introduced on the assembly line to replace hand labor. In small, specialized operations, however, they often appear instead as instruments that enlarge the field of available data, project a number of alternative possibilities, and require some considerable, "creative" problem-solving ability on the part of their users. Rather than machine operatives assigned to repetitive task performance, employees become the skilled knowledge workers who occupy Hage and Powers's attention, and who expect and demand control over the determination of what counts as a "task" in the first place. Knowledge workers in this sense must be highly educated, and they must assume that their education will be a continuing process as situations change and still newer technologies become available. As educated workers, they will likely be educated consumers as well, which can lead to dissatisfaction with mass-produced, standardized goods of all kinds, and thus to an increasing demand in other sectors for the sort of specialized goods and services they themselves oversee at work. In such an account, new technologies aren't assumed as the "cause" of a change from mass production to specialized production, any more then they cause higher levels of education. Their function in Hage and Powers's argument is more like an available code that permits a translation back and forth among different variables of change.

On the one hand, the concept of complexification thus yields a positive narrative of economic and cultural change made visible across the development of new technologies. On the other hand, however, Hage and Powers's refocusing of sociological attention toward this positive dynamics of knowledge growth and away from the unequal distribution of wealth and power that preoccupied earlier sociologists (such as Weber) makes the persistence of social inequalities seem virtually incomprehensible, as they are finally forced to admit: "The mechanisms of exploitation, which have produced a great underclass and denied large segments of society a realistic opportunity to develop to their human capital potential have simultaneously denied society the contributions these people are capable of making. A society that easily discards millions of people is unlikely to succeed in PI [postindustrial] competition. That path is so obviously dysfunctional that ignoring the problems of the underclass seems incomprehensible" (209). The route by which Hage and Powers arrive at that conclusion is similar to the arguments of human resources management consultants like Fernandez, who likewise express astonishment at the "dysfunctional" myth that would justify the "discarding" of millions. What from Weber's perspective seems obviously the inherent costs in human terms of the controlling profit dynamic of the corporation, for Hage and Powers as for Fernandez becomes merely a surviving relic of past beliefs and assumptions whose "dysfunctional" effects will soon become apparent even to the most obdurate corporate representatives.

Thus while perhaps not strictly technological determinists, Hage and Powers—and a great many other theorists of a postindustrial society—nevertheless tend to locate "solutions" to the "problem" of persistent inequalities within a recognizable tradition of technocratic thinking. As William Leiss puts it: "The concepts of 'information revolution,' 'information economy,' and 'information society' constitute an important new stage in the tradition of technocratic thinking in modern society. In large part their importance lies precisely in how perfectly they represent this tradition. They enable us to see clearly what role public policy is thought to have in the interaction between technology and society: namely, to 'soften up' public opinion so that a compliant response to a new technology may be delivered" (283–84). Theorists of a knowledge-driven information society would thus function, in a familiar phrase from Gramsci, as "experts in legitimation" for shaping a politics of consent. Whatever "solutions" they might offer are a matter of better adaptation to an inexorable "logic" of events, determined ultimately by changes in technologies.

Yet Leiss does not stress nearly enough how recent theorizing represents "an important new stage in the tradition of technocratic thinking." In that tradition, public policy remains reactive. Given the assumed inevitability of technological change, the most significant policy question is expressed in terms of how best to "adjust" to it. In this "important new stage," however, public policy also has an important role in creating conditions that make technological innovation possible. That is, public policy assumes a directive rather than a reactive role. In the context of public policy direction, postindustrial society theorizing functions as propaganda that helps create conditions that assign high priorities to and rewards for innovative technological developments. Public policy in this sense is where such theorizing intersects with the work of management consultants like Fernandez, who stress the human resources necessary to implement these developments, and sociologists like Hage and Power, who describe the shifting role requirements of knowledge growth and complexification. At the intersection of these currents of thought, the aim of public policy is the *creation* of new human resources rather than, as Leiss speculates, the reactive management of an "underclass."

In Hage and Powers's view, this new directive role of public policy implies that the dynamic of change no longer needs to preserve the equilibrium of "top" and "bottom." The basic task of creating new human resources must occur across the entire spectrum of the social formation, regardless of what might currently exist as "top" or "bottom." Similarly, "managing diversity," as consultants like Fernandez and Thomas understand it, is not a matter of "assimilating" traditionally excluded groups into an existing corporate culture. It's about changing corporate culture to maximize new human resources. The pedagogical function of a directive public policy thus must be directed not at an underclass unwilling to change, but first of all at now "dysfunctional" attitudes found in reactionary corporate management.

What this "new stage" preserves from the tradition of technocratic thinking Leiss identifies is a certain perception of inevitability, of inexorable "forces" at work, now embodied in "knowledge growth" or simply "information" as well as in technology itself. While in the past agency had been understood as a question of individual choice, Hage and Powers argue "that this conceptualization is inappropriate for our times" (210). The individual can no longer appear the determinate node of agent choice: "We demonstrate that knowledge growth, and more specifically the ways in which new knowledge is implanted in minds, in machines, and in patterns of social organization, determines the structural need for the exercise of agency as a functional prerequisite to flexible adaptation in the face of uncertain and changing conditions" (211). The curiously passive construction—"the ways in which new knowledge is implanted"—squatting in the midst of this discussion of "agency" signals not only the persistence of a technocratic assumption of inevitability, but also, and equally important, a change in the very notion of "change."

Although prominently associated with a theorizing of radical changes toward a postindustrial society, Daniel Bell responds with irritation to the endlessly repeated reminder that "change" has accelerated: "We have heard much of the acceleration of the pace of change. It is seductive but ultimately a meaningless idea other than as a metaphor. For one has to ask, 'Change of what?' and, 'How does one measure the pace?' There is no metric that applies in general, and the word change is ambiguous" (96). All that can be said with some certainty, he continues, "is that the scale of change has widened . . . the growth of an enterprise, for example, requires specialization and differentiation and very different kinds of control and management systems when the scales move from, say, $10 million to $100 million to $1 billion" (97). In other words, for Bell no independent measure exists by which relative rates of change might be assessed; the fundamental characteristic of change in the present is to absorb more and more surrounding territory that thereby becomes unavailable to function as a stable point of reference for rate. Counterpoised against Hage and Powers's discussion of agency, Bell's comments suggest that "inevitability" now has less to do with the linear progress and acceleration rates emphasized by technocratic thinking in the past and more to do with structural saturation. For "$10 million to $100 million to $1 billion" is not a measure of rate or even movement, but an index of completeness, of "spread" across a field. Bell's perception registers change by reference to scale alterations of the whole.

It shouldn't be surprising that "agency" in Hage and Powers's discussion likewise appears as a matter of "scale" rather than as some autonomous, unilateral exercise of choice at a determinate, causal node. Agency is distributed across a process requiring "negotiation and co-determined agreement among people who must cooperate" (210). Much of the analysis in *Post-Industrial Lives* thus has to do with networks and their role structures, as the ensemble of occasions that links the inevitable scale enlargements across the social formation with cooperatively negotiated powers of agency at any given point anywhere in the social field: "We predict that the fluid network will be the defining form of social organization in the PI era" (204), a form that reconstructs "the society from the bottom up" (205).

This reversal of a more traditional vision of change moving from the top down in every sector (with public policy functioning to "soften up" the bottom to accept change) explains why it is that the persistence of massive social inequalities, together with "ignoring the problems of the underclass," should seem so "obviously dysfunctional" as to be "incomprehensible" (206). It flies in the face of the inevitability of scale saturation. A linear vision of rapidly accelerating change could easily accept the social disjunction that emerges between a few leaders and a great many left behind, even when it might portend a "society that easily discards millions of people." Change as scale enlargement, in contrast, assumes the inevitability of permeating the entire social formation, wherever it might begin.

Over the last two decades, however, the rhetoric of corporate restructuring invokes a rather direct vocabulary of "scaling down" rather than the steady spread of scale implied by Bell's comments. Downsizing, flattened management hierarchy, flexible specialization, precision concentration on critical points in the value-added stream, regionally autonomous operating units, implemented automation, and so on, are all expressive of *reductions* of scale. Relatively sanguine information society theorists like Benjamin Compaine dismiss the fears about job loss, the replacement of workers with machines, the "information gap" between rich and poor and between nations, and the disparities in the availability of new technologies which have resulted from these forms of restructuring, by appealing once again to inevitabilities of scale, in even broader terms: "As seen in the figures representing the constant dollar price of electricity, automobiles, telephone service and television sets, the combination of declining costs, thanks to improvements in technology, and a wealthier work force, has lessened the difference in life style between the poorer and richer in society. Today, with many manufacturing jobs being transferred to the developing industrial nations, there are signs that a similar process is taking place on a global scale" (189–90). Thus in Compaine's vision at least, what worries Hage and Powers as an "incomprehensible" persistence of inequalities appears as a problem only because the scale of their own analysis is simply not wide enough.

As Bell reminds us, however, changes in scale are rarely uniform across the social formation of any specific country, let alone globally. The long historical curve plotted by Compaine not only ignores "local" disruptions, but depends on a structural schematic possessed by the analyst that conveniently permits a synchronicity of "before" and "after" at any given moment in the process of change. Bell argues in contrast that public policy in the form of deliberate political decisions must intervene to compensate for uneven developments: "The problem for future information societies is to match the scales between political and economic institutions and activities" (97), crudely, between an information *society* and an information *economy*. Even if one took, for example, the statistics generated in Marc Porat's massive nine-volume study in 1977, *The Information Economy*, as a QED for the existence of an economy driven primarily by "information work" in some form or another, Bell's point is that nothing would warrant assuming an egalitarian information society as an automatic corollary, as Compaine implies.

More radically, Herbert Schiller argues in *Who Knows: Information in the Age of the Fortune 500* that the more complete the scale of economic transformation toward an international, information-based capitalism, the more it becomes necessary to recognize that we live in a society of deliberately calculated *mis*information about social inequalities that have in fact been widened and intensified by the organization of an information economy. That is, in Schiller's argument there is a growing gap between information "haves" and "have-nots," and public policy has deliberately encouraged the dissemination of misinformation calculated to maintain the gap. Thus Bell's hope of "matching scales" would be merely a familiar utopian fantasy of liberal political "tinkering." It ignores both the investment of dominant interests in preserving inequalities, and the power of controlling the availability of information on which to base the political decisions Bell would urge as necessary. For Schiller, the existence of a genuine information society—with equal access to, and possibilities of empowerment by, information skills and knowledges—would make the current form of an information economy with its controlling interests an impossibility.

Schiller's arguments have not gone unanswered, of course. In one of the more careful responses, however, Jorge Reina Schement points out that Schiller has rather too quickly assimilated the organization and control of informational activities to a uniform development of capitalism: "They [Schiller, Vincent Mosco, and others] can explain the role played by capitalism in the formation of the pattern of informational activities, but they are unable to distinguish the relative influence of industrialization, apart from capitalism. By examining only the dynamics of capitalism, their critique remains incomplete" (37). As Schement goes on to argue, capitalism and industrialism can't be understood as necessarily synonymous: "The United States was already a capitalist society before entrepreneurs began adapting the industrial system to the pursuit of profit" (41). Likewise, while an information economy may indeed be capitalistic, there's no reason to assume that "adapting" the control of information "to the pursuit of profit" will yield exactly the same results as industrial capitalism. Understanding social inequalities requires analysis of the specific conditions of an information economy rather than simply assigning inequalities to some uniform "dynamics of capitalism" as an underlying cause.

Schement's argument also suggests good reasons to question Hage and Powers's perception of the now obsolete survival from the past of "rationalized," routine work practices. In an information economy, even flexibly specialized manufacturing involves creating *new*, local sectors of "routine" work existing in isolation from other and "complex" work sectors, and also—as subcontracted or leased—isolated from the organization and location of any central corporate structure. In other words, such local forms of routine work are not holdovers from a now vanishing form of rationalized production, as Hage and Powers imply, but are indispensable to and produced by the current requirements of "complex" work and its ends. Even if capitalism in some sense remains in place, structural patterns of inequalities and forms of exploitation will differ significantly.

To a great extent the "secular vocations" in the humanities that Robbins analyzes have projected a self-understanding of work in the humanities as occupying a kind of critical space "outside" this entire complex of changing marketplace forces and forms of economic exploitation. In practice, however, this distance translates into little more than the perpetuation in current circumstances of that familiar and frustratingly ineffective role of keeping a brief on these guys from a distance as proof that "we" at least haven't been fooled by this latest version of capitalism with a human face. While perhaps this is now a familiar picture of intellectual work, it is a picture that must be altered considerably in turning to consider the work, affiliations, and positions of consultants like Fernandez or business sociologists like Hage and Powers in current economic conditions.

Like scientific management planners earlier, human resources analysts understand their work as directly engaged on behalf of corporate objectives. "True, all groups will benefit," R. Roosevelt Thomas argues in *Beyond Race and Gender*, "whether they are different in terms of age, lifestyle, gender or race. But their benefit is not the driving motivation. Managing diversity presumes that the driving force is the manager's, and the company's, self-interest" (168). That "self-interest," Fernandez reminds us, is typically expressed as "rewards in traditional dollars-and-cents terms" (206). Given this admitted commitment to corporate profit objectives, Hage and Powers's assertion that they are theorizing change "from the bottom up,"; Fernandez's concern for the necessity to educate everybody, and to eliminate the disadvantages faced by people of color; and Thomas's argument that managing diversity requires a radical change in "corporate culture," rather than attempts to assimilate "others" into an existing culture, are all likely to seem hollow claims, nothing but a mask for economic business as usual.

Nevertheless, if in the past "traditional" corporate profit objectives didn't seem to require much attention to "diversity," then something must have changed significantly to have occasioned the current ensemble of linkages. The answer supplied by management diversity theorizing lies in demographics. Dramatized in the Hudson Institute's 1987 report, *Workforce 2000*, corporations will face a radical shortage in skilled labor and a labor force growth rate fueled overwhelmingly by white women and people of color in circumstances where "quality and innovation," as Hage and Powers argue, "are now more important in the marketplace than price" (35). Quality and innovation come from the availability of more and more highly skilled people educated to produce and take advantage of changing conditions rather than from an "efficiently" organized mass of relatively unskilled workers.

Likewise, in terms of marketing, the success of flexibly specialized production depends on the identification of very specifically targeted consumer "needs." And what from the side of production looks like a shortage of skilled labor and an influx of white women and people of color into the work force, looks from the marketing side like a shortage of knowledge about how to target goods and services to this influx. With respect to both production and marketing, demographics is intended to supply the reality check of hard data that reveals how profit potential must be linked with an attention to diversity. At the same time, however, demographics also projects a powerful politics of selection that alters fundamentally the very conditions of "incorporation" as a public citizen of a democracy. It is in terms of this politics of selection that the potential "redundancy" involved in how both educational institutions and corporations address the pedagogical process of developing human resources assumes a crucial and contested importance.

❖

The dream of a universal public education system involved a claim to create uniform, fair, public standards for the enormously complicated process of identifying appropriately qualified people for different occupational positions. Schools were the location where the interests of "private" enterprise intersected with the interests of the State as representative of the general public, with ideologies of merit—the best person for the requirements of any given position—providing a shared set of norms. The State's responsibility was to maintain an educational system that could ensure equal access to and equal opportunity for training to everyone; private enterprise was assumed to be driven by its own interests to hire the best available people emerging from educational training programs; educators in the schools, meanwhile, were simultaneously charged with carrying out the process of training and positioned at the controls of finely tuned discriminations of respective "merit" among the student population whose work they monitored.

In practice, of course, this double process of training and merit determination always seemed flawed, the indices skewed, corrections and adjustments a continual necessity, "exceptions" more and more obvious. Further, as critics pointed out with increasing frequency, determinations of merit were no more race- or gender- or class-blind than the actual selection decisions made at workplaces. In relation to occupational stratification, merit seemed little more than a complicated form of ideological legitimation. Even such ideological critiques of merit, however, tend to ignore how merit and workplace selection implied fundamentally distinct grounds of decision making. For all that the results often looked similar in the exclusions imposed on specific population groups, merit directly addresses the identification of differences among people against the background of a public discourse that invoked ideally knowable, uniform standards of educational achievement. Thus it was at least possible that once shown to be skewed, discriminatory or exclusionary in practice, both actual decisions and the norms of public discourse could be modified.

The process of workplace selection, in contrast, begins not with the assumption of differences among individuals, but with the organization of work itself, with differences among tasks. Workplace selection, that is, observes what Marx had identified as "the Babbage principle" of a division of labor, grounded in the differentiation and distribution of tasks in any specific process of production or marketing. At the upper levels of occupation—prestigious professions, corporate management, and so on—these two distinct fields of merit and workplace selection could appear to coalesce, insofar as in such circumstances the "quality" of the person and the precise nature of the work tasks performed seemed mutually defining. But the further down the scale of occupational stratification you go, the more visible the disjunction becomes, not only in terms of the fit between personal qualities and task-determined work responsibilities, but also with respect to the relative indices of differentiation to which individuals are subjected.

Relative to workplace selection, person X with a high-school diploma and two years of community college working as a convenience store clerk is not only overeducated and underemployed, as the familiar refrain has it. From management perspective at the workplace, person X is also "overmerited," as it were, having been the subject of far too many and "redundant" merit decisions than would be "necessary" to determine via workplace selection practices an "appropriate" worker at a convenience store. Thus educational theorists Samuel Bowles and Herbert Gintis, for example, argue in *Schooling in Capitalist America* that the real function of school-generated merit decisions is instead psychological. It has little directly to do with workplace selection, but rather with the necessity to convince large numbers of the population to accept the "fact" that they don't really have what it takes to occupy better-paying and more prestigious positions. In a great many cases the persuasion may take some considerable time. Person X may be one of those for whom four years of high school humiliation wasn't enough; however "redundant" from the perspective of workplace requirements at a convenience store, the two extra years of community college may well have been psychologically necessary to complete the "education."

While perhaps accurate enough as far as it goes, however, such reasoning underestimates the way in which in practice ideologies of merit also contributed powerfully to another psychology, involving workplace *rights* to be selected. Two years of community college may finally have persuaded person X that she or he really is too dumb to succeed, but there's nothing that automatically prevents the possibility that in specific combinations of circumstances person X would be convinced instead that she or he had immense untapped potential finally being realized. If merit decisions can effectively "cool off" student expectations, the authority invested in merit decisions to accomplish that aim can also yield a potentially "dangerous" psychology should the student come to feel "empowered" rather than "cooled off" by such merit decisions. The disjunction between indices of merit and indices of workplace selection, necessary in order for merit to function as ideological legitimization, carries with it a potential for disruption. It is of course that potential that is targeted by conservative social theorists as if it portended some massive and general "breakdown of standards" in educational systems. Perhaps the most typical dilemma now faced by school boards across the nation arises out of this double valence of merit decisions: "every parent" seems to want higher standards, but no parent assumes their children will fail to meet those standards.

Unlike conservative social theorists, however, corporations who see themselves presently facing a shortage of highly skilled labor worry less about the breakdown of standards and its effects on large numbers of the school population than about the training required for skilled positions. Corporate management fears, that is, focus at the top of the job ladder, where merit decisions and selection practices can seem to coalesce under the name of "human resources." Thus corporate human resources analysts occupy a stress point between what Robert Reich identifies as the necessarily *global* field of reference for the work of what he calls symbolic analysts, employed by transnational corporations, and the educational and occupational expectations of a potential *domestic* work force in the process of training.

For the former, global mobilities require continually learning new work skills and ways of adapting to unfamiliar conditions in both marketing and production. Human resources programs have an important role in this continual process of retraining. The so-called environmental scans produced by resources management professionals contribute to the identification of global market potential as well as feasibility projections for relocating or opening new corporate units. But environmental scanning also functions to isolate demographic factors that might yield a locally available source of new, highly educated workers. Thus the presence of a major research university, for example, whose programs are addressed to a large multicultural population, offers an attractive incentive for opening a new regionally autonomous corporate unit that would have immediately available a source of qualified workers. Human resources professionals who help define for the corporation what counts as "qualifications" are simultaneously engaged in defining educational goals for those in school at particular locations. Likewise, the globally tuned assessments of the desirability of specific regional locations, produced by human resources analysis, affect people's choice of school in the first place.

Seen through the lens of merit, selection procedures had seemed a generalized process, ideally answerable everywhere to uniform, known, public standards, and if necessary enforceable by public policies such as affirmative action. That is, and regardless of the realities of how actual decisions were made, an ideal of merit-based fairness functioned as a kind of double mediation. If very broadly and imprecisely, the ideal nevertheless constrained actual decisions at some limit of plausibility; selection decisions couldn't yield results likely to seem blatantly "unfair" to all other interested parties. Perhaps more important, an ideal of merit-based fairness embodied in public knowledge supplied, when necessary, the terms of legitimization for selection decisions. However they were made "in reality," decisions had to be justified in a language congruent with ideals of merit-based fairness. Decisions, again, were doubly mediated by an ideal of fairness that registered in general, public terms.

In this new scenario, however, selection from an available pool of educated workers at any given location is dependent entirely on a corporate management "read" of immediate conditions, produced by the demographic technologies of environmental scanning and the like. Conceptions of merit don't disappear, but the constitutive matrix grounding specific merit determinations is dislocated from any projection of a general, public set of shareable norms and values and reinscribed within the terms of demographic studies by corporate human resources analysis. Both the parameters of plausibility for actual decisions and the rhetoric of legitimization for those decisions are grounded in the assumable "fit" between corporate needs and demographic data. Demographics thus makes possible a certain "privatization" of the very conception of merit, insofar as corporate-generated demographic data substitute for a projection of shared public norms of merit-based fairness as the mediating principle of selection decisions. That privatization, in turn, portends the possibility of eliminating the "redundancy" between merit decisions entrusted to educational institutions and workplace selection practices entrusted to corporate employees. This would depart from the imagining of both forms of decision as ultimately answerable to some ideal of shared, public norms of fairness; they would now appear as two different orders of decision altogether, with the university order of decision making something that could be eliminated as redundant, as having no efficacy or rationale to be imported into a corporate world of selection decisions.

The expansion of private education is often viewed by conservative social theorists as a welcome alternative to the "radical" ideologies that have infiltrated public education systems and corrupted their standards of merit for "private" political ends. In such a conservative account, that is, if paradoxically, "private" education comes to seem the best hope for preserving "public" norms of merit-based fairness. In the sense I've been describing, however, corporations have already been engaged in a massive expansion of "private" education based on a privatization of conceptions of merit. For what's "private" about "private enterprise" in this vision is not really its economics, which human resources analysts acknowledge to be everywhere intricated with a vast public pool, precisely, of general human resources. It's rather the authority to control the constitutive ground of merit itself, relative to the data made available through the technologies of demographic studies.

Despite claims that demographics function as a reality check to spur corporate commitments to genuine diversity in the work force, Avery Gordon has explained how the "reality" supplied by demographics involves a rather remarkable sleight-of-hand: "For example, diversity management rarely attributes increased rates of white female labor force participation to the economic crisis of the mid-1970s, preferring the more idealistic explanation of heightened feminine consciousness" (16). In larger terms, diversity as a "new" reality made visible by demographics "allows the corporation to ignore the fact that it was instrumental in keeping American business more homogeneous than American society" (16). Demographics can thus project diversity management as politically progressive only "because in effect it has no history, only progress and the future" (16). Whatever may have been the case in the past, and for whatever reasons, demographics keeps the focus resolutely on meeting the challenges of the future, and identifies diversity management as the best tactical means for aligning progressive political reform with newly redesigned corporate business practices and inclusive forms of corporate culture.

Thus in R. Roosevelt Thomas's understanding, for example, managing diversity is a more effective form of "empowerment" for employees than general public policy dictates such as affirmative action because it "doesn't seek to give relief to a system's negative consequences by adding supplementary efforts" (26). That is, Thomas's quarrel with affirmative action as public policy is neither with its politics nor with its "intrusion" of politics into economics, but with its ineffectuality, the failure of affirmative action mandates to create conditions where "nontraditional" employees can thrive. Managing diversity, in contrast, "is a holistic approach to creating a corporate environment that allows all kinds of people to reach their full potential in pursuit of corporate objectives" (167). It involves an internal process of cultural education that leads to the "natural creation of a diverse work force," and a "natural upward mobility for minorities and women" (28) within the corporation.

As Gordon points out, Thomas's work is explicitly couched in the cultural terms of corporate reorganization, in ways that often seem oblivious to the social history of corporations in the United States. Nevertheless, the scope of his argument is informed by a powerful historical vision. The "corporate environment," as Thomas describes it, appears to be almost a laboratory situation for rethinking a great many fundamental premises of liberal democracy, much as John Dewey had imagined schools as a laboratory for social innovation and change. The difference is that this "laboratory" is now recentered around the *corporate* citizen rather than the publicly educated citizen of the State. Managing diversity as a cultural education is also a political education in citizenship, and ultimately corporate selection practices identify a process of incorporation into a body politic. Managing diversity, however, must nevertheless function within the privacy of the selection process for a corporate work force. And while the political role of human resources analysts may be imagined by Thomas and others as one of oppositional commitment to new, more open and democratic forms, their function as economic agents is already circumscribed by the politics of newly emergent divisions between public and private. Thus the "problem" is not that human resources analysts are also economic agents and hence inevitably "compromise" their politics, allow their work to be "co-opted." It's that the privatization of selection within corporate control also demarcates which zones of political power are available to which economic agents. Privatization, that is, makes the process of incorporation into a work force synonymous with political incorporation as citizens. Managing diversity is finally about the political management of citizenship, centered not in the State but in the corporation. Likewise, from the other side, being *subjected to* a workplace process of selection is made to appear synonymous with the process of becoming a political citizen.

In such circumstances, there seems much to be recommended in what is already well underway as a strategic rethinking of "outdated" conceptions like State and nation, even something approaching a renewal of a universalistic rhetoric of general public education. As the so-called welfare state has been progressively dismantled, for example, it's also become much clearer just how much had been leveraged to benefit people's lives by way of that now "obsolete" conception. Likewise, what had seemed in the heyday of sixties radicalism to be an unconscionable affiliation between educational institutions and the state might now seem instead a final barrier of protection against the massive forces set in motion by corporate "leaning" and "downsizing."

Nevertheless, before proceeding further with such rethinking, even "strategically," it's important to recognize that what I've been calling privatization doesn't really involve some new assertion of "the private sector" against a public domain organized around the structure of the welfare state and its public educational system. More exactly, the privatization I'm describing functions as a challenge to the assumption of some necessary symbiosis between two clearly demarcated spheres of private-sector economics and state-directed public policy. Rather than such clearly marked zones, and a gray area of lateral affiliations between them, what emerges from a process of privatization are serially linked fields of force. Within each field, the relative autonomy of decision-making simultaneously projects variable ratios of access to a position within the field and accountability to other fields. These variable ratios in turn constitute necessarily flexible norms that determine, on the occasion, zones of effect of specific decisions.

One result, as I remarked above, is that corporate control over selection decisions also identifies which economic agents can generate what range of political effects. Those effects don't occur across an already constituted dividing line between internal corporate control and an externally imposed public policy—rights to assess job candidate qualifications versus affirmative action mandates, for example. Rather, effects are produced within an ensemble of relations that admits no prior determination of what exactly is private and what public domain. Any process of rethinking older concepts of the State and of the public domain thus comes into play within this ensemble of relations. That is, such efforts are very much part of what's already at stake in the process of corporate change. This doesn't mean they are condemned to ineffectuality. But rather than using strategic leverage from "outside" to redefine the field of selection decisions, they occur in the midst of many often competing strategies of redirection.

As I argued in Chapter 2, however, the "flattening" of management hierarchy and the development of regionally autonomous units of the contemporary corporation have occurred concurrently with the proliferation of a so-called informal economy in country after country of the "developed" world no less than in traditionally "underdeveloped" nations. Thus the complicated directions of corporate change I've been describing, as they redefine the relations of public and private domains, face the surviving large-scale structures and institutions of the state as those structures and institutions are likely undergoing a process of reinvention. Perhaps even more important, the directions of corporate change also encounter a diversity of *economic* practices and markets by no means necessarily oriented toward the "self-interest" of corporations, however that self-interest is newly defined by human resources analysis.

Thus while transnational corporations in particular go in search of already capitalized sectors of an informal economy, university educators in

contrast can learn to look to the political expectations of diverse groups involved in the colonized economics of informal sectors. That is, if as university educators it's not necessary to be constrained by a vision like
Thomas's of allowing "all kinds of people to reach their full potential in
pursuit of corporate objectives" (167), then it's possible to attend more
closely to how emergent political definitions of "objectives" are embedded
in the complexities of colonized economic practices. In corporate eyes, of
course, any form such a process might take would seem a redundancy indeed, as if it were simply another and unnecessary parallel path to the incorporation already promised by the corporate management of diverse
multicultural populations as human resources. But a conception of human
resources can be understood instead to translate into a politics of incorporation as citizens *against* the defining terms of corporate demographic technologies, selection practices, and that now familiar search for already capitalized informal sectors of the economy to incorporate within a transnational web of capital politics.

Whether as redundant or conflicted, these forms of engagement with
informal, colonized economies meet in the organizations of markets—as I
argued in Chapter 4, understood to be complex ensembles of cultural, political, and economic practices everywhere involved in the distribution of
resources. Thus rather than identifying the point of insertion into an implacable, globalizing advance of transnational capital, human resources
managers as economic agents in the fields of market politics can identify
an "organic" point of connection to the political expectations of colonized
groups. As I will argue in my concluding section, that connection creates
conditions for understanding cultural studies work as an economic reeducation of the university.

❁

I argued in *Throwaways* that the growth and diversity of services is a dis-
tinctive feature of recent economic trends in the United States. Services of
all kinds, however, are increasingly sold within the terms of a complex
symbolic system designating service workers as professional providers. Business cards, to take a simple example, once limited to relatively traditional
and prestigious fields such as law, are now a feature of almost any service
transaction, from periodontal specialists to fitting room technicians at major department stores, mechanics at K-Mart, and housecleaning personnel.
They're a sign that signifies a "professional" level of service. A quick glance

at any phone book yellow pages will reveal not only dozens of usages of "professional" on every page, but also a remarkable proliferation of accreditation guarantees attesting to the professional level of service.

This emergent symbolic system may seem at best a rather shopworn marketing ploy and at worst merely a source of humor, as in the seemingly endless versions of late-night talk-show jokes about the transformation of garbage collectors into sanitation engineers, and so on. But such a dismissal ignores how, with respect to a growing number of symbolically designated professions, what "the public" seems to value most are not necessarily the services supplied by the profession and the opportunity to purchase those services, but rather an opportunity to become oneself a professional. That is, in larger terms, the dismissal fails to register that in the current circumstances of diverse and proliferating trajectories of market politics, a conception of "profession" (and "professional work") has begun to occupy a special role in the mutation of a so-called middle class and the social expectations defining a middle-class life in the United States. A profession no longer appears as an automatic sign of upward mobility within the terms of a specific set of assumptions about competency and training in a few very visible fields. The designation of "professional" functions instead to leverage a complex of economic practices into a claim for publicly recognized authority. "Profession" identifies a constructed pathway of incorporation by which agents engaged in market-organized economic practices can attempt to secure some visible and effective political position in a public world. For professional services are not only sold as market-appropriate resources, but are also intricated everywhere with an imaginary of general public value.

This shifting complex of meanings associated with professional position seems to me to raise a rather different set of issues than what has emerged in by now familiar debates over whether, and to what extent, literary study in the university can be identified as a distinct profession like law or medicine. In current circumstances, the status of literary study as a profession depends less on resemblances to such traditionally prestigious professional fields than on the complexities of the social relations configured across the multiple, diverse market fields of service providers claiming a designation as professional. It's true enough that there now exists a greater diversity of population groups entering literary study, and the discipline of English generally, than in the past. But I'm more immediately interested in how "profession" might be understood as a term that links university work practices in English to expectations of political incorporation, rather than as a means of distinguishing a culturally elite body of educators.

With his expanded definition of intellectuals in the *Notebooks*, Gramsci wasn't really setting out to identify under the name of "intellectual" a philosopher and historian such as Croce with a midlevel accountant. Among other things, his rethinking of the term was intended as a way to foreground complex ensembles of "organic" affiliations across the political formation. Likewise, in suggesting reasons for expanding an understanding of how "profession" now functions, I have no intention of identifying faculty and graduate students in English with all that vast diversity of often self-designated professional service providers. My point is to relocate an understanding of the multiple connections that organize emergent fields of social relations—in this case, around that contested term "professional" as a narrative of political incorporation. Thus rather than asking what public those of us with professional positions in English address in our work, I'm interested in how and in what ways positions in English are already affiliated with specific publics depending on how claims for professional status are made and realized in specific ensembles of practices.

No one can hope to plot in advance the effects of the many proposed directions of educational reform proposals nor the outcome of newly reconstituted forms of university-corporate symbiosis. And, obviously, the often contradictory imperatives that come with a professional, academic position are not likely to disappear into some clearly demarcated and "genuinely oppositional" political direction. Nevertheless, the encounters with multiple publics possible to such positions encourage the development of new tactical maneuvers that involve economic no less than cultural practices. Educators must be educated, as Gramsci always reminds us, and as professions multiply before our eyes we can learn new possibilities for making use of an economic agency in struggles for political change.

Programs for "managing diversity" such as those offered by Thomas and other human resources analysts are likely to seem suspect, but nevertheless there remains an indispensable lesson from their work as well. Like it or not, anyone positioned with any degree of power as an economic agent will represent the interests of a great many people. It's silly to overestimate the potential authority of such a position in the humanities, relative even to the work of corporate consultants like Fernandez, let alone those who shape the larger parameters of public policy. But it's a mistake to imagine that it's possible to avoid "speaking for" anyone else, somehow Edenically free from the contaminations of representation in all its forms.

Despite the name, it is true enough that cultural studies work is not necessarily well positioned to represent the cultural practices of marginalized and disenfranchised groups within the terms of academic study. Concerns about academic "colonialization" no less than critiques of cultural studies by feminist and African American theorists offer good reasons to suspect such familiar forms of positional representation. But if, as I suggested, it's possible to take advantage of the "redundancy" of university positioning, in order to engage with multiple economic practices across the organizations of markets in the social field, then these representations can also be made to function in very different terms as part of a process of economic education within the university. They would be directed first at the parameters and policies of universities, at making universities an alternative politics of human resources and incorporation whose allegiances to "diversity" begin in the economics of the colonies. Thus rather than imagining cultural studies as incorporating the cultures of excluded groups into the university, representing "their" cultural practices in the terms of academic study, cultural studies work would function instead by representing alternative directions for the determination of university policy. University resources would be made to figure the extension and legitimation of economically colonized groups, thereby incorporating the university into the political struggles of the colonized.

Such an economic reeducation must be a long and considerable task, and not only because of the intricate lines of power that affiliate the institutional structures and research programs of universities to different corporate and political ends that continue to marginalize programs like cultural studies. It's difficult because it also requires a profound reorientation of cultural studies politics and positioning. Hall's statement about the political desire expressed in the term "organic intellectual," what he calls the "nostalgia or will or hope . . . that at some point we would be prepared in intellectual work for that kind of relationship, if such a conjuncture ever appeared" (281), ignores how actual political conjunctures rarely oblige the terms of such desire, whether as nostalgia or will or hope. Recognizing the diversity of economic practices in the colonies as a vehicle of political desire is perhaps rare indeed. But it's in the complex of such economic practices that the possibility of conjuncture exists and functions to ground the concrete task of university re-education and incorporation into the resources of colonized populations.

Further, there's no reason to imagine that the formation of political alliances must occur within the terms of university groups, set in opposition to corporate human resources management. If it's true enough that reconstituted forms of university-corporation symbiosis can anticipate the outsourcing of sectors of a university faculty to corporate ends, it's at least plausible to imagine a counter-recruitment effort in effect that would align some sectors of corporate management with an economic education of the university toward the end of incorporation with the economic politics of colonized populations. In commenting on the "Corporate Culture" essays in *Social Text* I introduced for the issue, James Livingstone argues that while consultants like Thomas may seem our "monstrous doubles," it's "because his 'background and allegiances' do *not* differ from ours" (63; Livingstone's emphasis). Those backgrounds and allegiances, Livingstone goes on to suggest, are typical of academics as well, "at least of those who still hope to reconstruct or reconstitute the 'public sphere'" (63). I think Livingstone perhaps overstates his case, but surely he's right to recognize that in the complicated and shifting relations of both university and corporate cultures, it's a mistake to equate institutional location with political direction. Nor is it possible to maintain that because they are caught up in the market economics of the corporation, whatever radical politics are initiated with corporations are automatically compromised.

This is not a good time to give up on economics. It's not a good time to refuse the necessary politics of working to change irrevocably the parameters of capitalist common sense in a nation that still bills itself as the privileged global subject of a now international capitalism. It's not at all a good time to abandon whatever leverage is possible from within shifting conditions of professional work in the university. I've suggested ways in which I think the position of "human resources management," as outsourced to university humanities intellectuals, can be made to yield local sectors of leverage. Using that leverage depends on recognizing the configurations and colonizing powers of transnational capital politics. It depends on taking advantage of the "organic" affiliations possible with the economics of the colonies. Leverage involves developing the complex ensemble of relations that articulates expectations of political incorporation and multiplies both "professional" and "public" designations and positions. It means redirecting the representations of cultural practices toward the ends of what I would call an economic countereducation of universities.

It's clear in any case that universities are currently being "re-educated" in all kinds of ways economically. Debates over the increase in so-called temporary positions and the recent furor about tenure instigated by the University of Minnesota's president are perhaps only the most familiar recent examples of universities setting new economic priorities. In the context I've been describing, however, tenure must be understood in rather different terms than as an issue of free speech, protecting the right of un-encumbered research directions, and so on. Tenure, after all, is one sign of professional incorporation. It can stake a political agency with at least a limited power of producing effects that can change the parameters of social configuration in multiple sectors. As such, it stands in dramatic contrast to the vulnerability of a "temporary" work force whose incorporation in any sense depends not only on economic conditions, but even more fundamentally on the complex of selection practices and the "management" of diversity that, as I argued, shape a corporate politics. That is, minimally, tenure is not a distinct issue, but is everywhere linked to the economics of a temporary work force and to the widespread corporate and university privatization of selection. Thus in contrast to the relentless future orientation of demographics and its affiliated technologies of selection, every specific "tenure case" forces a complex history into view within the terms of that general concept of tenure.

No one in the academy "earns" tenure individually, simply as a reflection of having done the work any qualified evaluator would recognize as "tenurable" quality. One's tenure is more directly a result of an institutional history of tenure decisions, and also of how other people have worked to create conditions of possibility for doing specific kinds of work at all, as much in their everyday practices and behaviors as in their own research and scholarship. If you widen the scope a little further, it's necessary to recognize how tenure decisions implicate often a wide range indeed of prior political initiatives, both within and outside the tenuring institution, and an entire collective ensemble of market forces and relations. The circumscribing of tenure around issues of individual qualification is a particularly malignant shorthand, insofar as it not only imposes pathologies of inadequacy even on "successful" candidates, but more importantly precludes necessary working knowledges of the wide-ranging processes at stake.

As one sign of an incorporated agency, tenure also becomes a microcosm of educational politics, at once a historical process and a visible goal of countless itineraries of educational training. Thus it shouldn't come as a surprise that attacks on tenure occur at a certain conjuncture of two otherwise very different political directions. The more familiar of these directions, for academics at least, involves a new conservative agenda targeting tenure as a form of social protection for the ideologically corrupting forces at work in higher education. This attack is more dangerous than sometimes imagined, for it helps make possible a remarkable mobilization that maps a number of currents of anti-intellectual prejudice onto a potentially far more explosive anti-elitism. That is, such mapping positions "radical" university educators as engaged not only in a defense of social privilege unavailable to "ordinary citizens," but, more important, in a spearheading of elitist political directions antithetical to the hopes and expectations of those "ordinary citizens." In the context of this positioning, a defense of tenure as necessary to academic freedom appears at best a perversion of democratic ideals of free speech, and at worst a cynical misuse of cultural authority symmetrically comparable to the misuses of economic power by which "the rich" avoid all the burdens of a suddenly volatile and threatening general climate of economic change.

The other, and in many ways significantly different, direction of attack on tenure is involved in those programs of "managing diversity" that articulate a privatization of corporate selection practices as marking the socially necessary path of incorporation as public citizens. A challenge to tenure in these terms has relatively little to do with any politics of "resentment" directed at the university, nor is the freedom to speak or to participate in "radical" or "experimental" research at issue. The confluence occurs because, for this no less than for new conservative directions, tenure identifies a certain permanence of political agency. In the language of my earlier chapter, tenured agents are "irreplaceable"; they can't be made to disappear under the technologies of shifting demographic projections or environmental scanning.

To the extent tenure as a social positioning is made doubly visible at the point of confluence between these different directions of attack, it should be clear why more is at stake in the concept of tenure than what is implied by issues of academic freedom, important as those are in specific aspects of university work. Understood as educational goal and as part of a historical process, tenuring articulates one version of a narrative of expectations for political incorporation that occurs in many different forms throughout the mazy intricacies of informal sector economic practices, ad hoc organizations of outsourced workers, the movements of migrating populations—the whole complex of activities in the economic colonies of transnational capital. It's by no means the largest, most important, or most contested version, nor is it in any way a paradigmatic form that would comprehend all other versions. It's simply that the complexity of the tenuring process provides a means of connection with a large ensemble of social relations, what Stuart Hall would refer to as a point of articulation occurring at the intersections of a great many varied interests.

At this point of articulation, more often than not appearing around the

symbolic currency of "professional," the tenuring process can i
rection for a countereducation of the university, as a way for ur
participate in the educative formation of political agency. Tl
than some individual reflection of merit earned, tenure as a specific academic form of political incorporation might well function as a first step in
learning how to construct other and altogether different processes of formation of political agency within a "diversity" of populations. As countereducation, this learning process would commit the university to a prac-
tical role in the economic politics of the colonies. Thus one considerable
danger in limiting struggles over tenure to issues of academic freedom is
that it also limits an avenue of access to the larger work of constructing
political alliances across the multiple "organic" connections that should be
foregrounded in a countereducation of the university.

This is not a good time to give up on economics, to consign the intricacies of economic practices and the multiple ensembles of market politics
to the vast imaginary of a triumphant global capitalism. Economic practices are perhaps the surest indicators of what's happening otherwise in
countless intricated sectors of the colonies, "here" no less than in more culturally "exotic" regions worldwide. Thus it seems to me that whatever potential for social change might lie in the process of countereducating universities can be realized because of and not despite an emergent positioning
of humanities instruction as economic agency within the terms of "human resources." Whether this also means finally giving up on that long-
standing dream of the liminal formation of an authentic cultural vanguard,
as persistent in cultural studies as in its academic predecessors, remains to
be seen. But I suspect the specifically cultural distinctiveness so much a
part of that dream has already migrated into more immediately promising
configurations of political direction.

Reference Matter

Works Cited

Amariglio, Jack, and David Ruccio, "The Transgressive Knowledge of 'Ersatz' Economics," in Rob Garnett, Jr., ed., *Economic Knowledges: Producers, Consumers, Consequences* (forthcoming).

Angus, Ian, and Sut Jhally, eds. *Cultural Politics in Contemporary America.* New York, 1989.

Baker, Wayne. "The Social Structure of a National Securities Market." *American Journal of Sociology* 89 (Jan. 1984).

Barrett, Michèle. *The Politics of Truth.* Stanford, Calif., 1991.

Bell, Daniel. "Communication Technology: For Better or for Worse?" in Jerry Salvaggio, ed., *The Information Society.*

Blackmur, R. P. "Toward a Modus Vivendi." *The Lion and the Honeycomb: Essays in Solicitude and Critique.* New York, 1955.

Block, Fred. *Postindustrial Possibilities: A Critique of Economic Discourse.* Berkeley, Calif., 1990.

Bourdieu, Pierre. *Distinction: A Social Critique of the Judgment of Taste.* Trans. Richard Nice. Cambridge, Mass., 1984.

Bowles, Samuel, and Herbert Gintis. *Schooling in Capitalist America: Educational Reform and the Contradictions of Economic Life.* New York, 1976.

Compaine, Benjamin. "Information Gaps: Myth or Reality?" in Benjamin Compaine, ed., *Issues in New Information Technology.* Norwood, N.J., 1988.

Crawford, Richard. *In the Era of Human Capital: The Emergence of Talent, Intelligence, and Knowledge as the Worldwide Economic Force and What It Means to Managers and Investors.* New York, 1991.

Dalla Costa, Mariarosa, and Giovanna F. Dalla Costa, eds. *Paying the Price: Women and the Politics of International Economic Strategy.* Atlantic Highlands, N.J., 1995.

De Soto, Hernando. *The Other Path: The Invisible Revolution in the Third World.* Trans. June Abbott. New York, 1989.

Dicken, Peter. *Global Shift: The Internationalization of Economic Activity*. New York, 1992.

Dirlik, Arif. "The Postcolonial Aura: Third World Criticism in the Age of Global Capitalism." *Critical Inquiry* 30 (winter 1994).

Epstein, Gerald, Julie Graham, and Jessica Nembhard, eds., *Creating a New World Economy: Forces of Change and Plans for Action*. Philadelphia, 1993.

Etzioni, Amitai. *The Moral Dimension: Toward a New Economics*. London, 1988.

Fernandez, John P. *Managing a Diverse Work Force: Regaining the Competitive Edge*. Lexington, Mass., 1991.

Fernandez, John, and Jacqueline Dubois. "Managing a Diverse Workforce in the 1990s," in Manuel London, Emily Bassman, and John Fernandez, eds., *Human Resource Forecasting and Strategy Development*.

Garnett, Rob, Jr., ed. *Economic Knowledges: Producers, Consumers, Consequences* (forthcoming).

Gibson-Graham, J. K. *The End of Capitalism (As We Knew It): A Feminist Critique of Political Economy*. Oxford, 1996.

Gordon, Avery. "The Work of Corporate Culture: Diversity Management." *Social Text* 44 (fall/winter 1995).

Graham, Julie. "Multinational Corporations and the Internationalization of Production: An Industry Perspective," in Gerald Epstein, Julie Graham, and Jessica Nembhard, eds., *Creating a New World Economy: Forces of Change and Plans for Action*.

Granovetter, Mark. "Economic Action and Social Structure: The Problem of Embeddedness." *American Journal of Sociology* 91 (Nov. 1985).

Green, James R. *The World of the Worker: Labor in Twentieth-Century America*. New York, 1980.

Grossberg, Lawrence, Cary Nelson, and Paula Treichler, eds., *Cultural Studies*. New York, 1992.

Hage, Jerald, and Charles Powers. *Post-Industrial Lives: Roles and Relationships in the 21st Century*. Newbury Park, N.J., 1992.

Hall, Stuart. "Cultural Studies and Its Theoretical Legacies," in Lawrence Grossberg, Cary Nelson, and Paula Treichler, eds., *Cultural Studies*.

Hirsch, Fred. *Social Limits to Growth*. Cambridge, Mass., 1976.

Jameson, Fredric. *Postmodernism, or, The Cultural Logic of Late Capitalism*. Durham, N.C., 1991.

Laclau, Ernesto, and Chantal Mouffe. *Hegemony and Socialist Strategy*. London, 1985.

Lathen, Emma. *Murder to Go*. New York, 1969.

Leiss, William. "The Myth of the Information Society," in Ian Angus and Sut Jhally, eds., *Cultural Politics in Contemporary America*.

Livingston, James. "Corporations and Cultural Studies." *Social Text* 44 (fall/winter 1995).

London, Manuel, Emily Bassman, and John Fernandez, eds. *Human Resource Fore-*

casting and Strategy Development: Guidelines for Analyzing and Fulfilling Organiza-tional Needs. New York, 1990.

Mandeville, John J., and Ab Sidewater, eds., *The Complete Dog Book*, official publi-cation of the American Kennel Club. 17th edition. New York, 1985.

Marx, Karl. *Capital: A Critique of Political Economy*. Trans. Ben Fowkes and David Fernbach. New York, 1981.

McClintock, Anne. "The Angel of Progress: Pitfalls of the Term 'Post-Colonialism.'" *Social Text* 31/32 (1992).

Meehan, Eileen R. "Why We Don't Count: The Commodity Audience," in Patricia Mellencamp, ed., *Logics of Television*.

Mellencamp, Patricia, ed., *Logics of Television: Essays in Cultural Criticism*. Bloom-ington, Ind., 1990.

Mercer, Kobena. "'1968': Periodizing Postmodern Politics and Identity," in Lawrence Grossman, Cary Nelson, and Paula Treichler, eds., *Cultural Studies*.

Miyoshi, Masao. "A Borderless World? From Colonialism to Transnationalism and the Decline of the Nation-State." *Critical Inquiry* 19 (summer 1993).

Moraga, Cherrie, and Gloria Anzaldua, eds. *This Bridge Called My Back: Writings by Radical Women of Color*. New York, reprint, 1983.

Newfield, Christopher. "Corporate Pleasures for a Corporate Planet." *Social Text* 44 (fall/winter 1995).

————. "What Was Political Correctness? Race, the Right, and Managerial Democracy in the Humanities." *Critical Inquiry* 19 (1993).

Peters, Tom. *Liberation Management: Necessary Disorganization for the Nanosecond Nineties*. PBS broadcast, 1993.

Piore, Michael, and Charles Sabel. *The Second Industrial Divide: Possibilities for Pros-perity*. New York, 1984.

Porat, Marc. *The Information Economy*. 9 vols. Special Publication 77–12. Washing-ton, D.C.: Office of Telecommunications, 1977.

Pynchon, Thomas. *The Crying of Lot 49*. New York, 1966.

Reich, Robert. *The Work of Nations: Preparing Ourselves for 21st Century Capitalism*. New York, 1991.

Robbins, Bruce. *Secular Vocations: Intellectuals, Professionalism, Culture*. New York, 1993.

Ross, Robert J. S., and Kent Trachte. *Global Capitalism: The New Leviathan*. Albany, N.Y., 1990.

Quijano, Anibal. "A Different Concept of the Private Sector, a Different Concept of the Public Sector: Notes for a Latin American Debate." *CEPAL Review* 35 (1988).

Salvaggio, Jerry, ed. *The Information Society: Economic, Social and Structural Issues*. Hillsdale, N.J., 1989.

Schement, Jorge Reina. "The Origins of the Information Society in the United States: Competing Visions," in Jerry Salvaggio, ed., *The Information Society*.

Schiller, Herbert. *Who Knows: Information in the Age of the Fortune 500.* Norwood, N.J., 1981.

Sklar, Martin. *The United States as a Developing Country: Studies in U.S. History in the Progressive Era and the 1920s.* New York, 1992.

Smith, Barbara, and Beverly Smith. "Across the Kitchen Table: A Sister-to-Sister Dialogue," in Cherrie Moraga and Gloria Anzaldua, eds., *This Bridge Called My Back.*

Távara, José. "Development Strategies in Latin America: Which Way Now?" in Gerald Epstein, Julie Graham, and Jessica Nembhard, eds., *Creating a New World Economy.*

Thomas, R. Roosevelt, Jr. *Beyond Race and Gender: Unleashing the Power of Your Total Workforce.* New York, 1991.

Tokman, Victor. "The Process of Accumulation and the Weakness of the Protagonists." *CEPAL Review* 26 (1987).

Wector, Dixon. *The Age of the Great Depression.* New York, 1948.

Watkins, Evan. *Throwaways: Work Culture and Consumer Education.* Stanford, Calif., 1993.

Index

In this index an "f" after a number indicates a separate reference on the next page, and an "ff" indicates separate references on the next two pages. A continuous discussion over two or more pages is indicated by a span of page numbers, e.g., "57–59." *Passim* is used for a cluster of references in close but not consecutive sequence.